GRAMMAR EXPLORER 1A

Daphne Mackey
Series Editors: Rob Jenkins and Staci Johnson

NATIONAL GEOGRAPHIC LEARNING

Australia • Brazil • Canada • Mexico • Singapore • United Kingdom • United States

Grammar Explorer 1A

Daphne Mackey

Publisher: Sherrise Roehr
Executive Editor: Laura Le Dréan
Senior Development Editor: Mary Whittemore
Assistant Editor: Vanessa Richards
Senior Technology Product Manager: Scott Rule
Director of Global Marketing: Ian Martin
Marketing Manager: Lindsey Miller
Sr. Director, ELT & World Languages: Michael Burggren
Production Manager: Daisy Sosa
Content Project Manager: Andrea Bobotas
Senior Print Buyer: Mary Beth Hennebury
Cover Designer: 3CD, Chicago
Cover Image: George F. Herben/National Geographic Creative
Compositor: Cenveo® Publisher Services

© 2015 Cengage Learning, Inc. ALL RIGHTS RESERVED.

WCN: 01-100-364

No part of this work covered by the copyright herein may be reproduced or distributed in any form or by any means, except as permitted by U.S. copyright law, without the prior written permission of the copyright owner.

"National Geographic", "National Geographic Society" and the Yellow Border Design are registered trademarks of the National Geographic Society ® Marcas Registradas

For permission to use material from this text or product, submit all requests online at **cengage.com/permissions**

Further permissions questions can be emailed to **permissionrequest@cengage.com**

Grammar Explorer 1A: 978-1-111-35097-0

National Geographic Learning
5191 Natorp Boulevard
Mason, OH 45040
USA

Locate your local office at **international.cengage.com/region**

Visit National Geographic Learning online at **ELTNGL.com**
Visit our corporate website at **www.cengage.com**

Printed in China
Print Number: 08   Print Year: 2024

CONTENTS

Acknowledgments vii
Inside a Unit viii

UNIT 1 People 2

The Verb *Be*

LESSON 1: Simple Present of *Be*; Contractions with *Be* 4
  Reading: *Say hello!* 4
    1.1 Simple Present of *Be*: Affirmative Statements 6
    1.2 Contractions with *Be* 7

LESSON 2: *Be* + Singular Noun; *Be* + Plural Noun 11
  Reading: *Dereck and Beverly Joubert* 11
    1.3 *Be* + Singular Noun 13
    1.4 *Be* + Plural Noun 14
    1.5 Simple Present of *Be*: Negative Statements 16

LESSON 3: Descriptive Adjectives 21
  Reading: *Tank the Bear* 21
    1.6 Descriptive Adjectives 23

LESSON 4: Possessive Adjectives; Possessive Nouns 28
  Reading: *Sami Reindeer Herders* 28
    1.7 Possessive Adjectives 30
    1.8 Possessive Nouns 31

Review the Grammar 35
Connect the Grammar to Writing: Write about Two Family Members 38

UNIT 2 Celebrations 40

The Verb *Be*: Questions

LESSON 1: Simple Present of *Be*: Yes/No Questions 42
  Reading: *Happy name day!* 42
    2.1 Simple Present of *Be*: Yes / No Questions 44
    2.2 Simple Present of *Be*: Short Answers 45

LESSON 2: Prepositions of Place; Questions with *Where + Be* 50
  Reading: *Eiffel Tower Tour* 50
    2.3 Prepositions of Place 52
    2.4 Questions with *Where + Be* 54

LESSON 3: Questions about Time and Weather 58
  Reading: *New Year's Celebrations around the World* 58
    2.5 Questions about Time 60
    2.6 Questions with *When*; Prepositions of Time (Part 1) 61
    2.7 Questions about the Weather 63

LESSON 4: *This, That, These, Those* 66
  Reading: *Holi Festival* 66
    2.8 *This, That, These, Those* 68
    2.9 Questions and Answers with *This, That, These, Those* 69

Review the Grammar 73
Connect the Grammar to Writing: Write about a Celebration 76

UNIT 3 Work 78
Simple Present: Part 1

LESSON 1: Simple Present: Affirmative Statements 80
  Reading: *Doctor Bugs* 80
  3.1 Simple Present: Affirmative Statements 82
  3.2 Simple Present Spelling Rules:
       -s and -es Endings 83
  3.3 Irregular Verbs: *Do, Go,* and *Have* 84

LESSON 2: Simple Present: Negative Statements and Contractions 88
  Reading: *Life on the Space Station* 88
  3.4 Simple Present: Negative Statements 90
  3.5 Prepositions of Time (Part 2) 91
  3.6 *Like, Need,* and *Want* + Infinitive 92

LESSON 3: Verbs + Objects 97
  Reading: *Elephant Keepers* 97
  3.7 Verb + Object / Verb + Preposition + Object 99
  3.8 Object Pronouns 100

LESSON 4: Imperatives 104
  Reading: *How to Get a Job in Game Design* 104
  3.9 Imperatives: Affirmative 106
  3.10 Imperatives: Negative 107

Review the Grammar 111
Connect the Grammar to Writing: Write about a Job 114

UNIT 4 Lifestyles 116
Simple Present: Part 2

LESSON 1: Simple Present: *Yes/No* Questions and Short
           Answers 118
  Reading: *The People from the Nicoya Peninsula* 118
  4.1 Simple Present: *Yes/No* Questions 120
  4.2 Simple Present: Short Answers to *Yes/No* Questions 121

LESSON 2: Frequency Adverbs and Expressions 125
  Reading: *Night Markets* 125
  4.3 Frequency Adverbs 127
  4.4 Frequency Expressions 128

LESSON 3: Simple Present: *Wh-* Questions 131
  Reading: *The Amish* 131
  4.5 Simple Present: *Wh-* Questions 133
  4.6 *Who* Questions about a Subject 134

Review the Grammar 139
Connect the Grammar to Writing: Write about Someone's Daily Life 142

UNIT 5 Food and Hospitality 144
Count and Non-Count Nouns

LESSON 1: Count and Non-Count Nouns; Articles 146
  Reading: *At the Grand Hotel* 146
  5.1 Count and Non-Count Nouns 148
  5.2 Using *A/An* with Count Nouns 149
  5.3 *A/An* vs. *The* 150

LESSON 2: Measurement Words; *Some, Any* 154
  Reading: *Erik's Food Blog* 154
  5.4 Measurement Words 156
  5.5 *Some, Any* 157

LESSON 3: *Much, Many, A Lot of; A Few, A Little* 163
  Reading: *The Hadza People* 163
  5.6 *Much, Many, A Lot Of* 165
  5.7 *A Few, A Little* 166
  5.8 Questions with *How Much* and *How Many* 166

Review the Grammar 171
Connect the Grammar to Writing: Write about an Event 174

UNIT 6 Homes and Communities 176
There Is/There Are

LESSON 1: *There Is/There Are* 178
  Reading: *Side Trips from Shanghai* 178
  6.1 *There Is/There Are*: Statements 180
  6.2 *There Is/There Are*: Yes/No Questions and Short Answers 181
  6.3 *How Much . . . Is There? / How Many . . . Are There?* 182

LESSON 2: *Too Much/Too Many; Enough/Not Enough* 187
  Reading: *Home Design* 187
  6.4 *Too Much/Too Many* + Noun 189
  6.5 *Enough/Not Enough* + Noun 190

LESSON 3: Indefinite Pronouns 193
  Reading: *Dune Shacks* 193
  6.6 Indefinite Pronouns: *Nothing, Anything, Something, Everything* 195
  6.7 Indefinite Pronouns: *No One, Nobody, Anyone, Anybody, Someone, Somebody, Everyone, Everybody* 197

Review the Grammar 201
Connect the Grammar to Writing: Write Your Opinion about a Place 204

UNIT 7 Extremes 206
Present Progressive

LESSON 1: Present Progressive: Statements 208
   Reading: *Highliners* 208
   7.1 Present Progressive: Affirmative Statements 210
   7.2 Present Progressive: Negative Statements 212
   7.3 Spelling Rules: *-ing* Forms 213

LESSON 2: Present Progressive: Questions 218
   Reading: *An Interview with Stephen Alvarez* 218
   7.4 Present Progressive: *Yes/No* Questions and Short Answers 220
   7.5 Present Progressive: *Wh-* Questions 222
   7.6 *Wh-* Questions with *Who* 223

LESSON 3: Simple Present vs. Present Progressive 228
   Reading: *Tornado!* 228
   7.7 Simple Present vs. Present Progressive 230
   7.8 Non-Action Verbs 231

Review the Grammar 235
Connect the Grammar to Writing: Write about the Activities in Your Life 238

Appendices A1
Glossary of Grammar Terms G1
Index I1
Credits C1

ACKNOWLEDGMENTS

The authors and publisher would like to thank the following reviewers and contributors:

Gokhan Alkanat, Auburn University at Montgomery, Alabama; **Dorothy S. Avondstondt**, Miami Dade College, Florida; **Heather Barikmo**, The English Language Center at LaGuardia Community College, New York; **Kimberly Becker**, Nashville State Community College, Tennessee; **Lukas Bidelspack**, Corvallis, Oregon; **Grace Bishop**, Houston Community College, Texas; **Mariusz Jacek Bojarczuk**, Bunker Hill Community College, Massachusetts; **Nancy Boyer**, Golden West College, California; **Patricia Brenner**, University of Washington, Washington; **Jessica Buchsbaum**, City College of San Francisco, California; **Gabriella Cambiasso**, Harold Washington College, Illinois; **Tony Carnerie**, English Language Institute, University of California San Diego Extension, California; **Whitney Clarq-Reis**, Framingham State University; **Julia A. Correia**, Henderson State University, Arkansas; **Katie Crowder**, UNT Department of Linguistics and Technical Communication, Texas; **Lin Cui**, William Rainey Harper College, Illinois; **Nora Dawkins**, Miami Dade College, Florida; **Rachel DeSanto**, English for Academic Purposes, Hillsborough Community College, Florida; **Aurea Diab**, Dillard University, Louisiana; **Marta Dmytrenko-Ahrabian**, English Language Institute, Wayne State University, Michigan; **Susan Dorrington**, Education and Language Acquisition Department, LaGuardia Community College, New York; **Ian Dreilinger**, Center for Multilingual Multicultural Studies, University of Central Florida, Florida; **Jennifer Dujat**, Education and Language Acquisition Department, LaGuardia Community College, New York; **Dr. Jane Duke**, Language & Literature Department, State College of Florida, Florida; **Anna Eddy**, University of Michigan-Flint, Michigan; **Jenifer Edens**, University of Houston, Texas; **Karen Einstein**, Santa Rosa Junior College, California; **Cynthia Etter**, International & English Language Programs, University of Washington, Washington; **Parvanak Fassihi**, SHOWA Boston Institute for Language and Culture, Massachusetts; **Katherine Fouche**, The University of Texas at Austin, Texas; **Richard Furlong**, Education and Language Acquisition Department, LaGuardia Community College, New York; **Glenn S. Gardner**, Glendale College, California; **Sally Gearhart**, Santa Rosa Junior College, California; **Alexis Giannopolulos**, SHOWA Boston Institute for Language and Culture, Massachusetts; **Nora Gold**, Baruch College, The City University of New York, New York; **Ekaterina V. Goussakova**, Seminole State College of Florida; **Lynn Grantz**, Valparaiso University, Indiana; **Tom Griffith**, SHOWA Boston Institute for Language and Culture, Massachusetts; **Christine Guro**, Hawaii English Language Program, University of Hawaii at Manoa, Hawaii; **Jessie Hayden**, Georgia Perimeter College, Georgia; **Barbara Inerfeld**, Program in American Language Studies, Rutgers University, New Jersey; **Gail Kellersberger**, University of Houston-Downtown, Texas; **David Kelley**, SHOWA Boston Institute for Language and Culture, Massachusetts; **Kathleen Kelly**, ESL Department, Passaic County Community College, New Jersey; **Dr. Hyun-Joo Kim**, Education and Language Acquisition Department, LaGuardia Community College, New York; **Linda Koffman**, College of Marin, California; **Lisa Kovacs-Morgan**, English Language Institute, University of California San Diego Extension, California; **Jerrad Langlois**, TESL Program and Office of International Programs, Northeastern Illinois University; **Janet Langon**, Glendale College, California; **Olivia Limbu**, The English Language Center at LaGuardia Community College, New York; **Devora Manier**, Nashville State Community College, Tennessee; **Susan McAlister**, Language and Culture Center, Department of English, University of Houston, Texas; **John McCarthy**, SHOWA Boston Institute for Language and Culture, Massachusetts; **Dr. Myra Medina**, Miami Dade College, Florida; **Dr. Suzanne Medina**, California State University, Dominguez Hills, California; **Nancy Megarity**, ESL & Developmental Writing, Collin College, Texas; **Joseph Montagna**, SHOWA Boston Institute for Language and Culture, Massachusetts; **Richard Moore**, University of Washington; **Monika Mulder**, Portland State University, Oregon; **Patricia Nation**, Miami Dade College, Florida; **Susan Niemeyer**, Los Angeles City College, California; **Charl Norloff**, International English Center, University of Colorado Boulder, Colorado; **Gabriella Nuttall**, Sacramento City College, California; **Dr. Karla Odenwald**, CELOP at Boston University, Massachusetts; **Ali Olson-Pacheco**, English Language Institute, University of California San Diego Extension, California; **Fernanda Ortiz**, Center for English as a Second Language, University of Arizona, Arizona; **Chuck Passentino**, Grossmont College, California; **Stephen Peridore**, College of Southern Nevada, Nevada; **Frank Quebbemann**, Miami Dade College, Florida; **Dr. Anouchka Rachelson**, Miami Dade College, Florida; **Dr. Agnieszka Rakowicz**, Education and Language Acquisition Department, LaGuardia Community College, New York; **Wendy Ramer**, Broward College, Florida; **Esther Robbins**, Prince George's Community College, Maryland; **Helen Roland**, Miami Dade College, Florida; **Debbie Sandstrom**, Tutorium in Intensive English, University of Illinois at Chicago, Illinois; **Maria Schirta**, Hudson County Community College, New Jersey; **Dr. Jennifer Scully**, Education and Language Acquisition Department, LaGuardia Community College, New York; **Jeremy Stubbs**, Tacoma, Washington; **Adrianne Thompson**, Miami Dade College, Florida; **Evelyn Trottier**, Basic and Transitional Studies Program, Seattle Central Community College, Washington; **Karen Vallejo**, University of California, Irvine, California; **Emily Young**, Auburn University at Montgomery, Alabama.

From the Author: It has been a pleasure to work with such talented people on this project. I would like to thank Mary Whittemore for her dedication, her sense of humor, and her wonderfully diplomatic way of giving negative feedback. I have enjoyed working with Laura Le Dréan and the team at National Geographic Learning as well as fellow authors Sammi Eckstut, Amy Cooper, and Paul Carne. Lastly, I would like to thank Daria Ruzicka for her hard work and contributions on the initial stages of the project and Diane Piniaris for her outstanding work on the final stage.

Dedication: With love to George and Caroline

INSIDE A UNIT

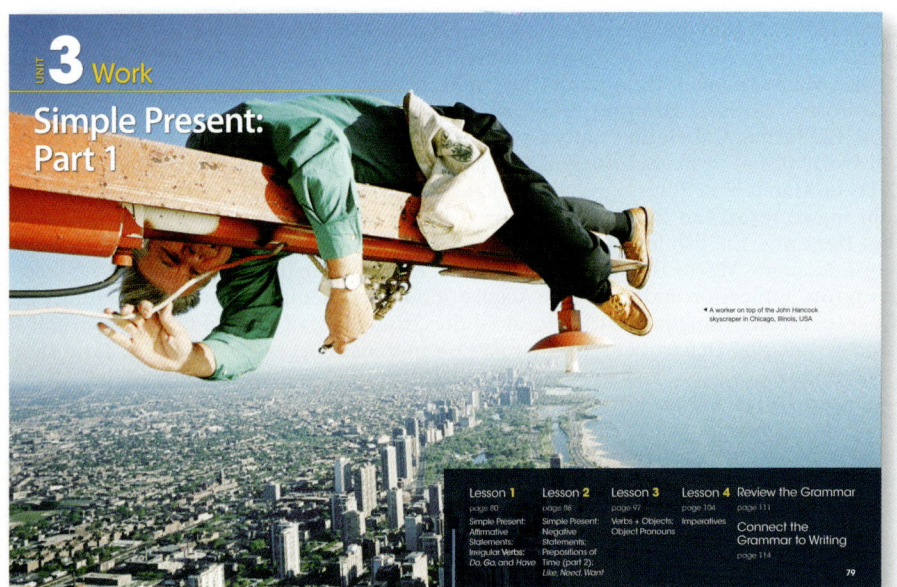

National Geographic images introduce the unit theme—real world topics that students want to read, write, and talk about.

Units are organized in **manageable lessons**, which ensures students **explore, learn, practice**, and **apply** the grammar.

INSIDE A UNIT

Each lesson begins with the *Explore* section, featuring a captivating National Geographic article that introduces the target grammar and builds students' knowledge in a variety of academic disciplines.

INSIDE A UNIT   ix

INSIDE A UNIT

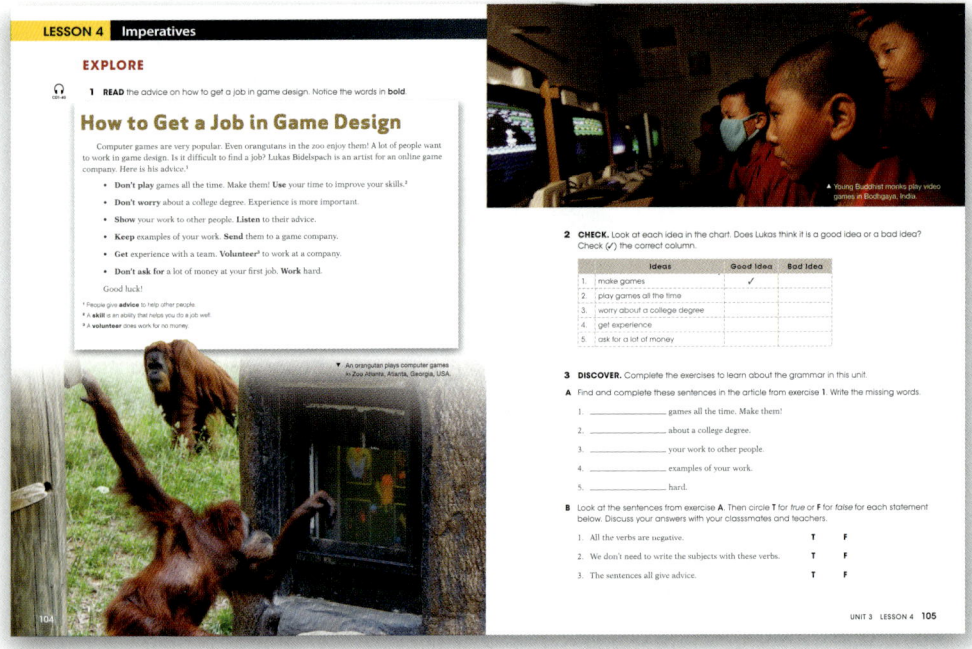

In the **Explore** section, students discover how the grammar structures are used in the readings and in real academic textbooks.

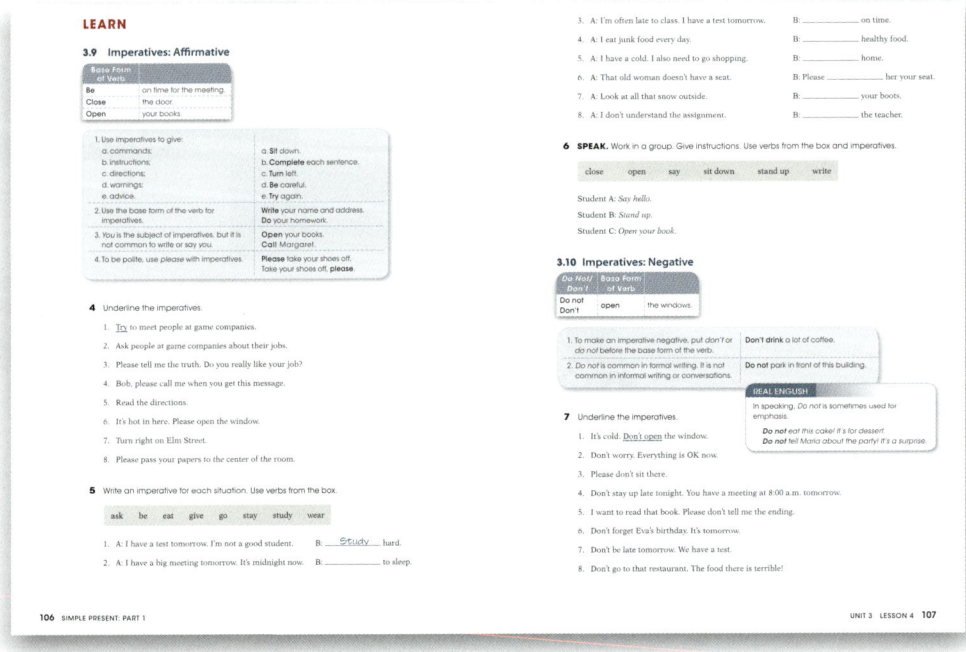

The **Learn** section features clear grammar charts and explanations followed by controlled practice of the grammar forms.

INSIDE A UNIT

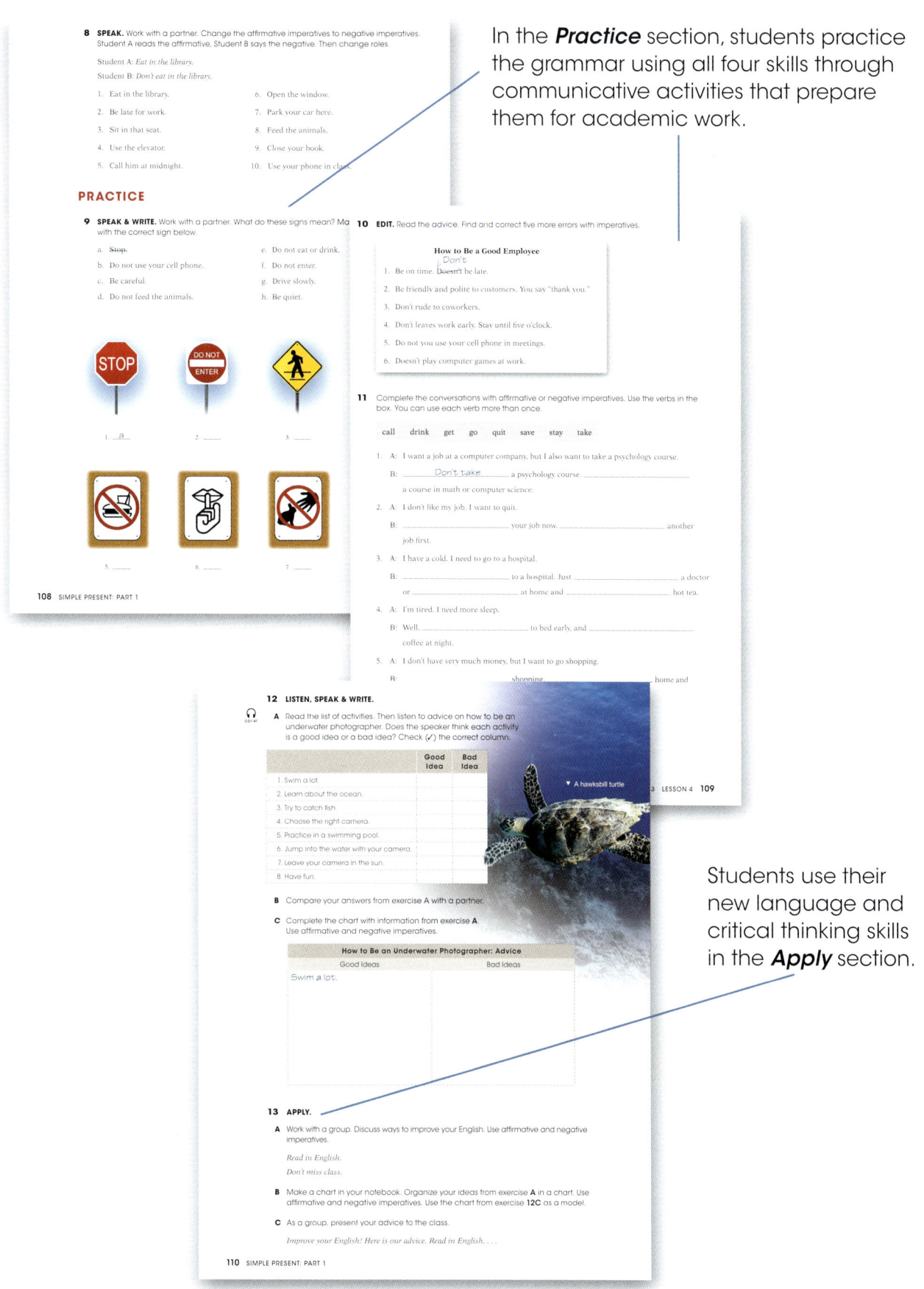

In the **Practice** section, students practice the grammar using all four skills through communicative activities that prepare them for academic work.

Students use their new language and critical thinking skills in the **Apply** section.

INSIDE A UNIT **xi**

INSIDE A UNIT

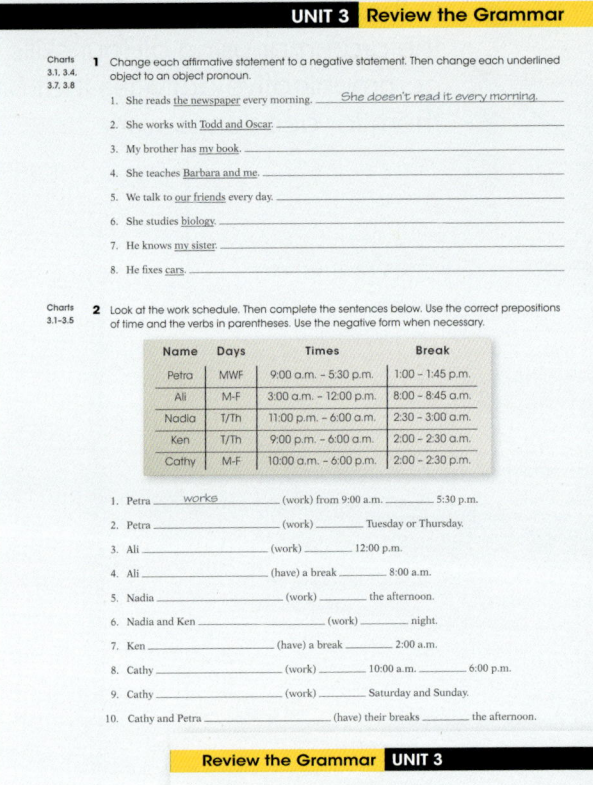

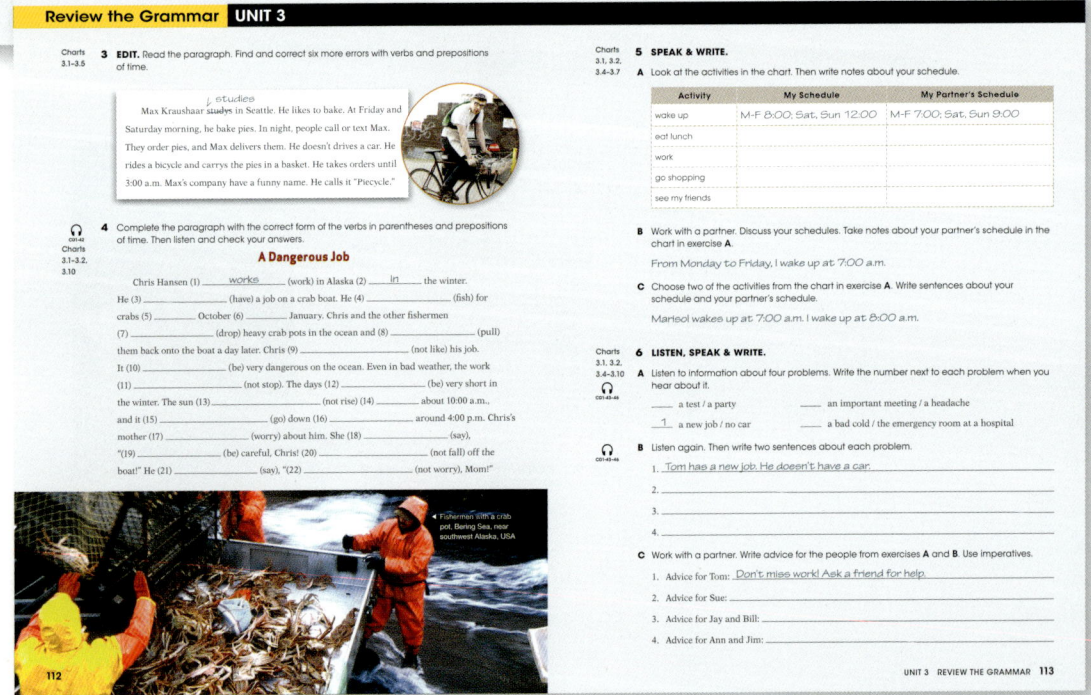

Review the Grammar gives students the opportunity to consolidate the grammar in their reading, writing, listening, and speaking.

INSIDE A UNIT

Connect the Grammar to Writing

1 READ & NOTICE THE GRAMMAR.

A Read the paragraph. What is the writer's advice for new teachers? Discuss with a partner.

My Job as a Teacher

I am a teacher. I work from 8:00 a.m. to 1:30 p.m. I teach four English classes. In class, I write on the board. I ask a lot of questions. I use pictures when I teach vocabulary. I don't arrive late. At home, I plan my lessons. I correct homework and tests. My advice for new teachers – learn your students' names on the first day.

GRAMMAR FOCUS

In the paragraph in exercise **A**, the writer uses the simple present to talk about habits or routines and schedules.

I **work** from 8:00 a.m. to 1:30 p.m.
I **don't arrive** late.

B Read the paragraph in exercise **A** again. Underline the verbs in the simple present. Circle the imperative. Then compare your answers with a partner.

C Complete the chart with information from the paragraph in exercise **A**. What does a teacher do in class? At home?

The Job of a Teacher	
In Class	At Home
She asks a lot of questions.	

Advice: Learn your students' names.

114 SIMPLE PRESENT: PART 1

Write about a Job

2 BEFORE YOU WRITE. Complete the chart with information about your job as a student. What do you do in class? At home? What advice do you have for new students? Use the chart from exercise **1C** as a model.

My Job as a Student	
In Class	At Home

Advice:

3 WRITE a paragraph about your job as a student. Give advice for new students. Use the information from your chart in exercise **2** and the paragraph in exercise **1A** to help you.

WRITING FOCUS — Indenting Paragraphs

Good writers indent the first line of a paragraph. To indent, begin the first line of a paragraph five spaces to the right.

   I am a teacher. I work from 8:00 a.m. to 1:30 p.m. I teach four English classes. In class, I write on the board. I ask a lot of questions.

4 SELF ASSESS. Read your paragraph. Underline the verbs in the simple present. Then use the checklist to assess your work.

☐ I did not put *be* in front of other verbs in the simple present. [3.1, 3.3]
☐ The verbs in the simple present are spelled correctly. [3.3]
☐ I used the base form of the verb for imperatives. [3.9, 3.10]
☐ The first line of my paragraph is indented. [WRITING FOCUS]

UNIT 3 CONNECT THE GRAMMAR TO WRITING 115

Connect the Grammar to Writing provides students with a clear model and a guided writing task where they first notice and then use the target grammar in one of a variety of writing genres.

UNIT 1 People
The Verb *Be*

▲ A father and son ride a bike to school, Uttar Pradesh, India.

Lesson 1
page 4

Simple Present of *Be*: Affirmative Statements; Contractions with *Be*

Lesson 2
page 11

Be + Singular/Plural Noun; Simple Present of *Be*: Negative Statements

Lesson 3
page 21

Descriptive Adjectives

Lesson 4
page 28

Possessive Adjectives; Possessive Nouns

Review the Grammar
page 35

Connect Grammar to Writing
page 38

LESSON 1   Simple Present of *Be*; Contractions with *Be*

EXPLORE

1 READ the conversation about greetings. Notice the words in **bold**.

Say hello!

Teacher:	Some people bow. Some people shake hands. How do *you* say hello? Please tell us. Also, please tell us your name and country.
Miyo:	Hello. **My name is** Miyo. **I'm** from Japan. In Japan, people bow.
Marie:	Hello, everyone. **It's** nice to meet you. **I'm** Marie. **I'm** from France. In France, we shake hands and kiss two times on the cheek!
Aran:	**My name is** Aran. **I'm** from Thailand. We put our hands together, like this.
Martin:	**I'm** Martin. This is Greta. **We're** from Germany. We usually shake hands.
David:	Nice to meet you! **I'm** from Italy. We shake hands, too. And in my family, we hug and kiss.
Teacher:	**It's** nice to meet you! **You're** all from different countries, and **your customs are** very interesting!

2 CHECK. Match each name with the correct country.

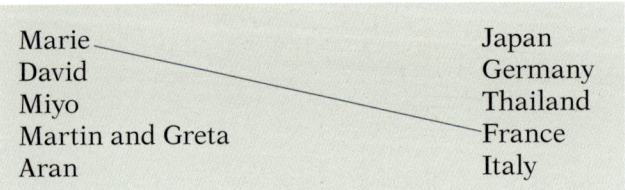

3 DISCOVER. Find these sentences in the conversation from exercise **1**. Write the missing words or letters. Then work with a partner and compare answers.

1. My name _____ Miyo.

2. I'_____ Marie.

3. You'_____ all from different countries, and your customs _____ very interesting.

◀ A Sikh boy from India gives a greeting.

LEARN

1.1 Simple Present of *Be*: Affirmative Statements

Singular			Plural		
Subject	Be		Subject	Be	
I	am	from Italy.	We Dave and I	are	from Italy.
You	are		You You and Anna		
He Mario The boy	is		They Mario and the girl The cars		
She Marie The girl					
It The car					

1. A sentence needs a subject and a verb.	Marta **is** from Mexico. Subject Verb ✓ Jon **is** from Canada. ✗ Jon from Canada.
2. The verb *be* has three forms in the present: *am, is, are*.	I **am** from Peru. She **is** from Spain. They **are** from Japan.
3. Subject pronouns can take the place of a noun as subject. Do not use a subject pronoun after a subject noun.	Rodrigo is Brazilian. **He** is from Recife. ✓ He is from Brazil. ✗ Rodrigo he is from Brazil.
4. *You* is for one person or more than one person.	Ed, **you** are late. (one person) Ed and Al, **you** are late. (more than one person)
5. Use *and* to join two nouns in the subject position.	Lucas **and** Ana are from Brazil. The boy **and** girl are from Brazil.

4 Circle the subject(s) in each sentences. Underline the verb *be*.

1. Hello. My name is Miyo.
2. Marie and Jean are from France.
3. I am from New York.
4. Chile is a country.
5. We are students.
6. Jim and Alex are teachers.
7. I am Japanese.
8. You are from Thailand.

5 Complete each sentence with *am*, *is*, or *are*.

1. I <u>am</u> a student.
2. They _____ from China.
3. Toronto _____ a city.
4. My name _____ Allen.
5. We _____ friends.
6. Tom _____ from my city.
7. Anna and I _____ friends.
8. I _____ from Mexico.
9. You _____ teachers.
10. She _____ from Colombia.

6 SPEAK. Work with a partner. Talk about yourself.

Hello. My name is . . . I'm from . . .

1.2 Contractions with *Be*

Full Form		
I	am	
You	are	
He		
Pierre		
She	is	from Canada.
Megan		
It		
We		
You	are	
They		

Contraction	
I'm	
You're	
He's	
Pierre's	
She's	from Canada.
Megan's	
It's	
We're	
You're	
They're	

1. A contraction is a short form. Contractions are used in conversation and informal writing.	A: Hello. My name's Larry. B: Nice to meet you. I'm Maria.
2. Use contractions with pronouns, nouns, and proper nouns. Proper nouns are names of specific people, places, and things.	**He's** from Mexico. My **name's** Lisa. **Yumiko's** from Japan. **Montreal's** a city in Canada. The **Burj Khalifa's** a building in Dubai.
3. The contraction *you're* is for one person or more than one person.	Ed, **you're** late. (one person) Ed and Al, **you're** late. (more than one person)

7 Complete the sentences. Use subject pronouns and contractions.

1. Carmela is from Italy. _She's_ Italian.
2. Tomas and Felix are from Mexico. _____ Mexican.
3. You and I are in class. _____ classmates.
4. I am from Beijing. _____ Chinese.
5. You are a student. _____ in class now.
6. The photograph is interesting. _____ on page 7.
7. Pablo is Spanish. _____ from Madrid.
8. The hotels are in Lima. _____ in Peru.

🎧 **8** Complete the conversations. Use contractions. Then listen and check your answers.
CD1-3

1. A: Hi. My name _'s_ Ali. I _'m_ from Saudi Arabia.

   B: Hi, Ali. It ____ nice to meet you. I ____ Maria.

2. A: Hello. I ____ Ted.

   B: Nice to meet you. My name ____ Chris. I'm from Vancouver.

   A: Oh, you ____ Canadian! I ____ from Canada, too. Toronto's my hometown.

3. A: Hello. We ____ in the same English class.

   B: Hi. You ____ Ricardo, right? I ____ Martin.

   A: That's right. You ____ from Germany.

   B: Yes, I am. How about you?

   A: I ____ from Mexico.

PRACTICE

9 Complete the sentences. Use *am*, *is*, or *are* in the first sentence. Use a subject pronoun and the correct contraction of *be* in the second sentence.

1. She __is__ Brazilian. _She's_ from Rio.
2. Aran and I _____ Thai. _____ from Bangkok.
3. I _____ Italian. _____ from Rome.
4. Emily _____ our teacher. _____ in class now.
5. Marc _____ from Montreal. _____ Canadian.
6. They _____ in the same class. _____ classmates.
7. He _____ Korean. _____ from Seoul.
8. You _____ my classmate. _____ in my English class.
9. My name _____ Olga. _____ Russian.
10. Quebec _____ a city. _____ in Canada.

10 Look at the class list. Then complete the paragraph below. Use information from the class list. Use contractions when possible.

English Conversation 101B: Class List

	Name	Nationality	Country	City
1.	Kyoko Takana	Japanese	Japan	Tokyo
2.	Abdul Al Dosari	Saudi	Saudi Arabia	Jeddah
3.	Marta Ramos	Mexican	Mexico	Puebla
4.	Feng Chen	Chinese	China	Beijing
5.	Diego Ruiz	Mexican	Mexico	Mexico City

My (1) __name's__ Kyoko. (2) _____ from Japan. (3) _____ a student in English Conversation 101B. My classmates (4) _____ from many different countries. Abdul is from Saudi Arabia. He (5) _____ from Jeddah. (6) _____ Chinese. He's from Beijing. Marta and Diego (7) _____ from Mexico. Marta's from Puebla, and (8) _____ from Mexico City. My teacher's name is Lisa. She's Canadian. (9) _____ from Toronto. I like my class. Lisa's a good teacher, and my classmates (10) _____ friendly and interesting.

11 LISTEN & SPEAK.

A Listen to students at a registration desk. Fill in the identity cards.

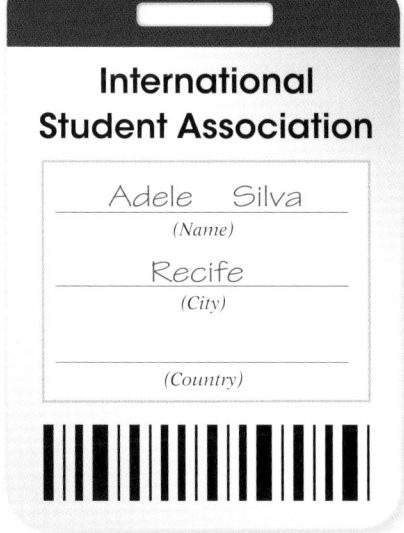
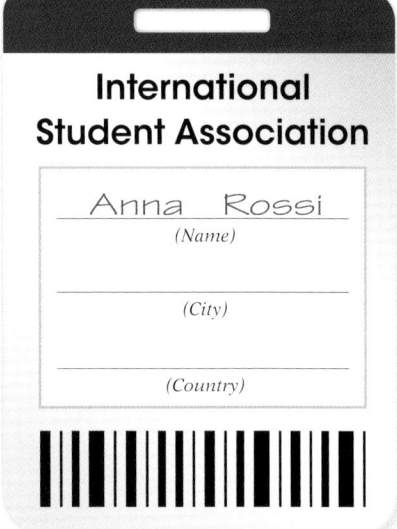

B Work with a partner. Say sentences about the students from exercise **A**.

Adele is from Brazil.

12 **EDIT.** Read the paragraph. Find and correct five more errors with subjects and *be*.

My name ⌄is Adele Silva. I from Recife. Is a city in Brazil. I a student in Boston. It a city in the United States. Is in Massachusetts.

13 **WRITE & SPEAK.**

A Complete the identity card with information about yourself.

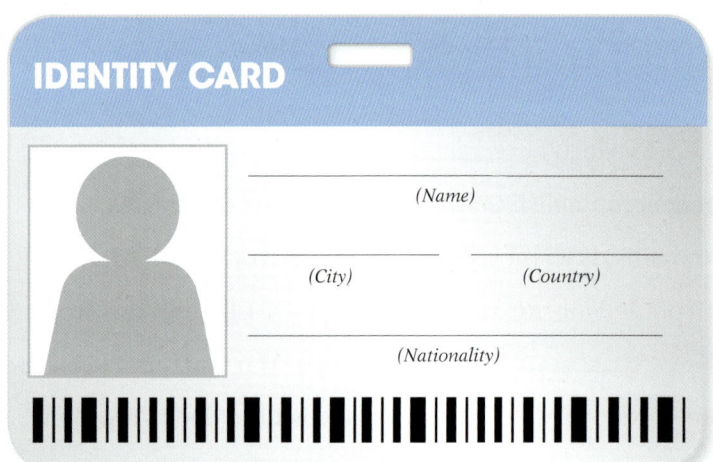

B Work with a partner. Share the information on your identity card from exercise **A**.

C Form a group with another pair of students. Introduce your partner.

This is Derya. She's from Turkey. . . .

> **REAL ENGLISH**
>
> Use *This is . . .* to introduce a person.
>
> **Hana:** *Nick, **this is** my brother, Hiro.*
> **Nick:** *Nice to meet you, Hiro.*
> **Hiro:** *Nice to meet you, too.*

14 **SPEAK.** Form a group with four or five other students. Student 1 introduces himself or herself to the group. Student 2 introduces himself or herself, then introduces Student 1. The next student introduces himself or herself and Students 1 and 2. The last student in the group introduces everyone.

Student 1: *Hi. My name's Yousef.*

Student 2: *Hello. My name's Luis, and this is Yousef.*

Student 3: *Hello. My name's Leyla. This is Yousef, and this is Luis.*

Student 4: *Hi. My name's Takeshi. This is Yousef, this is Luis, and this is Leyla.*

Student 5: *Hello. My name's Barbara. This is Yousef, this is Luis, ...*

15 **APPLY.** Write a paragraph about yourself in your notebook. Use the corrected paragraph in exercise **12** as a model.

Be + Singular Noun; *Be* + Plural Noun | **LESSON 2**

EXPLORE

 1 **READ** the article about two National Geographic explorers. Notice the words in **bold**.

Dereck and Beverly Joubert

Dereck and Beverly Joubert **are explorers** for National Geographic. For them, every day **is an adventure**. They explore Africa with their cameras. They **are filmmakers**. Beverly **is** also **a photographer**. They often work together. *The Last Lions* **is** one of their projects. It**'s a film** about a mother lion and her family. *The Last Lions* **is a book**, too. Dereck and Beverly **are authors**. They write many books about animals in Africa.

Beverly and Dereck are married. They live and work in Botswana, but they aren't from Botswana. They're from Johannesburg. It**'s a city** in South Africa.

▼ Filmmaker Dereck Joubert with his camera and a leopard

2 CHECK. Choose the correct information to complete each sentence about Dereck and Beverly Joubert.

1. Beverly Joubert is ____.   a. a photographer   b. a teacher
2. Johannesburg is ____.   a. a book   b. a city
3. Dereck and Beverly are from ____. a. South Africa   b. Botswana
4. *The Last Lions* is ____.   a. a magazine   b. a film and a book
5. Beverly and Dereck are ____.   a. married   b. single

3 DISCOVER. Complete the exercises to learn about the grammar in this lesson.

A Find these sentences in the reading from exercise **1** on page 11. Write the missing words.

1. For them, every day is ____ adventure.
2. Beverly is also ____ photographer.
3. It's ____ film about a mother lion and her family.

B Look at the sentences from exercise **A**. Then choose the correct rule below. Discuss your answers with your classmates and teacher.

1. Rule: Use *a* or *an* before a singular noun. (singular = one)
2. Rule: Use *a* or *an* before a plural noun. (plural = more than one)

▼ Photographer Beverly Joubert takes a photo of lions.

12 THE VERB *BE*

LEARN

1.3 Be + Singular Noun

Subject	Be	Singular Noun
I	am	a student.
South Africa	is	a country.
A lion	is	an animal.
You	are	an explorer.

1. *Singular* means *one*. Use *a* or *an* before a singular noun.	1 student = **a** student 1 apple = **an** apple
2. *A* and *an* have the same meaning. Use *a* before nouns beginning with a consonant sound. (Consonants = *b, c, d, f, g, h*, etc.)	She is **a** photographer. It is **a** book.
Use *an* before nouns beginning with a vowel sound. (Vowels = *a, e, i, o, u*)	He is **an** author. She is **an** explorer.
3. Do not use *a* or *an* before proper nouns.	✓ Lisa is **a** teacher. ✗ A Lisa is **a** teacher. ✓ Mexico is **a** country. ✗ A Mexico is **a** country.

> **REAL ENGLISH**
>
> Use *a* before nouns that begin with a vowel, but have a consonant sound.
>
> **a** university
>
> Use *an* before nouns that begin with a silent *h*.
>
> **an** hour

4 Complete each sentence with *a* or *an*.

1. Dereck is __a__ filmmaker.
2. He is _____ explorer.
3. *The Last Lions* is _____ film.
4. A lion is _____ animal.
5. Botswana is _____ country.
6. Tokyo is _____ city.
7. The Pacific is _____ ocean.
8. Yale is _____ university.
9. I am _____ student.
10. You are _____ artist.
11. Photography is _____ profession.
12. Angelina is _____ author.

5 Use the words to write sentences. Add the correct form of *be* and *a* or *an*.

1. Beverly / photographer _Beverly is a photographer._
2. A leopard / animal _____
3. Africa / continent _____
4. Harvard / university _____
5. She / professor _____
6. He / student _____
7. You / engineer _____
8. Photography / profession _____
9. Carmen / author _____
10. It / article _____

1.4 *Be* + Plural Noun

Subject	Be	Plural Noun
Beverly and Dereck	are	explorers.
You and Sam	are	engineers.
English and French	are	languages.
Botswana and South Africa	are	countries.

1. Plural means *more than one*. To make most nouns plural, add -*s*.	book–book**s** pen–pen**s** explorer–explorer**s**
2. To make nouns that end in -*ch*, -*sh*, -*ss*, -*x*, and -*z* plural, add -*es*.	class–class**es**, box–box**es**
To make nouns that end in *consonant* + -*y* plural, change the -*y* to -*i* and add -*es*.	city–cit**ies**, story–stor**ies**
3. Some plural nouns are irregular. They do not end in -*s*.	one man–two **men** one child–two **children** one woman–two **women** one person–two **people**
4. Use *are* after nouns joined by *and*.	Ken **and** Amy **are** students. Sandra **and** I **are** doctors.

See page **A1** for a list of spelling rules for plural nouns and a list of common irregular plural nouns.

6 Complete each sentence with *are* and the plural form of the noun in parentheses.

1. (explorer) Beverly and Dereck Joubert _____are explorers_____.
2. (woman) Many National Geographic explorers _____.
3. (animal) Leopards and lions _____.
4. (university) Oxford and Yale _____.
5. (student) We _____.
6. (class) English 101 and Biology 201 _____.
7. (country) Mexico and Brazil _____.
8. (continent) Africa and Asia _____.
9. (city) Toronto and Montreal _____.
10. (language) Arabic and Japanese _____.

7 **PRONUNCIATION.** Read the chart and listen to the examples. Then complete the exercises.

PRONUNCIATION — Plural Nouns: -s and -es Endings

The endings of regular plural nouns have three sounds: /s/, /z/, /əz/.

1. Say **/s/** after nouns that end with /f/, /k/, /p/, /t/, and /θ/ sounds.
   photographs   books   cups   students   baths
2. Say **/z/** after nouns that end with /b/, /d/, /g/, /l/, /m/, /n/, /ŋ/, /r/, /v/ sounds and vowel sounds (a, e, i, o, u).
   labs   beds   bags   calls   exams   pens   things   cars   gloves   shoes
3. Say **/əz/** after nouns that end with /tʃ/, /ks/, /dʒ/, /ʃ/, /s/, and /z/ sounds.
   watches   boxes   pages   dishes   classes   buzzes

See page **A4** for a guide to pronunciation symbols.

A Listen and circle the final sound you hear for each plural noun. Then listen again and repeat each word.

1. teachers   /s/ (/z/) /əz/
2. desks   /s/ /z/ /əz/
3. glasses   /s/ /z/ /əz/
4. cities   /s/ /z/ /əz/
5. languages   /s/ /z/ /əz/
6. stories   /s/ /z/ /əz/
7. things   /s/ /z/ /əz/
8. notebooks   /s/ /z/ /əz/
9. exercises   /s/ /z/ /əz/
10. universities /s/ /z/ /əz/
11. professions /s/ /z/ /əz/
12. photos   /s/ /z/ /əz/

B Listen again and repeat each word.

C Work with a partner. Student A, say a singular noun from the box. Student B, say the plural form of the noun.

actor	book	city	country	man	student
animal	box	class	lion	pen	teacher

Student A: *animal*

Student B: *animals*

1.5 Simple Present of *Be:* Negative Statements

Full Forms			Contractions		
I **am**			I**'m**		
You **are**			You**'re**		
He **is**			He**'s**		
She **is**	**not**	from India.	She**'s**	**not**	from China.
It **is**			It**'s**		
We **are**			We**'re**		
You **are**			You**'re**		
They **are**			They**'re**		

1. To make a negative statement, put *not* after *be* in the present.	I **am not** a photographer.
2. There are two negative contractions for *is* and *are* in the present.	**'s not = isn't** He**'s not** from Argentina. He **isn't** from Argentina. **'re not = aren't** They**'re not** sisters. They **aren't** sisters.
3. There is only one negative contraction for *am* in the present.	I**'m not** from Italy.

8 Complete the conversations. Use contractions and the words in parentheses. More than one negative form may be possible.

1.   A: Marc's a photographer.

   (a filmmaker) B: No, <u>he isn't a photographer. He's a filmmaker. OR he's not a photographer. He's a filmmaker.</u>

2.   A: They're from Botswana.

   (South Africa) B: No, _____.

3.   A: Justin and Costa are brothers.

   (friends)   B: No, _____.

4. A: It's a book.
   (film) B: No, _____.

5. A: He's a teacher.
   (a student) B: No, _____.

6. A: Rui and Tiago are from Brazil.
   (Portugal) B: No, _____.

7. A: She's a doctor.
   (an engineer) B: No, _____.

8. A: Julia is an author.
   (an artist) B: No, _____.

9. A: Sylvia is Canadian.
   (French) B: No, _____.

10. A: London is a country.
    (a city) B: No, _____.

11. A: The Amazon is an ocean.
    (a river) B: No, _____.

12. A: Botswana is a city.
    (a country) B: No, _____.

13. A: Asia and Africa are countries.
    (continents) B: No, _____.

14. A: Spanish and Chinese are countries.
    (nationalities) B: No, _____.

PRACTICE

9 Use the words to write negative statements. Use contractions. Add *a* or *an* if necessary. More than one negative form may be possible.

1. Korea / city _____ Korea isn't a city. _____
2. Nora and I / explorers _____
3. Seoul and Tokyo / countries _____
4. Nick / Brazilian _____
5. I / teacher _____
6. You / from Mexico _____
7. She / filmmaker _____
8. We / actors _____
9. He / from Japan _____
10. It / film _____

10 EDIT. Read the sentences. Find and correct five more errors with singular and plural nouns, *a/an*, and negatives.

1. Madrid, London, and Prague are cit~~y~~. (ies)
2. Europe aren't a country. It's a continent.
3. Iceland and Ireland is islands. Water is all around them.
4. The Rhine is river in Europe. It's in Germany.
5. The Alps aren't rivers. They're mountains.
6. The Atlantic isn't a river. It's a ocean.
7. Austria and Romania are countries.
8. Lisbon isn't in Spain. It in Portugal.

11 SPEAK. Work in a group. Look at the lists of words below. One word from each list does not belong. Talk about the lists of words with your group. Use the words from the box to help you. Use negative forms and *a* or *an* if necessary.

animals	continents	foods	people
cities	countries	languages	school supplies

A teacher, an actress, and a bus driver are people. A desk isn't a person.

1. teacher — bus driver — ~~desk~~ — actress
2. banana — pencil — pen — eraser
3. Ireland — Spain — Sweden — Rome
4. egg — apple — orange — book
5. French — English — Chinese — India
6. lion — dog — horse — notebook
7. London — Romania — Paris — Berlin
8. Europe — Asia — Tokyo — Africa

12 SPEAK, LISTEN & WRITE.

A Work with a partner. Look at the photos below and guess each person's profession.

B Listen to the conversations and write the correct profession for each person.

| doctor | musicians | professor |

1. Name: Larissa Santos
   Profession: _____
   Country of origin: _____

2. Name: Liz Stanford and Jude Wilson
   Profession: _____
   Country of origin: _____

3. Name: Chu Ying Liu
   Profession: _____
   Country of origin: _____

C Listen again. Write the correct country of origin for each person.

D Work with a partner. Compare your answers from exercises **B** and **C**.

E Use the words to write correct sentences about the people in exercise **B**. Use negatives if necessary.

1. Larissa / from England <u>Larissa isn't from England. She's from Brazil.</u>
2. Chu Ying / doctor _____
3. Jude and Liz / professors _____
4. Jude / from China _____
5. Liz / professor _____
6. Chu Ying / from China _____
7. Larissa / musician _____
8. Liz / from Brazil _____

13 APPLY. Write three true statements and two false sentences about students in your class. Use the verb *be*. Then read your sentences to a partner. Your partner will say "true" or "false" after each statement and correct the false statements.

Student A: *Carlos is a student.*

Student B: *True.*

Student A: *Ali is from China.*

Student B: *False. Ali isn't from China. He's from Saudi Arabia.*

Descriptive Adjectives | **LESSON 3**

EXPLORE

 1 READ the article about Tank the Bear and Doug Seus. Notice the words in **bold**.

Tank the Bear

Tank the Bear is a **huge** grizzly bear from Utah in the United States. He is also a **famous** television and movie star. He's in a lot of television shows and movies. Tank is **huge** and **heavy**, but he's not a **typical** grizzly bear. Most grizzly bears are **wild**[1] and **dangerous**, but Tank isn't. In fact, he's **gentle** and **friendly** with his trainer Doug Seus.

Doug and his wife Lynn are animal trainers. They work with many **different** animals at their home in Utah. Doug is a **brave** man. His job is **dangerous**. It is also **difficult**, but for Doug it's **fun**. He's **patient**[2] and **kind** with Tank. Tank is a member of his family!

[1] **Wild** animals live in nature.
[2] A **patient** person is calm and does not get angry easily.

▶ Animal trainer Doug Seus with a huge grizzly bear named Bart. Bart died in 2000.

UNIT 1   LESSON 3   **21**

2 CHECK. Read the list of adjectives in the chart. Who does each adjective describe? Put a check (✓) in the correct column. Then work with a partner and compare charts.

Adjective	Tank	Doug
brave		✓
kind		
famous		
patient		
friendly		
huge		
gentle		
heavy		

3 DISCOVER. Complete the exercises to learn about the grammar in this lesson.

A Find these sentences in the reading from exercise **1** on page 21. Write the missing words.

1. Tank is _____ and _____ , but he's not a typical grizzly bear.

2. Doug is a _____ man.

3. His job is _____ . It is also _____ , but for Doug it's _____ .

4. He's _____ and _____ with Tank.

B Read the statements. Circle **T** for *true* or **F** for *false*. Then discuss your answers with your classmates and teacher.

1. Adjectives describe nouns. T F

2. Adjectives describe pronouns. T F

◀ Douglas Chadwick, author, with Tank the bear.

LEARN

1.6 Descriptive Adjectives

Subject	Be	Adjective
I	am	tall.
He	is	strong.
We	are	happy.
They	are	late.

	Adjective	Noun
He is a	tall	man.
She is an	interesting	person.

1. Adjectives describe nouns or pronouns.	He is **patient**. They are **friendly**.
2. Adjectives often come after the verb *be*. They can also come before nouns.	We are **busy**. We are **busy** people.
3. The form of an adjective does not change. An adjective is the same for singular and plural nouns and pronouns.	✓ The room is **big**. ✓ The rooms are **big**. ✗ The rooms are bigs.
4. Use *a* or *an* before adjectives + singular nouns. Use *a* before an adjective beginning with a consonant sound. Use *an* with an adjective beginning with a vowel sound.	He's **a** good person and **an** excellent friend. She's **a** good doctor. He's **an** excellent teacher.

> **REAL ENGLISH**
>
> Two adjectives are often used to describe a noun or pronoun. Use *and* to connect two adjectives.
>
> He is tall **and** strong.
> Reika is smart **and** funny.
> It's a black **and** red book.

4 Underline the adjective in each sentence. Then draw an arrow to the nouns or pronouns they describe.

1. It is an <u>interesting</u> article.
2. Tank is famous.
3. Doug is brave.
4. They are friendly.
5. He is an excellent teacher.
6. Canada is a huge country.
7. She is funny.
8. Sandra is young.
9. I am late.
10. You are kind.

5 Put the words in the correct order to make sentences. Add *a* or *an* if necessary.

1. Sandra / amazing / is / artist _Sandra is an amazing artist._
2. big / Bears / are _____
3. am / I / happy _____
4. famous / Akira Kurosawa / filmmaker / is _____
5. engineer / David / is / good _____
6. is / new / My phone _____
7. Rome / city / is / interesting _____
8. are / We / tired _____
9. is / difficult / language / Chinese _____
10. am / excellent / I / student _____

PRACTICE

6 Complete the exercises.

A Look at the adjectives in the box. Check (✓) the adjectives you know. Ask your teacher for help with the adjectives you do not know.

☐ big	☐ difficult	☐ easy	☐ funny	☐ nice	☐ quiet	☐ small
☐ clean	☐ dirty	☐ friendly	☐ happy	☐ noisy	☐ serious	☐ smart

B Use the verb *be* and adjectives from exercise **A**. Complete each sentence. Add *a/an* if necessary.

1. Our teacher _is friendly_ .
2. My classmates _____ students.
3. This exercise _____ .
4. We _____ .
5. I _____ .
6. My friends _____ people.
7. English _____ language.
8. This classroom _____ .
9. This building _____ .
10. My hometown _____ .

7 EDIT. Read the paragraph. Find and correct four more errors with adjectives and *a/an*.

A Sherpa Climber

This is a photograph of a Sherpa climber on Mount Everest. It's a amazing photo. Mount Everest is beautiful mountain, but it's dangerous. Fura Gyaljen is Sherpa climber. He is strong. His job is difficult and dangerous. Sherpa climbers are braves people.

◀ Fura Gyaljen, a Sherpa climber, on an ice field on Mt. Everest in Nepal

8 SPEAK, LISTEN & WRITE.

A Work with a partner. Read the job advertisement. What kind of person is right for the job? Discuss with your partner. Check (✓) the adjectives in the box below.

A perfect person for this job is . . .

☐ busy	☐ funny	☐ nice	☐ retired
☐ experienced	☐ hardworking	☐ old	☐ smart
☐ friendly	☐ helpful	☐ patient	☐ young

B Listen to the messages. Which adjectives from exercise **A** does each person use to describe himself or herself? Take notes next to each photo.

Kevin

funny

Liz

Jane

C Write two sentences about each person. Use your notes from exercise **B**.

Kevin: _He is funny._

Liz: _____

Jane: _____

D Work with a partner. Make a decision. Who is the best person for the job? Who is not good for the job? Use adjectives to talk about each person from exercise **B**.

Kevin isn't a good person for this job. He is young. He isn't experienced.

26 THE VERB *BE*

9 SPEAK & WRITE.

A Work with a partner. Describe yourself. Use adjectives from exercise **8A** on page 25 and your own ideas to describe yourself.

I'm young and hardworking. . . .

B Complete the Venn diagram. One partner is Student A. One partner is Student B. Write your adjectives from exercise **8A** on page 25 on the correct side of the Venn diagram.

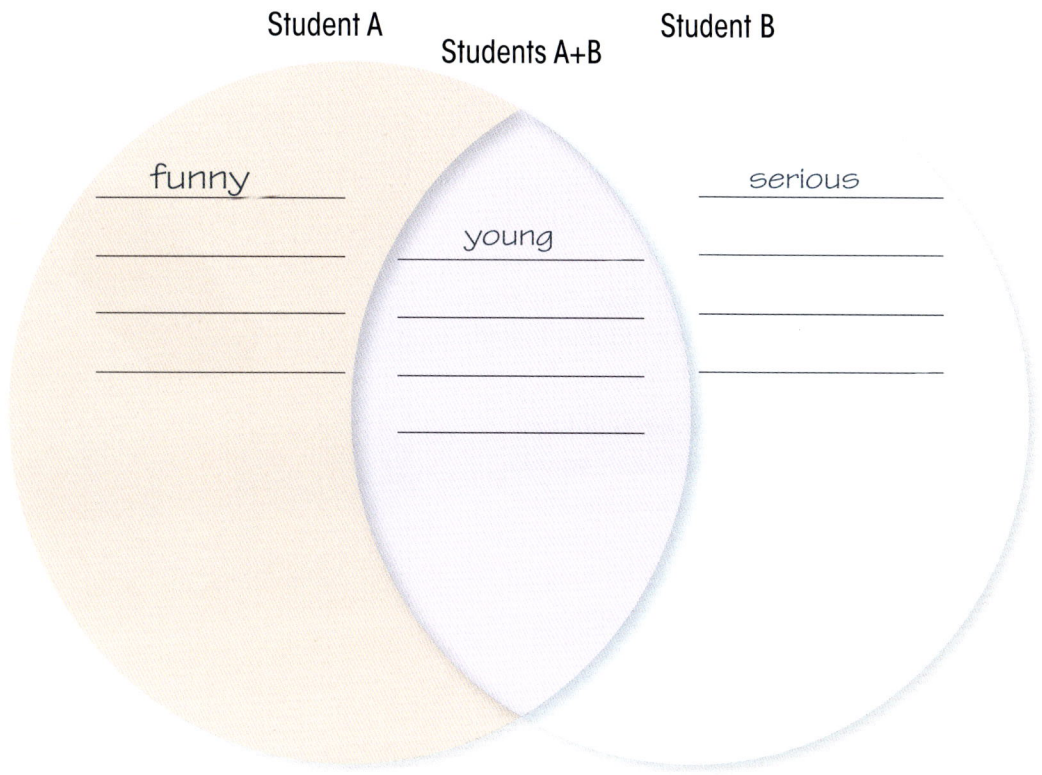

C Write sentences about you and your partner. Use the information from your Venn diagram in exercise **B**.

> I am funny.
> Alex is serious.
> We are both young.

> **REAL ENGLISH**
>
> Use *both* when something is true about two people or two things.
>
> *Yuri and Luisa are **both** good students.*
>
> *Russia and Canada are **both** huge countries.*

10 APPLY.

A Choose a person in your class. Write a short paragraph about him or her. Do not use his or her name. Use the model below to help you. Use adjectives from exercise **8A** on page 25 and your own ideas.

> She is friendly and kind. She's an excellent student. She's single. She's young. She is short and funny. Her name is _____.

B Read your paragraph from exercise **A** to your classmates. Do not say the person's name. Your classmates will guess.

LESSON 4 Possessive Adjectives; Possessive Nouns

EXPLORE

 1 READ the article about a family of reindeer herders. Notice the words in **bold**.

Sami Reindeer Herders

Nils Peder Gaup is from Norway, 200 miles (almost 322 kilometers) north of the Arctic Circle. It is very cold there. Gaup is a Sami reindeer herder. He looks after large groups of reindeer and uses them for food and clothing. **Gaup's** wife is a reindeer herder, too. **Her** name is Ingrid. **Their** five children also help.

A reindeer herder's job is not easy. Every year Gaup and **his** family travel a long way with the reindeer to find food. They leave **their** homes and live on snowy mountains and frozen lakes for long periods of time. They sleep in special tents called *lávuts*. The Gaups take good care of the reindeer. The Gaups love **their** work, but clearly, it is not just a job. It is **their** life.

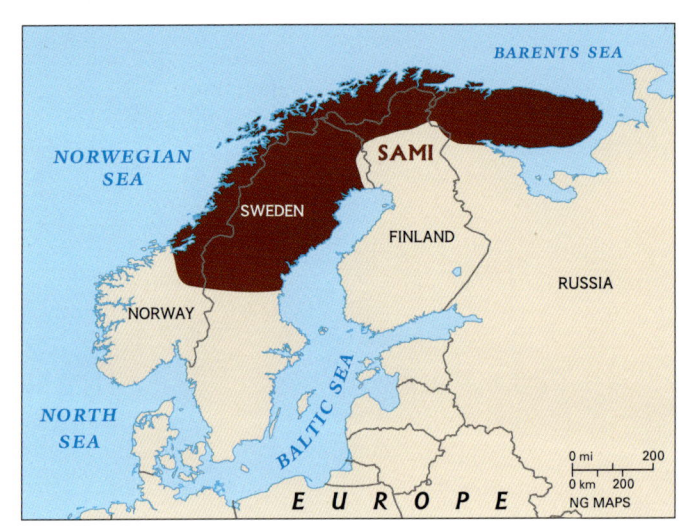

▼ Nils Peder Gaup with his reindeer

▶ TK

28 THE VERB *BE*

▸ Nils Peder Gaup's brother, Mahtta, with a herd of reindeer

2 CHECK. Read the statements. Circle **T** for *true* or **F** for *false*.

1. Nils Peder Gaup is from Sweden.   T   F
2. Ingrid is not a reindeer herder.   T   F
3. The job of a reindeer herder is difficult.   T   F
4. The Gaup children are reindeer herders, too. T   F

3 DISCOVER. Complete the exercise to learn about the grammar in this lesson.

A Find these sentences in the reading from exercise **1**. Write the missing words.

1. Gaup's wife is a reindeer herder, too. _____ name is Ingrid.
2. Every year Gaup and _____ family travel a long way with the reindeer to find food.
3. The Gaups love _____ work, but clearly, it is not just a job. It is _____ life.

B Look at the sentences from exercise **A**. Who does *her* refer to? Who does *his* refer to? Who does *their* refer to? Discuss with your classmates and teacher.

UNIT 1   LESSON 4   **29**

LEARN

1.7 Possessive Adjectives

Subject Pronouns	Possessive Adjectives	Example Sentences
I	my	I am from India. **My** name is Manik.
you	your	You are a student. **Your** class is in Room 209.
he	his	He is from Norway. **His** name's Lars.
she	her	She is married. **Her** husband is a scientist.
it	its	It is a friendly dog. **Its** name is Nanook.
we	our	We are French. **Our** home is in Paris.
you	your	You are great photographers. **Your** photos are beautiful.
they	their	They are actors. **Their** movie is funny.

1. Possessive adjectives show possession or relationships.	**Our** apartment is small. **My** brother is funny and smart.
2. Possessive adjectives come before nouns.	**His** <u>eyes</u> are brown. Nora is a scientist. **Her** <u>job</u> is very interesting.
3. Use *your* for one person or more than one person.	Max, **your** friend is here. Max and Jesse, **your** friend is here.

4 Underline the subject pronouns. Then complete each sentence with the correct possessive adjective.

1. <u>They</u> are reindeer herders. ___Their___ children are reindeer herders, too.

2. We are Spanish. Toledo is _____ hometown.

3. He is from India, but _____ home is in the United States.

4. You are a good cook, Maria. _____ soup is delicious!

5. I am a grandfather. _____ grandson is three years old.

6. We are students. _____ class is in Room 206.

7. She is tall. _____ brothers are tall, too.

8. You are good teachers. _____ students are very lucky.

9. She is married. _____ husband is Russian.

10. I am from Portugal. _____ name's Carlos.

11. He is an author. _____ books are interesting.

12. They are students. _____ teacher's name is Paula.

13. You are late. _____ seat is over there.

14. It's a nice car. _____ seats are comfortable.

1.8 Possessive Nouns

Singular	Plural
The **student's** last name is Ming.	The **students'** last names are Ming and Diaz.
My **neighbor's** house is small.	My **neighbors'** houses are small.

1. To make a singular noun possessive, add an apostrophe (') + -s to the end of the noun.	The **baby's** room is small. **Lisa's** car is green.
2. To make most plural nouns possessive, add an apostrophe (') after the -s.	The **babies'** room is small. My **brothers'** names are Ted and Jeremy.
3. To make an irregular plural noun possessive, add an apostrophe (') + -s to the end of the noun.	The **children's** room is small.

5 Circle the correct possessive form to complete each sentence.

1. Susan is **(Ken's)** / **Kens'** wife.
2. A **doctors'** / **doctor's** job is not easy.
3. My uncle Mike is my **fathers'** / **father's** brother.
4. My **sons'** / **son's** names are Sam and Leo.
5. The **girl's** / **girls'** dress is yellow.
6. My **mother's** / **mothers'** name is Lenka.
7. The **children's** / **childrens'** room is messy.
8. **Italys'** / **Italy's** flag is green, white, and red.

6 Write the correct possessive form of the word in parentheses to complete each conversation.

1. A: What's _____Aileen's_____ (Aileen) last name?

   B: It's Peterson.

2. A: Is this the _____ (women) room?

   B: No, it's the _____ (men) room!

3. A: Where is _____ (Kim) coat?

   B: It's over there.

4. A: Your _____ (roommates) names are Carl and Matt, right?

   B: No, their names are Kevin and Mike.

5. A: My _____ (husband) hometown is Prague.

   B: Oh, Prague is a beautiful city!

6. A: Where is your _____ (children) school?

   B: It's on Elm Street.

PRACTICE

7 Rewrite each sentence. Replace each possessive noun with a possessive adjective.

1. Nils Peder's job is dangerous. _His job is dangerous._
2. Ingrid's children are herders, too. _____
3. The workers' company is successful. _____
4. The children's grandfather is famous. _____
5. Elena's office is huge. _____
6. David's house is beautiful. _____
7. Maria's grandmother is 89 years old. _____
8. The hotel's rooms are small. _____

8 EDIT. Read the paragraph. Find and correct five more errors with possessive nouns and possessive adjectives.

> Teresa Pereira is from Portugal. She's Portuguese. Óbidos is ~~his~~ ↓her hometown. Her father name is Antonio, and her mother's name is Fatima. They are teachers. Teresas brother is an engineer. He name is Pedro. His wife name is Luisa. She's a doctor. They children's names are Rui and Eduardo.

◄ Óbidos, Portugal

9 SPEAK & WRITE.

A Look at the words for family members in the box. Check (✓) the words you know. Ask your teacher about any words you do not know.

- ☐ aunt
- ☐ brother
- ☐ brother-in-law
- ☐ cousin
- ☐ daughter
- ☐ grandparents
- ☐ husband
- ☐ nephew
- ☐ niece
- ☐ sister
- ☐ sister-in-law
- ☐ son
- ☐ uncle
- ☐ wife

B Look at the Perez family tree. Then complete the sentences that follow with the correct possessive adjectives and possessive nouns.

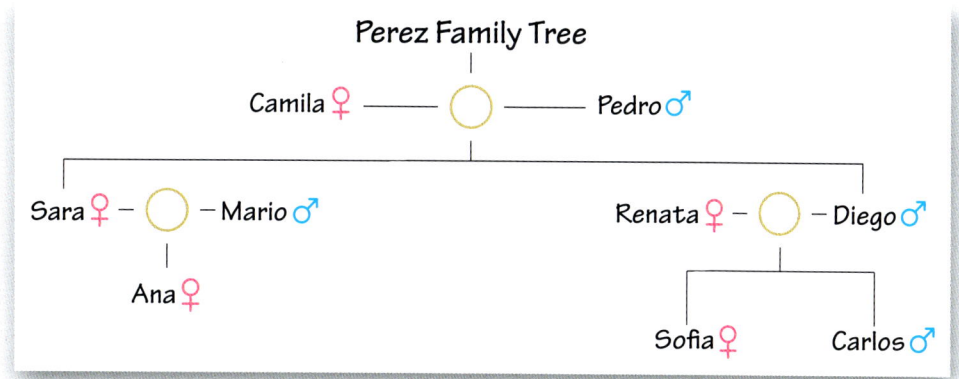

1. Camila and Pedro are married. _____Their_____ daughter's name is Sara. _____ son's name is Diego.

2. Diego is _____ brother.

3. Diego is married. _____ wife's name is Renata.

4. Sara is married, too. _____ husband's name is Mario.

5. Mario is not Diego's brother. He's _____ brother-in-law. He's _____ brother-in-law, too.

6. Sofia is Sara's niece, and Carlos is _____ nephew.

7. Carlos and Sofia are _____ cousins.

8. Diego is _____ uncle, and Renata is _____ aunt.

9. Renata is not Pedro's daughter. She's _____ daughter-in-law.

10. Camila and Pedro are not Ana's parents. They are _____ grandparents.

C Write two sentences about each person. Use possessive nouns and possessive adjectives. Use the Perez family tree from exercise **B** and the words from exercise **A** to help you.

Camila: _Camila is Pedro's wife._

Mario: _____

Carlos: _____

10 LISTEN & SPEAK.

A Listen to the information about another family and complete the family tree. Use the names from the box.

| Jena | Rylie | Tim | Doug |

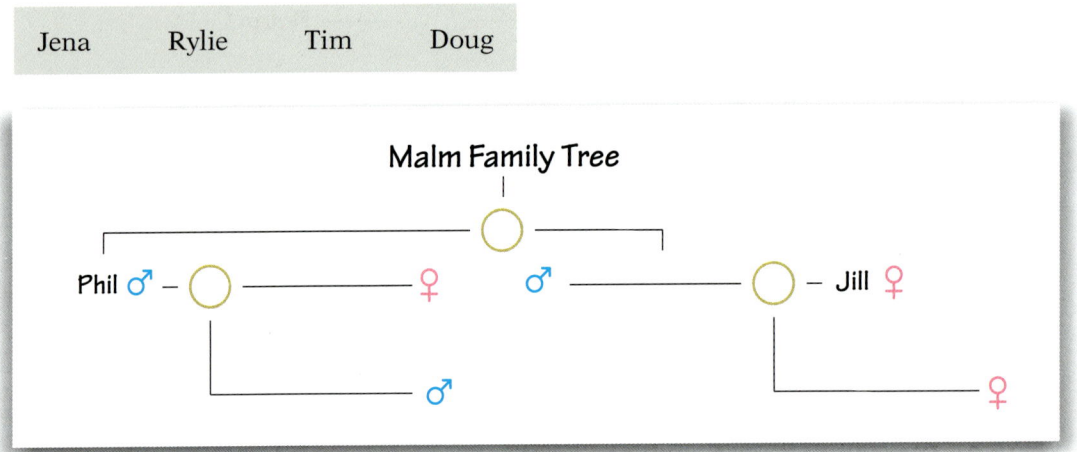

B Compare your answers from exercise **A** with a partner. Then make sentences about the Malm Family Tree.

11 APPLY.

A Draw your family tree in your notebook and include your family members' names. Use the Perez family tree from exercise **9B** on page 33 as a model.

B Work with a partner. Talk about your family tree. Talk about your family members' jobs and where they are from.

My father Alvaro is a farmer. His father is a farmer, too. They are from Venezuela. . . .

34 THE VERB *BE*

UNIT 1 Review the Grammar

Charts 1.1–1.8

1 Put the words and contractions in the correct order to make sentences.

1. Pat / 'm / I _____ I'm Pat.
2. name / My / Jim / is _____
3. sister / She / Pat's / is _____
4. parents / are / We / Carl's _____
5. Ken's / is / brother / tall _____
6. isn't / My / dangerous / job _____
7. friend / person / is / an / interesting / My _____
8. an / It / easy / 's / exercise _____

Charts 1.1–1.8

2 **LISTEN** and write the sentences you hear. (CD1-17)

1. I'm a teacher.
2. _____
3. _____
4. _____
5. _____
6. _____
7. _____
8. _____

Charts 1.1, 1.3, 1.4, 1.6

3 **WRITE & SPEAK.**

A Write sentences. Use one of the adjectives in parentheses and your own ideas. Use the correct form of *be*. Add *a* or *an* if necessary.

1. (famous / small) university _____ Harvard is a famous university.
2. (good / terrible) actor _____
3. (kind / funny) people _____
4. (great / scary / funny) movie _____
5. (excellent / terrible) cars _____
6. (small / huge / beautiful) country _____
7. (good / great) soccer player _____
8. (safe / dangerous / interesting) city _____

B Share your sentences from exercise **A** with a partner.

Review the Grammar   UNIT 1

Charts 1.1–1.8

4 Write a negative and then an affirmative statement. Use the words in parentheses and the correct form of *be*. Use a pronoun in the second sentence.

1. (Ed / funny / serious) _Ed's not funny. He's serious._
2. (You / late / early) _____
3. (My / car / old / new) _____
4. (She / from Mexico / from Chile) _____
5. (They / engineers / explorers) _____
6. (I / photographer / student) _____
7. (We / lazy students / hardworking students) _____
8. (My mother's father / my uncle / my grandfather) _____

Charts 1.1–1.7

5 Complete each sentence with *is/isn't* or *are/aren't* and the singular or plural form of words from the box.

| dangerous animal | easy language | interesting profession | small city |
| difficult class | good student | large country | warm continent |

1. Lions and bears _are dangerous animals_.
2. You and I _____.
3. Tokyo _____.
4. Geometry and Biology 101 _____.
5. French _____.
6. Actor and artist _____.
7. Belgium and Costa Rica _____.
8. Antarctica _____.

Charts 1.1–1.8

6 EDIT. Read the conversation. Find and correct five more errors with the verb *be* and *a/an*.

> I'm from Brazil. Brazil is ~~an~~ *a* big country. It's a beautiful country. My family's home are in Rio. We are all in different cities now. My mother and father is at our home in Rio. My sister and I aren't in Rio. We am students in London. My brother is in Boston. He's a architect. He is married with two children. My nephews are twins. They is six years old.

36   THE VERB *BE*

Charts 1.1–1.5

7 Complete the conversation with affirmative or negative forms of *be*. Add *a* or *an* if necessary.

Sally: This photo __is__ interesting.
Jim: Yes, it _____. He's ˅an amazing gymnast.
Sally: He _____ gymnast. He's acrobat.
Jim: Oh, right.
Sally: Chinese acrobats _____ famous.
Jim: That' _____ true. They' _____ very good.

▲ A juggler with dishes, Beijing, People's Republic of China

Charts 1.1–1.3, 1.5, 1.7, 1.8

8 LISTEN & WRITE.

CD1-18

A Listen and choose the best name for the school.

a. Ling High School
b. Ling School of Art
c. Ling School for Acrobats

CD1-18

B Listen again. Write each name from the box next to the correct person in the picture.

| Jing | Li | Min | Sheng | Wu |

C Write five sentences about the people in the picture. Use the words in the box and information from exercises **A** and **B**.

| Sheng | wife | grandmother | father | children |

1. _____
2. _____
3. _____
4. _____
5. _____

UNIT 1 REVIEW THE GRAMMAR 37

Connect the Grammar to Writing

1 READ & NOTICE THE GRAMMAR.

A Read the paragraph. Who are the writer's family members? Discuss with a partner.

Jay and Hayley

My brother's name is Jay. He's 29. He's married. Hayley is his wife. She's my sister-in-law. They're in Scotland. Jay is a teacher. Hayley isn't a teacher. She's a salesclerk. They're very kind.

GRAMMAR FOCUS

In the paragraph in exercise **A**, the writer uses the verb *be* to give information about family members.

Remember: Use *is* when the subject is singular. Use *are* when the subject is plural.

My brother's name **is** Jay.
She'**s** my sister-in-law.
They'**re** very kind.

B Read the paragraph in exercise **A** again. Underline affirmative and negative forms of the verb *be*. Then work with a partner and compare answers.

C Complete the chart with information about the writer's family members in exercise **A**.

Family Members		
Name	Jay	Hayley
Family member	Brother	
Age		X
Married / Single		
Job		
Other information		

Write about Two Family Members

2 BEFORE YOU WRITE. Complete the chart with information about two of your family members. Use the chart in exercise **1C** as a model.

Family Members		
Name		
Family member		
Age		
Married / Single		
Job		
Other information		

3 WRITE a paragraph. Use the information from your chart in exercise **2** and the paragraph in exercise **1A** to help you.

> **WRITING FOCUS   Capital Letters and Periods**
>
> A statement begins with a capital letter and ends with a period.
> *He's 29.*
> *She's a sales clerk.*

4 SELF ASSESS. Read your paragraph. Underline the verb *be* in your paragraph. Then use the checklist to assess your work.

☐ I used the correct form of *be*. [1.3, 1.4, 1.5]
☐ I used the correct possessive nouns and adjectives. [1.7, 1.8]
☐ I used a capital letter at the beginning of each statement. [WRITING FOCUS]
☐ I put a period at the end of each statement. [WRITING FOCUS]

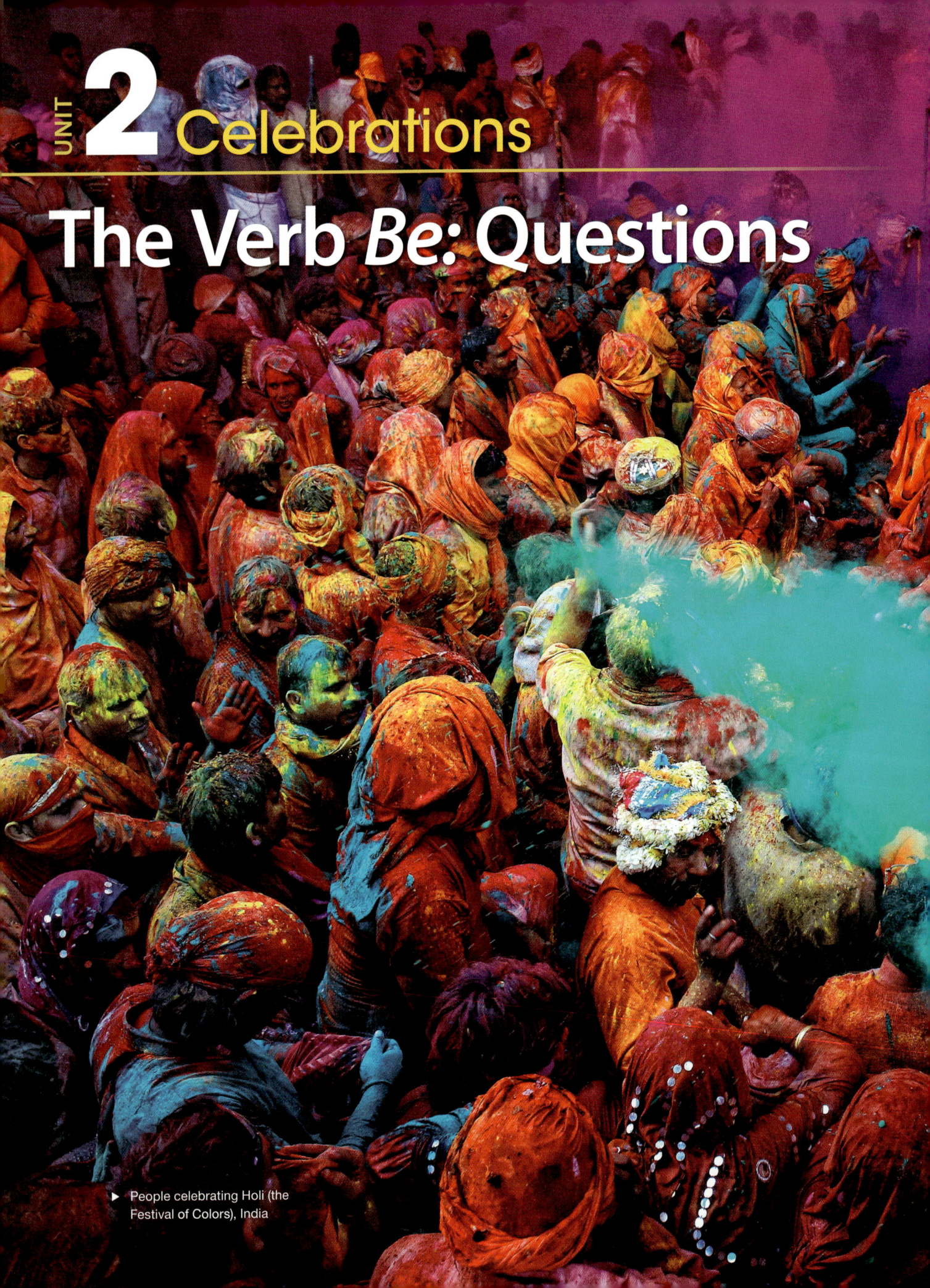

UNIT 2 Celebrations

The Verb *Be:* Questions

▶ People celebrating Holi (the Festival of Colors), India

Lesson 1
page 42

Simple Present of *Be*: Yes/No Questions

Lesson 2
page 50

Prepositions of Place; Questions with *Where* + *Be*

Lesson 3
page 58

Questions about Time and Weather; Prepositions of Time (Part 1)

Lesson 4
page 66

This, That, These, Those

Review the Grammar
page 73

Connect the Grammar to Writing
page 76

LESSON 1 Simple Present of *Be*: Yes/No Questions

EXPLORE

 1 READ the interview about name days. Notice the sentences in **bold**.

HAPPY NAME DAY!

TV host: Welcome to the show, Dimitris. **Are you from Greece?**

Dimitris: Yes, **I'm from Athens**.

TV host: Great. Well, today our show is about celebrations.¹ Tell us about a celebration in Greece.

Dimitris: OK. My favorite celebration is my name day.

TV host: **Is your name day your birthday?**

Dimitris: No, **my name day isn't my birthday**. It's different. My birthday is in September, but my name day is in October. Everyone with the name Dimitris celebrates on October 26.

TV host: Really? That's interesting! **Are name days common all over Europe?**

Dimitris: Yes, **they're common in many European countries**. They're also common in Latin America.

TV host: And how do you celebrate your name day?

Dimitris: Well, we have five Dimitrises in my family, so we have a big party. It's a lot of fun.

TV host: Five Dimitrises!? Wow!

¹ A **celebration** is a party or activity for a special day or occasion.

▶ The Acropolis, Athens, Greece

2 CHECK. Read the statements. Circle **T** for *true* or **F** for *false*.

1. Dimitris is from Greece. (T) F
2. The TV show is about celebrations. T F
3. Dimitris's name day is his birthday. T F
4. Dimitris's name day is in November. T F
5. Name days are common in other countries. T F

3 DISCOVER. Complete the exercises to learn about the grammar in this lesson.

A Find these questions and answers in the interview from exercise **1**. Write the missing words. Then underline the verb *be* and circle the subject in each question and answer.

Yes/No Questions	Answers (Statements)
1. <u>Are</u> (you) from Greece?	1. Yes, _____ from Athens.
2. _____ your birthday?	2. No, _____ my birthday. It's different.
3. _____ common all over Europe?	3. Yes, _____ common in many European countries.

B Look at the questions and answers from exercise **A**. Choose the correct answer to complete the statement below. Then discuss your answer with your classmates and teacher.

The word order is _____ in questions and statements.   a. the same   b. different

LEARN

2.1 Simple Present of *Be*: Yes/No Questions

Statements		
Subject	*Be*	
I	am	late.
He / She / It	is	from Greece.
You / We / You / They	are	from Greece.

Yes/No Questions		
Be	Subject	
Am	I	late?
Is	he / she / it	from Greece?
Are	you / we / you / they	from Greece?

1. The subject comes before the verb in a statement. A statement ends with a period (.).	The festival **is** in February. They **are** from Athens. I **am** from Greece.
2. The verb comes before the subject in a Yes/No question with *be*. A question ends with a question mark (?).	**Is** the festival in February? **Are** they from Athens? **Is** your name day in April?

4 Underline the subject and circle the verb *be* in each statement. Then complete each Yes/No question with *be* + subject.

Statements

1. Eleni ⓘs from Patras.
2. Alex is from Athens.
3. Athens and Patras are in Greece.
4. Eleni and Alex are married.
5. They are happy.
6. Costas is their last name.
7. Eleni and Alex are popular Greek names.
8. Eleni's name day is on May 21.

Yes/No Questions

1. _Is_ _Eleni_ from Patras?
2. ____ _____ from Athens?
3. ____ _____ in Greece?
4. ____ _____ married?
5. ____ _____ happy?
6. ____ _____ their last name?
7. ____ _____ popular Greek names?
8. ____ _____ on May 21?

5 Put the words in the correct order to make Yes/No questions.

1. you / Are / from Mexico Are you from Mexico?
2. in / Mexico city / Mexico / Is _____
3. common / name days / Are / in Latin America _____
4. they / from Brazil / Are _____
5. your birthday / in November / Is _____
6. you / a / student / Are _____
7. she / a / teacher / Is _____
8. Korean / Is / he _____

2.2 Simple Present of Be: Short Answers

Yes/No Questions			Affirmative Short Answers			Negative Short Answers	
Be	Subject			Subject	Be		Subject + Be + Not
Am	I	late?		you	are.		you're not.
Are	you	from Athens?		I	am.		I'm not.
Is	he she it	in Europe?	Yes,	he she it	is.	No,	he's not. she's not. it's not.
Are	we you they	happy?		we you they	are.		we're not. you're not. they're not.

1. Do not use contractions in affirmative short answers.	✓ Yes, she **is**. ✗ Yes, <u>she's</u>. ✓ Yes, they **are**. ✗ Yes, <u>they're</u>.
2. There are two forms of negative contractions for *is* and *are* in the present.	No, he's not / she's not / it's not. No, he **isn't** / she **isn't** / it **isn't**. No, we're not / you're not / they're not. No, we **aren't** / you **aren't** / they **aren't**.
3. There is only one negative contraction for *am* in the present.	No, I'm not.

6 Complete the short answer to each *Yes/No* question. Use contractions when possible.

1. Are name days common in Europe? Yes, _they are_____.
2. Is today Bill's birthday? No, _____.
3. Is he from Mexico? No, _____.
4. Is Madrid in Spain? Yes, _____.
5. Are we late? No, _____.
6. Is she a student? No, _____.
7. Am I in Room 207? Yes, _____.
8. Are they in the cafeteria? No, _____.

PRACTICE

7 Complete each *Yes/No* question with the correct form of *be*. Then write the correct short answer to each question. Use the photo and the photo caption to help you.

1. A: _Is_ Argentina in North America?
   B: _No, it isn't._

2. A: ____ Rio in Argentina?
   B: _____

3. A: ____ the man and the woman in Brazil?
   B: _____

4. A: ____ the tango a dance?
   B: _____

5. A: ____ they dancers?
   B: _____

6. A: ____ they in Argentina?
   B: _____

7. A: ____ our teacher from Argentina?
   B: _____

8. A: ____ you a good dancer?
   B: _____

▲ Tango dancers in Buenos Aires, Argentina

46 THE VERB *BE*: QUESTIONS

8 Complete the *Yes/No* questions and short answers in each conversation. Use only one word or contraction for each blank. Use contractions when possible. Then listen and check your answers.

1. A: It's noisy. (1) __Are__ __you__ at a party?

   B: No, (2) _____ _____. (3) _____ at a wedding.

   A: (4) _____ _____ fun?

   B: Yes, (5) _____ _____! (6) _____ a lot of fun!

2. A: (7) _____ our meeting at nine o'clock?

   B: Yes, (8) _____ _____. (9) _____ we late?

   A: No, (10) _____ _____. (11) _____ early. It's only 8:45.

3. A: Hi. (12) _____ _____ you at home?

   B: No, (13) _____ _____. (14) _____ at school. Carol and Ann say hello.

   A: Oh, (15) _____ _____ with you?

   B: Yes, they (16) _____.

9 SPEAK. Work with a partner. Practice the conversations from exercise **8**.

10 LISTEN & SPEAK.

A Read the questions. Then listen to the information about a special celebration for a girl named Isabel. Check (✓) *Yes* or *No* for each question.

	Yes	No
1. Is *quinceañera* an English word?	☐	✓
2. Is it a celebration for boys?	☐	☐
3. Is it popular in Latin America?	☐	☐
4. Is Isabel in Miami, Florida?	☐	☐
5. Is she 16 years old?	☐	☐
6. Is her dress white?	☐	☐

B Work with a partner. Ask and answer the questions from exercise **A**.

Student A: *Is* quinceañera *an English word?*

Student B: *No, it isn't.*

UNIT 2 LESSON 1

11 EDIT. Read the conversation. Find and correct six more errors with *Yes/No* questions and short answers.

                                                               Are you

Ken: Hi. ~~You are~~ at the hotel now?

Molly: Yes, I'm. I'm in the hotel restaurant.

Ken: Is it a nice hotel?

Molly: Yes, it is. It's beautiful! It's very busy here, too.

Ken: It is a business meeting?

Molly: No, it not. The women here are in long dresses.

Ken: Is they at the hotel for a wedding?

Molly: No, they aren't. The party is for a young girl.

Ken: It is a *quinceañera*?

Molly: Yes, it's.

12 READ, WRITE & SPEAK.

A Read the e-mail message. Then write *Yes/No* questions.

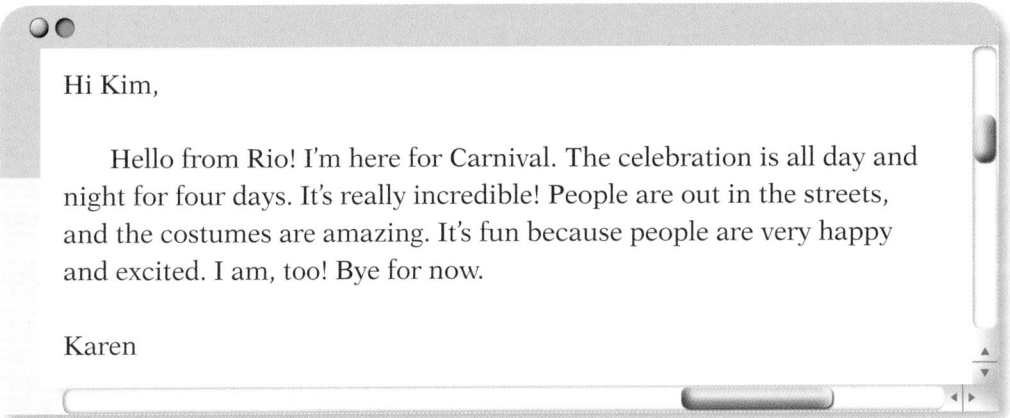

Hi Kim,

    Hello from Rio! I'm here for Carnival. The celebration is all day and night for four days. It's really incredible! People are out in the streets, and the costumes are amazing. It's fun because people are very happy and excited. I am, too! Bye for now.

Karen

1. _Is Karen in New York?_
2. _____
3. _____
4. _____
5. _____
6. _____

B Work with a partner. Ask and answer your questions from exercise **A**.

Student A: *Is Karen in New York?*

Student B: *No, she isn't.*

▶ A Samba School Parade during Carnival in Rio de Janiero, Brazil

13 APPLY.

A Work with a partner. Get ready to role-play a phone conversation about a celebration. First, choose a celebration from the box or your own idea.

| a birthday party | a name day celebration | a wedding |
| a graduation party | a *quinceañera* party | your idea: _____ |

B Read the model conversation. Then complete the conversation below for your role-play. Student B is at the celebration. Student A asks Student B questions about the celebration.

Student A: *Hi, Mario. Are you at home?*

Student B: *No, I'm not. I'm at my sister's graduation party.*

Student A: *Oh. Is it her high school graduation?*

Student B: *No, it's not. It's her college graduation.*

Student A: *Is it a fun party?*

Student B: *Yes, it is! My sister and her classmates are really happy and excited.*

> **REAL ENGLISH**
>
> *Really* is often used in conversation. It means *very*.
>
> A: *This is a **really** fun party.*
> B: *Yeah, it is!*

Student A: Hi, _____. Are you _____?

Student B: No, _____. I'm _____.

Student A: _____?

Student B: _____.

Student A: _____?

Student B: _____.

C Role-play your conversation from exercise **B** for the class.

LESSON 2 — Prepositions of Place; Questions with *Where* + *Be*

EXPLORE

 1 READ the advertisement for a tour of the Eiffel Tower in Paris, France. Notice the words in **bold**.

Eiffel Tower Tour

Visit the Eiffel Tower! Gustave Eiffel built it for the 1889 World's Fair and to celebrate the 100-year anniversary[1] of the French Revolution.

Take our exciting tour! Our first stop is for a photo of *you* **in front of** the Eiffel Tower. Next, we go to a secret room **under** the tower to learn about its history.

Our last stop is the top of the tower. The view **over** the city is amazing! The Seine River is **below**, and the beautiful Trocadero Park is **across** the river.

FAQs[2]

Where is the meeting place for the tour?
Meet the tour guide **next to** the statue[3] of Gustave Eiffel.

Where is the ticket office?
The ticket counter is **next to** the elevator.

See you **in** Paris!

---

[1] **anniversary:** a date that is remembered because something special happened on that day in an earlier year
[2] **FAQs:** Frequently Asked Questions
[3] **statue:** a large model made of stone or metal

▶ The Eiffel Tower, Paris, France

2 CHECK. Read the statements. Circle **T** for *True* or **F** for *False*.

1. The ad is for a bus tour of Paris. T F
2. The Eiffel Tower is 100 years old. T F
3. The first stop is a secret room. T F
4. Trocadero is a river. T F
5. The last stop is the top of the tower. T F

3 DISCOVER. Complete the exercises to learn about the grammar in this lesson.

A Find these sentences in the advertisement from exercise **1**. Write the missing words.

1. Our first stop is for a photo of *you* _____ the Eiffel Tower.
2. The view _____ the city is amazing!
3. Meet the tour guide _____ the statue of Gustave Eiffel.

B Look at the sentences from exercise **A**. Then choose the correct word to complete the statement below. Discuss your answer with your classmates and teacher.

We use *in front of, over, below, across from, under,* and *next to* to talk about _____.

a. time   b. place   c. people

LEARN

2.3 Prepositions of Place

The pen is **in** the glass.

The pen is **next to** the glass.

The pen is **in front of** the glass.

Room 301 is **across from** Room 302.

The pen is **under / below** the chair.

The pen is **on** the book.

The pen is **near** the glass.

The pen is **in back of / behind** the glass.

The pen is **between** the glasses.

The pen is **over / above** the glass.

1. Phrases with prepositions tell where something is.	Our class is **in** Room 502. My book is **on** my desk.
2. Use *at* with specific addresses and with places we visit in daily life.	She lives **at** 39 Main Street. He's **at** the supermarket. They're **at** the library.
3. Use *on* with streets, roads, avenues, and floors of a building.	Their office is **on** Park Street. We live **on** Maple Road. Her office is **on** the second floor.
4. Use *in* with cities, countries, and rooms.	The Eiffel Tower is **in** Paris. Paris is a city **in** France. Our class is **in** Room 215.

4 Complete each sentence with the correct preposition from the box.

| above | across from | behind | between | in | in front of | near | next to | on | under |

1. The light is _____above_____ the table.

2. The keys are _____ the books.

3. The pen is _____ the book.

4. The pen is _____ the glass.

5. The pen is _____ the book.

6. The keys are _____ the table.

7. The pen is _____ the glass.

8. The backpack is _____ the table.

9. The keys are _____ the book.

10. The red chair is _____ the green chair.

5 Complete each sentence with *at*, *in*, or *on*.

1. Paris is __in__ France.

2. The Eiffel Tower is _____ Paris.

3. Beijing is a city _____ China.

4. The doctor's office is _____ 21 Palmer Street.

5. The supermarket is _____ Mountain Avenue.

6. The Statue of Liberty is _____ New York City.

7. Our new house is _____ 141 Hillview Road.

8. Our meeting is _____ Room 210.

> **REAL ENGLISH**
>
> We don't need to use *the* before some common locations.
>
> I'm at **school**.
>
> We're at **home**.
>
> She's at **work**.

UNIT 2 LESSON 2 **53**

2.4 Questions with *Where* + *Be*

Questions			Answers
Where	*Be*	Subject	
Where	is	the exit?	**Next to** the stairs. It's **next to** the stairs.
Where	is	the post office?	**On** Park Street. It's **on** Park Street.
Where	are	Ben and Louisa?	**In** the park. They're **in** the park.

1. Use *Where* to ask questions about place.	A: **Where** is the library? B: It's next to the Science Building.
2. Put the verb before the subject in questions with *Where*.	✓ Where is the park? ✗ Where the park is?
3. *Where's* is the contraction of *Where* and *is*. Do not contract *Where* and *are*.	**Where's** the bus stop? ✓ Where are the books? ✗ Where're the books?

REAL ENGLISH

Use *Where* alone to clarify or get more information.

A: *They're in the park.*
B: ***Where****?*
A: *Over by the bridge.*
B: *Oh, OK. Now I see them.*

6 Put the words in the correct order to make questions.

1. our class / is / Where <u>Where is our class?</u>

2. is / the bathroom / Where _____

3. teacher / Where's / our _____

4. are / Where / our / books _____

5. your / home / Where / is _____

6. our / classmates / are / Where _____

7. classroom / our / Where's _____

8. you / are / Where _____

9. Chan and Meg / are / Where _____

10. your / Where's / office _____

7 SPEAK. Work with a partner. Ask and answer questions 1-8 from exercise **6**.

Student A: *Where's our class?*

Student B: *It's in Room 205.*

PRACTICE

8 READ & SPEAK.

A Look at the floor plan of an office building. Then choose the correct preposition of place to complete each statement.

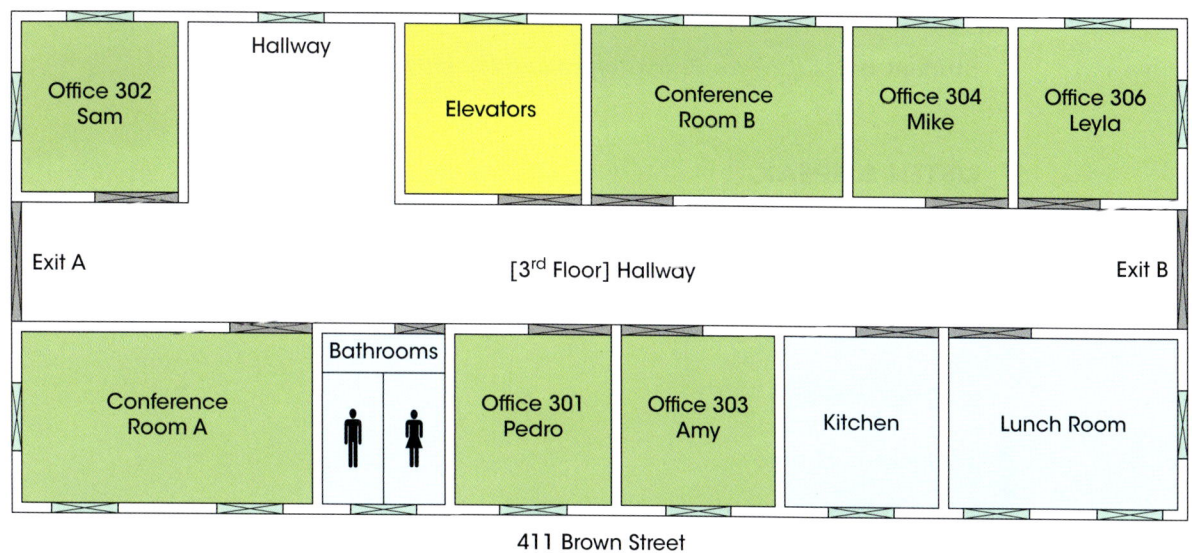

1. The office building is ___ 411 Brown Street. a. at b. in c. on
2. The office building is ___ Brown Street. a. in b. at c. on
3. These offices are ___ the third floor. a. in b. on c. at
4. The elevators are ___ Conference Room B. a. next to b. between c. in
5. Pedro's office is ___ Amy's office. a. in front of b. behind c. next to
6. The lunch room is ___ the kitchen. a. between b. next to c. behind
7. The parking lot is ___ the building. a. between b. near c. in
8. Mike is ___ Office 304. a. on b. in c. at
9. Leyla's office is ___ the lunch room. a. across from b. behind c. between
10. The kitchen is ___ Office 303 and the lunch room. a. between b. across from c. in front of

B Work with a partner. Ask and answer questions about the office building floor plan from exercise **A** on page 55. Use prepositions of place, *Yes/No* questions, and questions with *where + be*.

Student A: *Is Leyla's office next to Mike's office?*

Student B: *Yes, it is.*

Student A: *Where's Amy's office?*

Student B: *It's between Pedro's office and the kitchen.*

9 LISTEN & SPEAK.

CD1-23

A Look at the list of places in New Orleans. Then listen to a tour guide describe each place. Write the number of each place on the map.

1. The Cabildo Museum
2. The Cathedral
3. Jackson Square
4. The Pontalba Buildings (two places)
5. Statue of Andrew Jackson
6. The Café du Monde

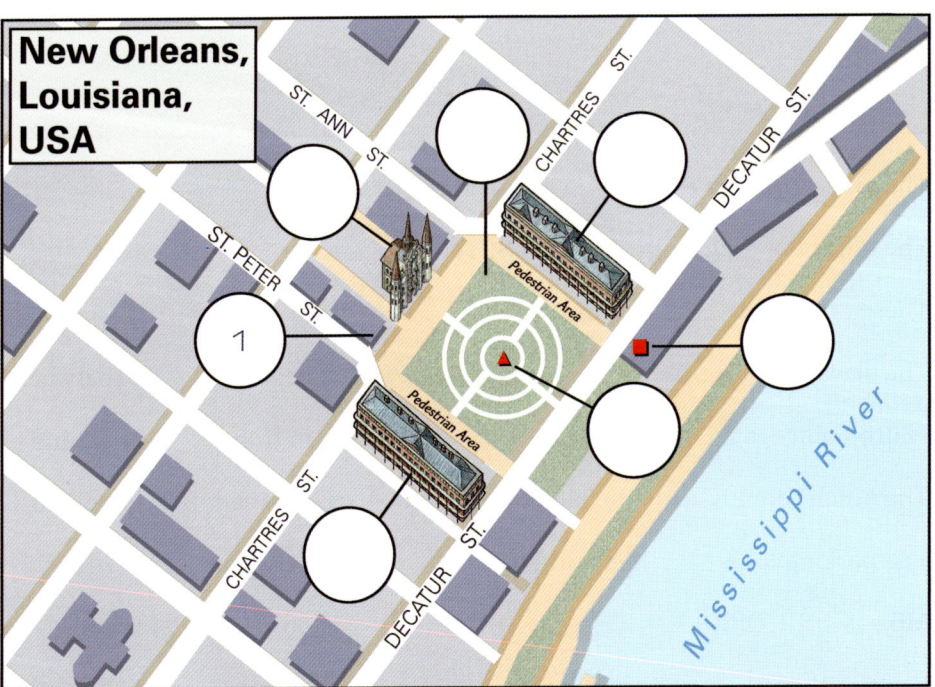

B Work with a partner. Ask and answer questions about the map from exercise **A**.

Student A: *Where is Jackson Square?*

Student B: *It's between the Pontalba Buildings.*

56 THE VERB *BE*: QUESTIONS

10 EDIT. Read the information about New Orleans. Find and correct six more errors with prepositions of place. Use the map in exercise **9A** to help you.

New Orleans

New Orleans is a city ~~on~~ ^in the United States. It is in the state of Louisiana. The French Quarter is a very old part of New Orleans. It is between the Mississippi River. Jackson Square is under Decatur Street and Chartres Street. The Café du Monde is in Decatur Street. It is across of Jackson Square. The Cathedral is on Chartres Street. It is above the Cabildo Museum. Apartments are under the stores and restaurants in the Pontalba Buildings.

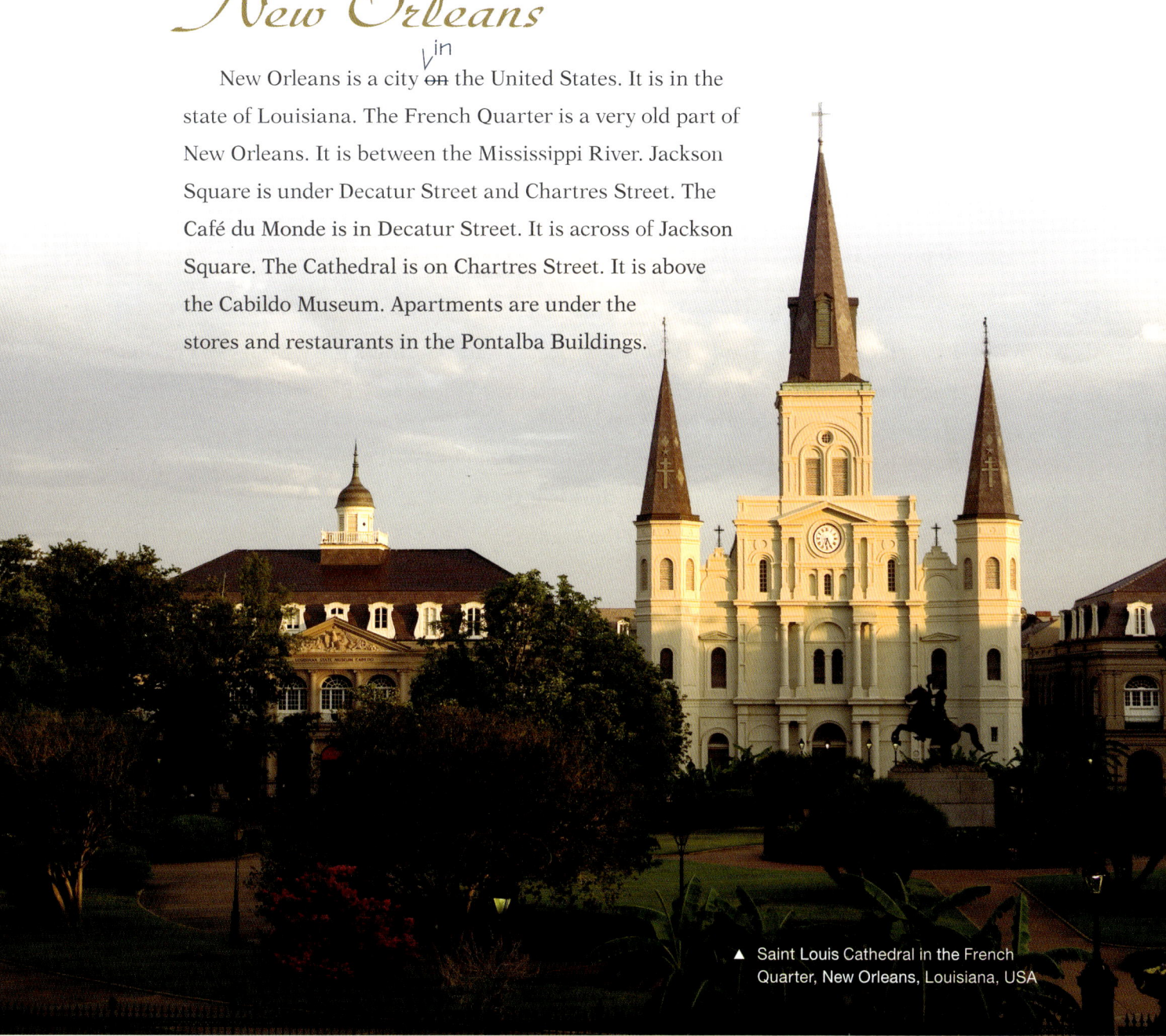

▲ Saint Louis Cathedral in the French Quarter, New Orleans, Louisiana, USA

11 APPLY.

A In your notebook, draw a map of a place you know with stores, parks, and interesting buildings (for example: a post office, a school, a library, a supermarket, a bank, etc). Then write a few sentences about it. Describe the location of the different buildings. Use prepositions of place.

> My apartment is at 51 Garden Street. It is between a park and a school . . .

B Work with a partner. Talk about places on your map from exercise **A**.

The park is on Garden Street. It's next to the shopping center.

LESSON 3 Questions about Time and Weather

EXPLORE

1 READ the news report. Notice the words in **bold**.

New Year's Celebrations around the World

Reporter 1:	5, 4, 3, 2, 1 . . . Happy New Year, London! **It's midnight on New Year's Eve**! This is Emily Michaels. I have our reporter[1] Philip Jones in New York on the line. Hi, Philip. Happy New Year!
Reporter 2:	Hello, Emily. Happy New Year to you, too! **How's the weather in London?**
Reporter 1:	**It's cool and rainy**, but people are in the streets. Everyone is very excited. **How is it in New York?**
Reporter 2:	**It's freezing[2] here! It's cold and snowy** . . . It's terrible!
Reporter 1:	That's too bad! **What time is it there**?
Reporter 2:	**It's seven o'clock in the evening**.
Reporter 1:	OK, thank you, Philip. Keep warm! Now, let's check in with our reporter in Sydney, Australia. Nicole, are you there?
Reporter 3:	Yes, hello. Happy New Year, everyone! **It's sunny and warm here**!
Reporter 2:	That's right—it's summer in Australia. **What time is it there?**
Reporter 3:	**It's eleven o'clock in the morning**.
Reporter 1:	Thanks, Nicole. Happy New Year! Now back to our celebration in London!

[1] **reporter:** someone who tells or writes about news   [2] **freezing:** very cold

2 CHECK. Complete the chart with information from the news report in exercise **1**.

	Time	Weather
London		cool and rainy
New York	seven o'clock	
Sydney		

3 DISCOVER. Complete the exercises to learn about the grammar in this lesson.

A Find and underline statements and questions with *it* in the news report from exercise **1**. Are they about time or weather? In the margin, write **T** for *time* and **W** for *weather*.

It's midnight on New Year's Eve. T   It's cool and rainy. W

B Work with a partner. Compare your answers from exercise **A**. Then discuss your answers with your classmates and teacher.

▲ Fireworks explode over Sydney Harbor, Sydney, Australia, January 1, 2000.

LEARN

2.5 Questions about Time

Questions		
What time		
What day	is	it?
What month		
What year		
What	is	the date today?
	's	today's date?

	Answers
It's It is	two o'clock. Monday. February. 2017. May 3rd.

1. Use *it* in questions with *What* + a time word.	**What time is it?** **What year is it?**
2. Do not use *it* in time questions with *What is/What's*.	✓ **What is the time?** ✗ What is it the time?
3. Put the verb *is* before the subject in questions about time.	✓ **What time is it?** ✗ What time it is? ✓ **What is the date today?** ✗ What the date is today?
4. Use *it* to answer questions about time.	**It's five-thirty.** **It's Thursday.**

4 Write the correct question for each answer. More than one answer may be possible.

1. A: <u>What month is it?</u>

   B: It's April.

2. A: _____

   B: It's two o'clock.

3. A: _____

   B: It's Saturday.

4. A: _____

   B: It's April 5th.

5. A: _____

   B: It's Monday.

6. A: _____

   B: It's November.

7. A: _____

   B: It's 2017.

8. A: _____

   B: It's nine-thirty.

5 Choose the correct answer for each question.

1. What time is it?   a. It's April 9th.   (b.) It's four o'clock.
2. What day is it?   a. It's Monday.   b. It's March.
3. What year is it?   a. It's September.   b. It's 2017.
4. What time is it?   a. It's ten-thirty.   b. It's 2017.
5. What month is it?   a. It's January.   b. It's Friday.
6. What's today's date?   a. It's October 14th.   b. It's Wednesday.
7. What day is it?   a. It's 2017.   b. It's Thursday.
8. What is the date today?   a. It's December.   b. It's December 2nd.

6 **SPEAK.** Work with a partner. Ask and answer the questions from exercise **5**.

Student A: *What time is it?*   Student B: *It's eleven-thirty.*

2.6 Questions with *When*; Prepositions of Time (Part 1)*

Questions		Answers		
			Preposition of Time	
When is / When's	your class?	My class is / It's	at	two o'clock.
			on	Monday night.
			in	the morning.

1. Use *When* to ask questions about time.	**When** is our meeting? **When's** your birthday?
2. *When's* is the contraction of *When* and *is*.	A: **When's** your soccer game? B: It's on Saturday afternoon.
3. Put the verb *is* before the subject in questions with *When*.	✓ When **is** <u>the test</u>? ✗ When <u>the test is</u>?
4. Phrases with prepositions tell when something happens.	The party is **on** Saturday.
5. Use *at* with clock times.	at <u>three-thirty</u> at <u>one o'clock</u> at <u>midnight</u>
6. Use *in* with years, months, seasons of the year, and times of the day (exception: *at night*).	in <u>2015</u> in <u>May</u> in <u>the summer</u> in <u>the morning</u> / <u>afternoon</u> / <u>evening</u>
7. Use *on* with dates and days of the week. *On* is also used with *the weekend*.	**on** June 29 **on** Sunday **on** the weekend

*For Prepositions of Time (Part 2), see Unit 3, Lesson 2.

7 Use the words in parentheses to write questions with *When*. Then complete the answers with *in*, *at*, or *on*.

1. (New Year's Eve)   A: <u>When's New Year's Eve?</u>

    B: It's ____ December 31st.

2. (her 21st birthday)   A: _____

    B: It's ____ 2020.

3. (your birthday)   A: _____

    B: My birthday's ____ June.

4. (St. Patrick's Day)   A: _____

    B: It's ____ March 17th.

5. (our English class)   A: _____

    B: It's ____ two o'clock.

6. (the party)   A: _____

    B: It's ____ Tuesday night.

7. (the exam)   A: _____

    B: It's ____ Monday.

8. (the winter festival)   A: _____

    B: The winter festival is ____ December.

8 Complete the conversations with the correct prepositions of time.

1. A: When's Mother's Day in the United States?
   B: It's <u>in</u> May. It's always ____ Sunday.

2. A: When's your name day?
   B: It's ____ September.

3. A: Is the party ____ Friday?
   B: No, it's not. It's ____ Thursday.

4. A: When's the music festival?
   B: It's ____ the summer.

5. A: When's his birthday?
   B: It's ____ December 3rd.

6. A: My class is ____ seven-thirty.
   B: Is it ____ the morning?
   A: No, it's ____ night.

9 SPEAK. Work with a partner. Ask questions about special days, holidays, and celebrations. Use the ideas from the box below or your own ideas.

| your birthday   Mother's Day in your country   New Year's Day   your class |

Student A: *When's your birthday?*   Student B: *It's on August 9th.*

2.7 Questions about the Weather

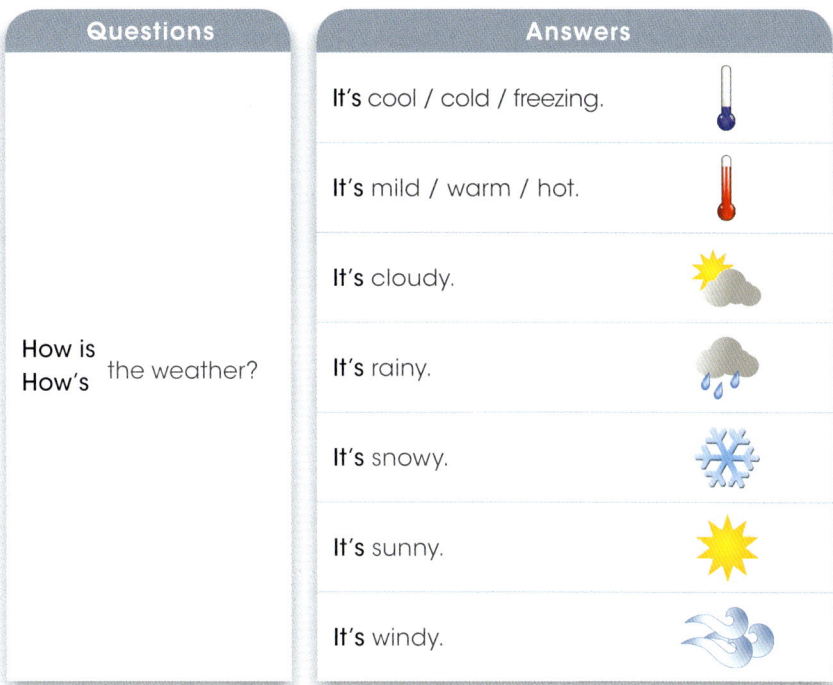

1. Use questions with *how* and answers with *it* to talk about the weather.	A: **How** is the weather in Madrid today? B: **It**'s warm and sunny.
2. *How's* is the contraction of *How* and *is*.	A: **How's** the weather in London? B: It's cool and rainy.
3. *What's the weather like* is also used to ask about weather.	A: **What's the weather like** in Chicago in the winter? B: It's cold and windy.
4. Use adjectives to describe the weather.	It's **hot** and **sunny**. It's **freezing**.

10 Complete each question. Then write the correct answer to each question.

1. A: ____How's____ the weather? B: (cold and windy) ____It's cold and windy.____

2. A: _____ the weather? B: (warm and sunny) _____

3. A: _____ the weather like? B: (rainy) _____

4. A: _____ the weather? B: (cold and snowy) _____

5. A: _____ the weather? B: (hot and sunny) _____

6. A: _____ the weather like? B: (cool and cloudy) _____

7. A: _____ the weather? B: (sunny and mild) _____

8: A: _____ the weather like? B: (freezing) _____

11 SPEAK. Work with a partner. Ask and answer questions about different places.

Student A: *What's the weather like in Hawaii?*   Student B: *It's hot and sunny.*

PRACTICE

12 Complete each conversation. Use contractions when possible. Then listen and check your answers. (CD1-25)

1. A: (1) ___What___ ___time___ is it?

    B: (2) ___It's___ one o'clock.

    A: Oh no! Are we late for the meeting?

    B: No, it's (3) _____ two o'clock.

2. A: Hi, Peter. (4) _____ the weather in Miami today?

    B: (5) _____ warm and sunny.

    A: You're lucky! (6) _____ cold and rainy here in Toronto.

3. A: Hmmm. (7) _____ the (8) _____ today?

    B: (9) _____ July 9th.

    A: Thank you.

4. A: (10) _____ the game?

    B: It's (11) _____ Saturday.

    A: Is it (12) _____ the morning?

    B: No, it's (13) _____ the afternoon. It's (14) _____ three o'clock.

13 EDIT. Read the conversations. Find and correct six more errors with questions about time and prepositions of time.

1. **Sam:** Hi, Mel. What time ~~it is~~ *is it*?

    Mel: It's nine-thirty.

    Sam: Oh no! I'm late!

2. **Ben:** When is your birthday?

    Mika: It's on June.

    Ben: Really? My birthday's in June, too. It's in June 24th.

3. **Nora:** What time is it?

    Chan: It seven o'clock.

    Nora: Oh, good! The movie is on 7:30.

4. **Toshi:** When Steve's graduation party?

    Maria: It's on Friday.

    Toshi: Is it in the afternoon?

    Maria: No, it's in night.

14 LISTEN & WRITE.

A Listen to the news report. Circle the holiday you hear.

a. Mother's Day   b. Valentine's Day   c. a name day

B Read the questions. Then listen to the news report again and write the answer to each question.

1. What time is it? _____

2. What day is it? _____

3. What month is it? _____

4. What's the date? _____

5. How's the weather? _____

15 APPLY.

A Choose a holiday or festival from your country. Then write notes for a news report below. Use the model to help you.

Notes
Holiday: Family Day
Date: April 6th
Weather: sunny and warm

Notes
Holiday:
Date:
Weather:

B Role-play your weather report for the class. Use your notes from exercise **A** and the model below to help you.

Good morning, Cape Town. It's nine o'clock on Monday, April 6.
It's Family Day today, and it's beautiful outside. It's sunny and warm.
Have a great day, families!

LESSON 4   This, That, These, Those

EXPLORE

 1 READ the conversation about the Holi Festival. Notice the words in **bold**.

Holi Festival

Scott: Hi, Dan. **Is this seat** free?

Dan: Oh, hi, Scott. Yeah, **it is**. Have a seat. How are you doing?

Scott: Good. **Is that** your new laptop?

Dan: Yes, **it is**. I'm really happy with it so far.

Scott: **What's that** on your screen? **Is that** your photo, or is it from the Internet?

Dan: Oh, **it's** a photo from my trip to India last month. **It's** the Holi festival of colors.

Scott: The Holi festival. **What's that**?

Dan: **It's** a Hindu holiday to celebrate spring. People of all ages are in the streets. They throw paint and water on each other.

Scott: Interesting. It looks like fun . . . Wow. Look at **those colors**. **Is that** paint in the air?

Dan: Yes. **It** was everywhere. Do you see **these people** here?

Scott: Yeah?

Dan: I was completely yellow thanks to them . . . Look, here are a few more photos of the Holi festival.

Scott: Wow! **Those are** amazing photos! You're a great photographer.

Dan: Thanks. **Is this** your stop?

Scott: Oh, yes, **it is**. See you, Dan.

Dan: OK. See you later, Scott.

◀ The Holi Festival, Mathura, Uttar Pradesh, India

▲ People throw paint and water at the Holi Festival, Mathura, Uttar Pradesh, India.

2 CHECK. Choose the correct word(s) to complete each sentence about the conversation.

1. This photograph is from _____.   a. Hollywood   b. India
2. Holi is the festival of _____.   a. paint   b. colors
3. On this holiday, people dance in _____.   a. the streets   b. their houses
4. _____ is a great photographer.   a. Dan   b. Scott

3 DISCOVER. Complete the exercises to learn about the grammar in this lesson.

A Find these statements and questions in the conversation from exercise **1**. Write the missing words.

1. Is _____ your new laptop?
2. Look at _____ colors.
3. Do you see _____ people here?
4. _____ are amazing photos!
5. Is _____ your stop?

B Circle the correct word to complete each statement. Then discuss your answers with your classmates and teacher.

1. We use *this* and *that* with **singular** / **plural** nouns.
2. We use *these* and *those* with **singular** / **plural** nouns.

LEARN

2.8 This, That, These, Those

Singular		
Subject	Verb	
This / That	is	a great photo.
This / That laptop	is	great.

Plural		
Subject	Verb	
These / Those	are	great photos.
These / Those laptops	are	great.

1. *This*, *that*, *these*, and *those* can be pronouns or adjectives.	**This** is a great photo. (pronoun) **This** photo is great. (adjective)
2. Use *this* and *that* with singular nouns. Use *these* and *those* with plural nouns.	**This** exercise is easy. **That** is Miguel's coat. **These** cookies are delicious. **Those** are expensive shoes.
3. Use *this*, *that*, *these*, and *those* to identify people or things.	**This** is my grammar book. **That**'s my house across the street. **Those** women are my classmates.
4. Use *this* and *these* for people or things that are near. Use *that* and *those* for people or things that are not near.	**This** is my wife, Erika. **These** are our children, Anna and Jason. **That** is my car over there. **Those** are my keys on the table.

REAL ENGLISH

Use *this* to introduce people. After you introduce the person, use a personal pronoun.

This is Arlene. *She's* my wife.

4 Circle the correct word to complete each sentence.

1. **This** / **(These)** photos are from my trip to India.
2. **That** / **Those** is an interesting photo.
3. **This** / **These** festival is a lot of fun!
4. **This** / **These** is my new camera.
5. **That** / **Those** men over there are teachers at my school.
6. **This** / **These** are Miguel's books.
7. **This** / **These** flowers are beautiful.
8. **That** / **Those** laptops are very expensive.
9. **This** / **Those** is my sister, Yoko.
10. **Those** / **That** is Hamid's backpack.

5 Complete each sentence with *this*, *that*, *these*, or *those*. Look at the information in parentheses (*near/not near*).

1. _____These_____ are photos of the festival. (*near*)
2. _____ man is from India. (*not near*)
3. _____ is a beautiful building. (*not near*)
4. _____ is my new phone. (*near*)
5. _____ students are in our class. (*not near*)
6. _____ classroom is cold! (*near*)
7. _____ books are heavy. (*near*)
8. _____ are Greg's parents. (*not near*)

2.9 Questions and Answers with *This*, *That*, *These*, *Those*

Yes/No Questions		Affirmative Short Answers	Negative Short Answer
Is	this your notebook? / that boy your son?	Yes, it is.	No, it isn't. / it's not.
Are	these scarves / those people from India?	Yes, they are.	No, they aren't. / they're not.

Questions with What		Answers	
What is	this? / that?	It's	a phone. / my new camera.
What are	these? / those?	They're	glasses. / apartment buildings.

1. For *Yes/No* questions with *this* and *that*, use *it* in the short answer.	A: Is **this** your notebook? B: Yes, **it** is. A: Is **that** building a museum? B: No, **it** isn't. **It's** a high school.
2. For *Yes/No* questions with *these* and *those*, use *they* in the short answer.	A: Are **these** your sunglasses? B: No, **they're** not. They're Mary's. A: Are **those** students from China? B: Yes, **they** are.
3. Use *What* to ask questions about things.	A: **What's** that? B: It's my <u>homework assignment</u>. A: **What** are these? B: They're <u>photographs</u> from my trip.

UNIT 2 LESSON 4

6 Put the words in order to make questions. Then write the correct answer for each question.

1. your camera / Is / that
   A: Is that your camera?
   B: Yes, it is.

2. Are / Bob's sons / those
   A: _____
   B: Yes, _____.

3. those cars / Are / expensive
   A: _____
   B: No, _____.

4. this / your jacket / Is
   A: _____
   B: Yes, _____.

5. Are / Cho's books / these
   A: _____
   B: No, _____.

6. Is / our bus / that
   A: _____
   B: No, _____.

7. is / What / that
   A: _____
   B: _____ my backpack.

8. those / What / are
   A: _____
   B: _____ notebooks.

9. these / are / What
   A: _____
   B: _____ earrings.

10. is / What / this
    A: _____
    B: _____ a scarf.

7 **LISTEN** and choose the correct answer for each question.

1. a. Yes, it is.   b. Yes, they are.
2. a. No, they aren't.   b. No, it isn't.
3. a. No, it isn't.   b. No, they're not.
4. a. Yes, it is.   b. Yes, they are.
5. a. Yes, they are.   b. Yes, it is.
6. a. No, they're not.   b. No, it's not.
7. a. Yes, they are.   b. Yes, it is.
8. a. Yes, they are.   b. Yes, it is.

PRACTICE

8 Circle the correct word(s) to complete each conversation.

1. A: Happy Birthday, Alberto! (1) **This** / **These** is a fun party.

   B: Thanks, Roberto.

   A: Alberto, (2) **this** / **these** is my wife, Amelia.

   B: Nice to meet you, Amelia.

2. A: (3) **That** / **Those** are amazing photos.

   B: Thank you. They're from Trocadero Park.

   A: Is (4) **that** / **those** in Belgium?

   B: No, (5) **it's** / **they're** not. (6) **It's** / **They're** in Paris, France.

3. A: Excuse me, is (7) **this** / **these** the Language Lab?

   B: No, (8) **it's** / **they're** not. (9) **It's** / **They're** in Room 410.

   A: Is (10) **that** / **those** on the fourth floor?

   B: Yes, (11) **it is** / **they are**.

4. A: (12) **That** / **Those** is a beautiful scarf. (13) **Is** / **Are** it from India?

   B: Yes, (14) **it is** / **that is**. (15) **This** / **These** earrings are from India, too.

9 EDIT. Read the conversation. Find and correct six more errors with *this, that, these,* or *those*.

THE MEDELLÍN FLOWER FESTIVAL

▶ The Medellín flower festival, Medellín, Colombia

Alicia: Wow! ~~These~~ **This** festival is amazing!

Ima: Yeah, it is. All of this flowers are beautiful.

Alicia: Are that roses over there?

Ima: Yes, it is.

Alicia: They're so colorful.

Ima: This big yellow flowers here are beautiful, too. I think they're sunflowers.

Alicia: Are that people over there farmers?

Ima: Yes, they are. They grow the flowers for these festival every year.

10 SPEAK. Work with a partner. Practice saying sentences and asking and answering questions about things in your classroom. Use *this, that, these, those, Yes/No* questions, and questions with *What*.

Student A: *That's a beautiful sweater.*

Student B: *Thanks.*

Student A: *What's that?*

Student B: *It's my phone.*

Student A: *Is that your backpack?*

Student B: *Yes, it is.*

11 APPLY.

A Work with a partner. Write a conversation about a party, festival, or celebration. Use the conversation from exercise **9** on page 71 to help you.

A: _____

B: _____

A: _____

B: _____

A: _____

B: _____

B Role-play your conversation from exercise **A** for the class.

▼ People with lanterns at the Kratong festival, Chiang Mai, Thailand

UNIT 2 Review the Grammar

Charts 2.1–2.9

1 LISTEN and choose the correct answer for each question.

1. a. No, I'm not.   b. Yes, she is.
2. a. Yes, they are.   b. Yes, you are.
3. a. No, they're not.   b. No, it's not.
4. a. It's in the morning.   b. It's in Conference Room B.
5. a. It's at 9 a.m.   b. It's 9:00 a.m.
6. a. It's in Room 203.   b. It's at 10:30.
7. a. They're flowers.   b. It's a flower.
8. a. Yes, it is.   b. It's cool and cloudy.

Charts 2.1–2.7

2 WRITE & SPEAK.

A Look at Angela's calendar. Then write four questions about the information.

February						
Sunday	Monday	Tuesday	Wednesday	Thursday	Friday	Saturday
12	13 Meeting Boston 10:00 a.m.	14 Jack's party 7:00 p.m. 21 Baker Street Valentine's Day	15 Soccer game 5:30 p.m.	16 Meeting Room 206 2:00 p.m. Marta's Birthday	17 Concert 21 Park Street 7:00 p.m.	18 Street fair 8th Street Alma and Ted's Wedding 4:00

Is Marta's birthday on Wednesday?
_____
_____
_____

B Work with a partner. Ask and answer your questions from exercise **A**.

Student A: *Is Marta's birthday on Wednesday?*
Student B: *No, it's not. It's on Thursday.*

Review the Grammar | UNIT 2

Charts 2.1–2.6

3 EDIT. Read the conversation. Find and correct six more errors with questions and prepositions of time and prepositions of place.

Delma: Hello?

Sara: Hi, Delma. Are you in Madrid now?

Delma: Yes, I am. It's beautiful here.

Sara: Where ^is your hotel is?

Delma: It's near to the Prado Museum.

Sara: Is it nice?

Delma: Yes, it is. It's really nice. What time is it at Boston now?

Sara: It's eight o'clock at the morning. What time it there?

Delma: It's at two o'clock at the afternoon here. It's time for lunch. I'm hungry!

Sara: OK. Well, enjoy your vacation!

Delma: Thanks! Bye.

Sara: Bye.

Charts 2.1–2.6

4 READ, WRITE & SPEAK.

A Read about the Harbin International Ice Festival. Then ask *Yes/No* questions and questions with *When, Where,* and *How*.

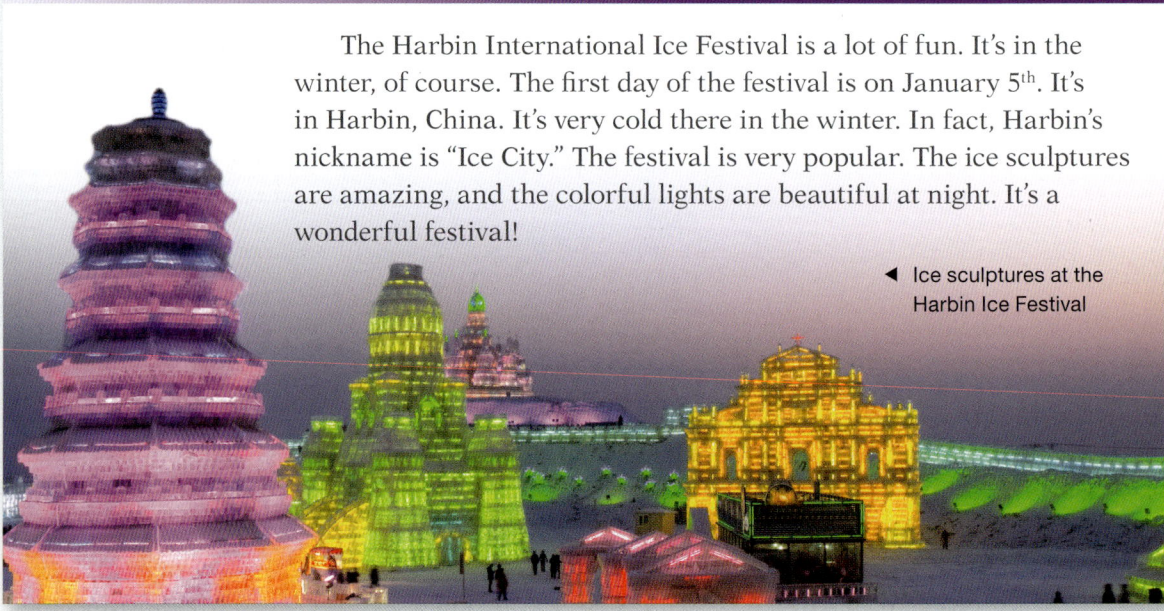

The Harbin Ice Festival

The Harbin International Ice Festival is a lot of fun. It's in the winter, of course. The first day of the festival is on January 5th. It's in Harbin, China. It's very cold there in the winter. In fact, Harbin's nickname is "Ice City." The festival is very popular. The ice sculptures are amazing, and the colorful lights are beautiful at night. It's a wonderful festival!

◀ Ice sculptures at the Harbin Ice Festival

Student A: *Is Harbin in China?*   Student B: *Yes, it is.*

◀ Buildings of ice at the Harbin Ice Festival, Harbin, China

B Think of a festival or celebration in your country or a country you know. Write sentences about the festival or celebration.

It's in Harbin, China.

It's in the winter.

_____

_____

_____

_____

C Work with a partner. Share your sentences from exercise **B**. Ask and answer questions.

Student A: *The festival is in China.*

Student B: *Is it in the summer?*

Student A: *No, it's not. It's in the winter.*

Connect the Grammar to Writing

1 READ & NOTICE THE GRAMMAR.

A Read the paragraph. What is the grandfather's favorite celebration? Discuss with a partner.

A Favorite Celebration

My grandfather's favorite celebration is his birthday. It's in September. His party isn't at a restaurant. It's at our home. The weather is often warm and sunny in September, so the party is outside in our yard. My grandfather is very happy on September 3rd. It's his special day, and it's a lot of fun!

GRAMMAR FOCUS

In the paragraph in exercise **A**, the writer uses phrases with prepositions to give information about time and place.

> It's **in September.**
> His party isn't **at a restaurant.**

B Read the paragraph in exercise **A** again. Underline the prepositions of time and place. Then work with a partner and compare answers.

C Complete the chart with questions and answers about the celebration in the paragraph in exercise **A**.

A Favorite Celebration		
	Questions	Answers
What	What is the grandfather's favorite celebration?	His birthday.
When		
Yes/No question	Is his party at a restaurant?	
How		
Yes/No question		

76   THE VERB *BE*: QUESTIONS

Write about a Celebration

2 BEFORE YOU WRITE.

A Write interview questions in the chart to ask someone about his or her favorite celebration. Use the chart from exercise **1C** as a model.

	_____'s Favorite Celebration	
	Questions	Answers
What	What is your favorite celebration?	
When		
Yes/No question		
How		
Yes/No question		

B Choose a person to interview. Ask him or her your interview questions from exercise **2A**. Take notes on his or her answers in your chart.

3 WRITE a paragraph. Use the information from your chart in exercise **2A** and the paragraph in exercise **1A** to help you.

> **WRITING FOCUS Paragraph Format**
>
> A paragraph is not a list of sentences. It has a special format.
>
> **A List of Sentences:**
>   My favorite celebration is the Kite Festival.
>   It is a celebration in Shirone, Japan.
>   It's in June.
>   It's warm and sunny then.
>
> **A Paragraph:**
>   My favorite celebration is the Kite Festival. It is a celebration in Shirone, Japan. It's in June. It's warm and sunny then.

4 SELF ASSESS. Read your paragraph. Underline the prepositions of time and place. Then use the checklist to assess your work.

- ☐ I used the correct form of *be*. [1.3–1.5]
- ☐ I used the correct prepositions of time. [2.6]
- ☐ I used the correct prepositions of place. [2.3]
- ☐ I used the correct format for my paragraph. [WRITING FOCUS]

UNIT **3** Work

Simple Present: Part 1

◀ A worker on top of the John Hancock skyscraper in Chicago, Illinois, USA

Lesson 1
page 80

Simple Present: Affirmative Statements; Irregular Verbs: *Do*, *Go*, and *Have*

Lesson 2
page 88

Simple Present: Negative Statements; Prepositions of Time (Part 2); *Like*, *Need*, *Want*

Lesson 3
page 97

Verbs + Objects; Object Pronouns

Lesson 4
page 104

Imperatives

Review the Grammar
page 111

Connect the Grammar to Writing
page 114

LESSON 1 Simple Present: Affirmative Statements

EXPLORE

1 READ the article about Doctor Bugs. Notice the words in **bold**.

Doctor Bugs

Most people don't like bugs, but Doctor Mark Moffett **loves** them! In fact, his nickname is Doctor Bugs. He's a photographer and an entomologist. An entomologist **studies** bugs.

Doctor Moffett's favorite bug is the ant. He **goes** all over the world to study ants. He **watches** them as they **eat**, **work**, **rest**, **sleep**, and **fight**.

He **takes** photographs of the ants. He **lies** on the ground with his camera and **waits** for the right moment. The ants and other bugs often **bite** him, but that doesn't stop Doctor Bugs. He **has** an interesting and unusual job, and he **loves** it!

▲ Doctor Mark Moffett

2 CHECK. Read the list of verbs in the chart. Who does each action? Check (✓) the correct column.

Verbs	Doctor Moffett	Ants
1. studies		
2. fight		
3. waits		
4. bite		

3 DISCOVER. Complete the exercises to learn about the grammar in this lesson.

A Look at the list of verbs in exercise **2**. Then find other verbs in the article from exercise **1**. Who does each action? Write each verb in the correct column.

Doctor Moffett	Ants
goes	eat

B Look at the charts from exercise **2** and exercise **A**. Choose the correct answer to complete each statement. Then discuss your answers with your classmates and teacher.

1. The verbs under *Doctor Moffett* **end in -s / do not end in -s**.

2. The verbs under *Ants* **end in -s / do not end in -s**.

◀ Leaf cutter ants

LEARN

3.1 Simple Present: Affirmative Statements

Subject	Verb		Subject	Verb	
I You We You They Tom and Sue	work	every day.	He She It My brother	works	every day.

1. Use the simple present to talk about habits or routines, schedules, and facts.	Habit or Routine: I **exercise** every day. Schedule: She **starts** work at eight. Fact: It **rains** a lot in April.	
2. Add -s to the verb for *he, she, it*, and singular subjects.	He **drives** to work. She **works** in an office. The bank **opens** at 9:00 a.m.	
3. Do not put *be* in front of another verb in the simple present.	✓ He works at a bank. ✗ He <u>is work</u> at a bank.	

4 Circle the correct form of the verb to complete each sentence.

1. Doctor Moffett **love** / **(loves)** his job.
2. He **study** / **studies** ants.
3. A salesperson **sell** / **sells** products for a company.
4. You and Anita **work** / **works** on weekends.
5. Nurses **help** / **helps** people.
6. We **write** / **writes** science books.
7. Our office **close** / **closes** at 7:00 p.m.
8. She **take** / **takes** classes at the business school.
9. You **walk** / **walks** to work every day.
10. I **start** / **starts** work at 8:00 a.m. every morning.

5 **WRITE & SPEAK.** List three activities you do often. Share your sentences with a partner. Then tell the class about your partner.

Student A: *I study. I play games. I talk with my friends.*

Student B: *Maria studies. She plays games. She talks with her friends.*

6 Complete each sentence with the correct form of the verb in parentheses.

1. A zookeeper ____feeds____ (feed) animals.
2. Computer programmers _____ (write) software.
3. Photographers _____ (take) photos.
4. A chef _____ (cook) food.
5. A firefighter _____ (fight) fires.
6. Musicians _____ (play) instruments.
7. A farmer _____ (work) on a farm.
8. A dancer _____ (dance).

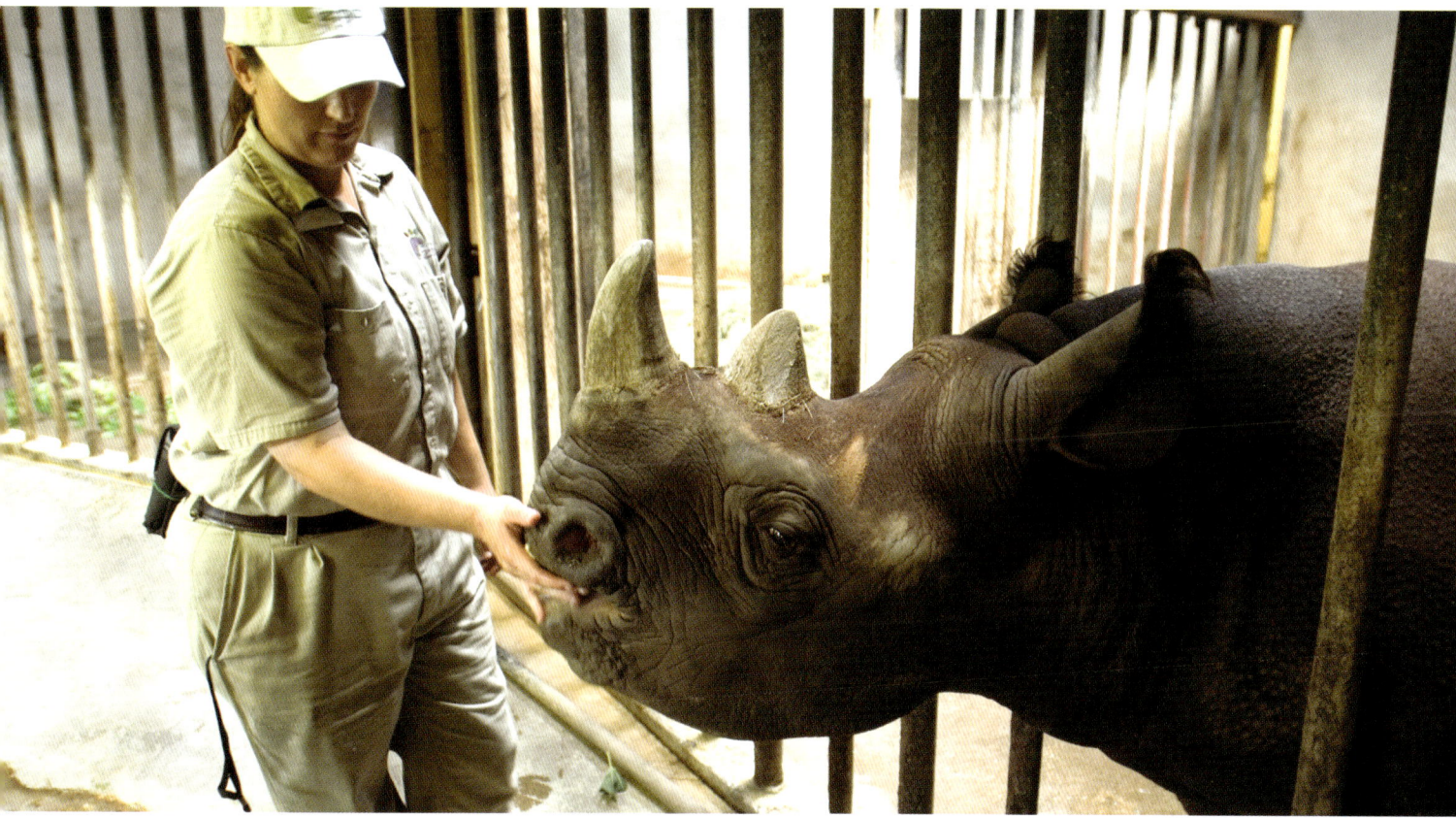

▼ A zookeeper feeds a rhino at the Sedgwick County Zoo in Wichita, Kansas, USA.

3.2 Simple Present Spelling Rules: -s and -es Endings

1. Add -s to most verbs.	close–close**s** dance–dance**s** exercise–exercise**s** feed–feed**s**	love–love**s** open–open**s** play–play**s** put–put**s**	stop–stop**s** take–take**s** write–write**s** work–work**s**
2. Add -es to verbs ending in -sh, -ch, -s, -x, and -z.	wash–wash**es** teach–teach**es**	dress–dress**es** relax–relax**es**	buzz–buzz**es**
3. Change -y to -i and add -es to verbs ending in a consonant + y.	carry–carr**ies**	copy–cop**ies**	study–stud**ies**

See page **A2** for additional spelling rules for -s, -es, and -ies endings.

7 Write each verb with the correct -s, -es, or -ies ending.

1. study _studies_
2. fish _____
3. pass _____
4. worry _____
5. explore _____
6. bite _____
7. buy _____
8. help _____
9. miss _____
10. fly _____
11. fix _____
12. watch _____
13. like _____
14. pay _____

3.3 Irregular Verbs: *Do, Go,* and *Have*

Subject	Verb		Subject	Verb	
I	do	the dishes every day.	He	does	the dishes every day.
You	go	to work at 7:00 a.m.	She	goes	to work at 7:00 a.m.
We			It		
You	have	dinner at 6:00 a.m.		has	dinner at 6:00 a.m.
They					

The verbs *do, go,* and *have* are irregular for *he, she, it,* and singular subjects.

She **goes** home at six-thirty.
He **has** a meeting at two-thirty.
John **does** the laundry on Sunday night.

8 Complete the paragraphs with the correct form of the verbs in parentheses.

Manuel and Lila Vega

Manuel and Lila Vega (1) ___have___ (have) a busy lifestyle. Manuel is a doctor at a hospital. He works at night, so he (2) _____ (go) to work at 7:00 p.m. and comes home at 7:00 a.m. His wife Lila works at a bank. She (3) _____ (go) to work at 8:00 a.m. and comes home at 6:00 p.m. They don't see each other a lot during the week.

Manuel and Lila also (4) _____ (have) two children, Luis and Carla. Every morning they all (5) _____ (have) breakfast together at 7:30. Then, Luis and Carla (6) _____ (go) to school, and Lila (7) _____ (go) to work. Manuel (8) _____ (do) the dishes, and then (9) _____ (go) to bed. Carla usually (10) _____ (do) her homework at a friend's house in the afternoon, and Luis (11) _____ (have) soccer practice. Manuel gets up at 4:00 p.m. At 6:00 p.m., he (12) _____ (have) dinner with Lila, Luis, and Carla. After dinner, he (13) _____ (go) to work. Manuel and Lila (14) _____ (have) a busy schedule during the week, but on weekends they relax.

PRACTICE

9 Complete the paragraphs with the correct form of the verbs in parentheses. Then listen and check your answers.

Bush Pilots

Bush pilots (1) ___have___ (have) interesting jobs. They (2) _____ (fly) special planes to Alaska's bush country. (This is a wild area, far away from cities with airports.) Bush pilots (3) _____ (carry) people or supplies in their bush planes. They also (4) _____ (help) rescue people.

Paul Claus is a famous bush pilot. He (5) _____ (have) a lot of experience, and he is an excellent pilot. Paul also (6) _____ (own) a hotel in Alaska. He (7) _____ (fly) customers to his hotel and (8) _____ (take) them on adventures. He (9) _____ (go) to interesting places with them. It's an exciting job!

▲ Bush planes on a glacier in Denali National Park, Alaska, USA

10 EDIT. Read the paragraph. Find and correct five more errors with the simple present.

Bill is a mechanic. He know^s a lot about cars. He work at a garage. He fix cars and talks to customers. They asks questions about their cars. Bill works from 8:00 a.m. to 6:00 p.m. every day. He haves a busy schedule, but he like his job very much.

11 PRONUNCIATION. Read the chart and listen to the examples. Then complete the exercises.

PRONUNCIATION	Simple Present -s and -es Endings		
The ending of third-person singular verbs has three sounds: /s/, /z/, /əz/	/s/ walks	/z/ pays	/əz/ fixes
1. Say /s/ after /p/, /t/, /k/, and /f/ sounds.	stop-stops	put-puts	work-works laugh-laughs
2. Say /z/ after /b/, /d/, /g/, /l/, /m/, /n/, /ŋ/, /r/, /v/, and /ð/ sounds, and after vowel sounds.	rub-rubs read-reads bag-bags feel-feels	come-comes spin-spins sing-sings hear-hears	love-loves bathe-bathes pay-pays go-goes
3. Say /əz/ after verbs that end in /s/, /z/, /ʃ/, /tʃ/, /dʒ/, and /ks/.	kiss-kisses buzz-buzzes	wash-washes watch-watches	judge-judges relax-relaxes

See page **A4** for a guide to pronunciation symbols.

A Read the sentences about Rick's schedule. Then listen and circle the sound you hear for the verb in each sentence.

Rick's Schedule

1. Rick **wakes** up at 6:15 a.m. every morning.	(/s/)	/z/	/əz/
2. He **jogs** for an hour in the park.	/s/	/z/	/əz/
3. Then he **takes** a shower.	/s/	/z/	/əz/
4. He **brushes** his teeth.	/s/	/z/	/əz/
5. He **eats** breakfast at 7:45.	/s/	/z/	/əz/
6. He **reads** the newspaper.	/s/	/z/	/əz/
7. He **washes** the dishes.	/s/	/z/	/əz/
8. Then he **drives** to work.	/s/	/z/	/əz/
9. He **starts** work at 8:30.	/s/	/z/	/əz/
10. He **goes** home at 5:30.	/s/	/z/	/əz/
11. He **relaxes** on Saturday and Sunday.	/s/	/z/	/əz/
12. He **loves** weekends!	/s/	/z/	/əz/

B Work with a partner. Practice reading the sentences from exercise **A**. Pay attention to the pronunciation of the –s and -es endings.

12 LISTEN & SPEAK.

A Look at the list of activities in the chart. Then listen to the conversation between two teachers. Who does each activity? Check (✓) the correct column(s).

	Alvaro	Galina
1. lives in Ecuador	✓	
2. lives in Russia		
3. teaches at a university		
4. teaches at a high school		
5. teaches biology		
6. gets up early		
7. goes home at 3:00 p.m.		
8. goes home at 6:00 p.m.		
9. meets with students after class		
10. relaxes on Saturday		

B Compare your answers from exercise **A** with a partner. Then practice saying sentences about Alvaro and Galina. Use the information from the chart.

Alvaro lives in Ecuador.

C In your notebook, write sentences about Alvaro and Galina. Use the chart from exercise **A** to help you.

Alvaro lives in Ecuador.

13 READ, SPEAK & WRITE.

A Read the e-mail about Rosa's new job. Guess her job. Then discuss your idea with a partner.

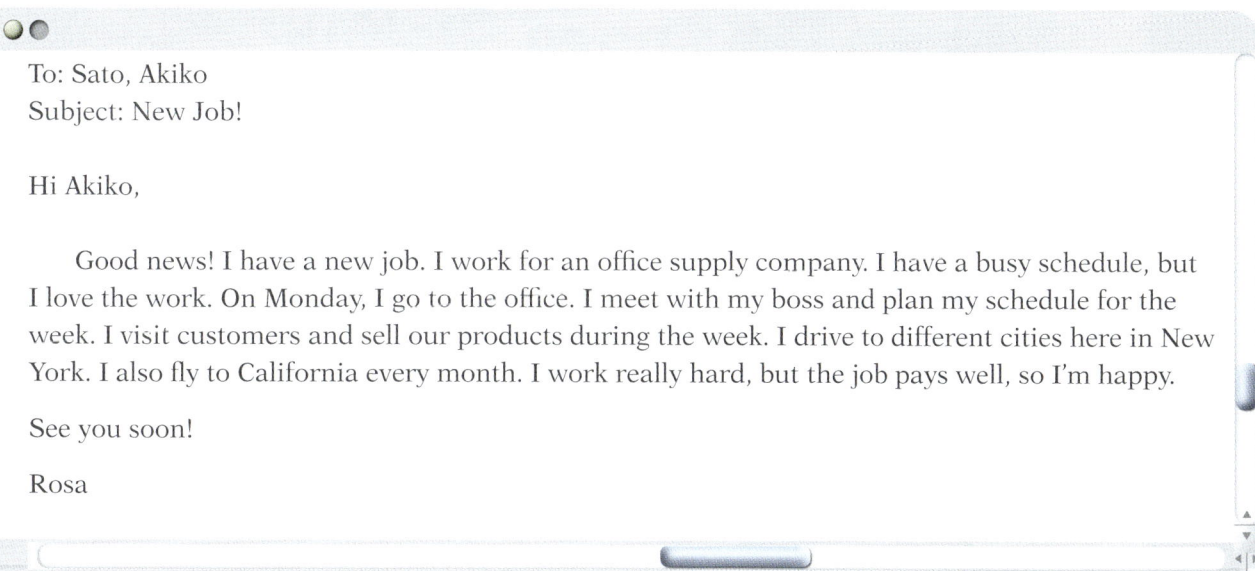

To: Sato, Akiko
Subject: New Job!

Hi Akiko,

Good news! I have a new job. I work for an office supply company. I have a busy schedule, but I love the work. On Monday, I go to the office. I meet with my boss and plan my schedule for the week. I visit customers and sell our products during the week. I drive to different cities here in New York. I also fly to California every month. I work really hard, but the job pays well, so I'm happy.

See you soon!

Rosa

B Write five sentences about Rosa's new job. Use the information from the e-mail in exercise **A**.

Rosa goes to the office on Monday.

14 APPLY. In your notebook, write a paragraph about a friend's or family member's job. Do not write the name of his or her job. Use the model to help you.

My cousin Maya has an interesting job. She has ballet class every morning. Then, she goes to the gym and exercises for two hours. She has a short break after lunch, and then she practices her dances. She gives performances on the weekends.

B Work with a partner. Exchange paragraphs and try to guess the person's job.

▶ A ballet dancer

LESSON 2 — Simple Present: Negative Statements and Contractions

EXPLORE

1 READ the article about life on the International Space Station. Notice the words in **bold**.

Life on the Space Station

Astronauts on the International Space Station have a busy schedule. Every day they wake up at 7:00 GMT.[1] **From 7:00 to 8:00,** they wash up and eat breakfast. **At 8:00 in the morning,** they call Ground Control[2] in their countries. After they talk to Ground Control, their workday begins. The astronauts **don't do** the same thing every day. Their schedules change every week.

The astronauts **don't work** all the time. Each day they exercise for an hour **in the morning** and an hour **in the afternoon**. After dinner, they have free time. Then, it's time to go to sleep. Sometimes this isn't easy because the sun rises and sets 16 times each day on the space station.

The astronauts' work **doesn't end** on Friday. They work a half day **on Saturday** and all day **on Sunday**. Astronauts are very busy people.

[1] **GMT:** Greenwich Mean Time
[2] **Ground Control:** People on Earth who work with astronauts in space.

◀ The International Space Station (ISS)

▼ The center of the Whirlpool Galaxy

2 CHECK. Match each of the astonauts' activities with the correct time.

1. They wash up and have breakfast. _d_
2. They talk to Ground Control. ____
3. They exercise. ____
4. They have some free time. ____
5. They need to work a half day. ____

a. at 8:00 in the morning
b. after dinner
c. on Saturday
d. from 7:00 to 8:00 in the morning
e. for an hour in the morning and an hour in the afternoon

3 DISCOVER. Complete the exercises to learn about the grammar in this lesson.

A Find these sentences in the article from exercise **1**. Write the missing words.

1. The astronauts don't _____ the same thing every day.
2. Astronauts don't _____ all the time.
3. The astronauts' work doesn't _____ on Friday.

B Look at the sentences from exercise **A**. Then circle **T** for *true* or **F** for *false* for each statement below. Discuss your answers with your classmates and teacher.

1. Use the base form of the verb after *don't*.   T   F
2. Add an *-s* to the base form of the verb after *doesn't*.   T   F

UNIT 3   LESSON 2   **89**

LEARN

3.4 Simple Present: Negative Statements

Subject	Do Not/ Don't	Base Form of Verb	Subject	Does Not/ Doesn't	Base Form of Verb
I You We You They	do not don't	work.	He She It	does not doesn't	work.

Be careful! In negative statements with *does not* or *doesn't*, do not add *-s* to the base form of the verb.

✓ She **doesn't exercise** every day.
✗ She doesn't exercise<u>s</u> every day.

4 Circle *doesn't* or *don't* to complete each sentence.

1. An astronaut on the International Space Station **(doesn't)** / **don't** have a lot of free time.
2. Astronauts **doesn't** / **don't** work all day on Saturday.
3. An astronaut **doesn't** / **don't** have the same schedule every day.
4. We **doesn't** / **don't** work on weekends.
5. I **doesn't** / **don't** work in an office.
6. My office **doesn't** / **don't** have a window.
7. She **doesn't** / **don't** travel for her job.
8. You **doesn't** / **don't** have a busy schedule.

5 Change each affirmative statement to a negative statement.

1. My brother has a job. _My brother doesn't have a job._
2. I drive to work. _____
3. Pilots fix planes. _____
4. Our teacher does homework. _____
5. I go to the gym in the morning. _____
6. We have class on Sunday. _____
7. You teach biology. _____
8. We have an exam on Saturday night. _____

6 SPEAK. Work with a partner. Make negative statements with the words below.

I …	work
My mother …	study
My father …	exercise
My …	drive to class/work

Student A: *I don't drive to class.*   Student B: *My mother doesn't study.*

3.5 Prepositions of Time (Part 2)

1. Many time expressions are prepositional phrases. A prepositional phrase is a preposition + a noun.	Preposition Noun **at** <u>three-thirty</u> **in** <u>the afternoon</u> **at** <u>night</u> **on** <u>Sunday</u>	
2. **Remember:** Use *at* with specific times and in the phrase *at night*.	The bank opens **at** nine o'clock. We relax **at** night.	
Use *in* with *morning, afternoon,* and *evening*.	We go to work **in** the morning. We eat dinner **in** the evening.	
Use *on* with days of the week and specific dates.	I don't work **on** Saturday. The meeting is **on** Monday afternoon. His birthday is on November 25th.	
3. To show when an activity begins and ends, use *from . . . to*.	She works **from** nine **to** five-thirty.	
4. Use *until* to talk about an activity that continues up to a specific time.	The bank is open **until** four o'clock.	
5. A sentence can have more than one prepositional phrase.	He wakes up <u>at five-thirty</u> <u>in the morning</u>.	

For Prepositions of Time (Part 1), see Unit 2, Lesson 3.

REAL ENGLISH

To be less specific, we use *around* and *about*.

*We usually eat dinner at **about** 8:00. (We don't eat exactly at 8:00 every night.)*

*I usually leave work at **around** 6:00. (I don't leave work at exactly 6:00 every night.)*

7 Underline the prepositional phrases in these sentences.

1. We have class <u>from 9:40 to 10:50</u>.
2. On Wednesday, I have class until 3:30.
3. The party is on Saturday night.
4. The meeting doesn't end until 3:00.
5. My workweek is from Monday to Friday.
6. I work from 9:00 to 7:00 on Tuesday and Wednesday.
7. I don't work on weekends.
8. She doesn't get home until 4:00 in the afternoon.

8 Complete each sentence with the correct preposition(s).

1. She works __at__ night.
2. The meeting is _____ Wednesday afternoon.
3. I sleep _____ 9:30 _____ the morning _____ Saturday.
4. I work _____ Monday _____ Friday.
5. Class starts _____ 8:30 _____ the morning.
6. We study _____ night.
7. The library is open _____ eleven o'clock _____ night.
8. I have lunch _____ 12:00 _____ 1:00 every day.
9. She goes to bed _____ 1:00 a.m. _____ Friday and Saturday.
10. We have a break _____ 10:30 _____ 10:45 _____ the morning.

9 WRITE & SPEAK. Complete the sentences with prepositional phrases of time. Use the prepositions from chart **3.5** on page 91. Then share your sentences with a partner.

1. I have breakfast __at 7:00.__
2. English class starts _____
3. We have class from _____
4. I have lunch _____
5. I have dinner _____

3.6 *Like, Need,* and *Want* + Infinitive

Subject	Verb	Infinitive	
I	like	to exercise	in the morning.
He	likes		
We	need	to relax	today.
She	needs		
They	want	to meet	every week.
He	wants		

1. An infinitive is *to* + the base form of the verb.	He likes **to play** soccer.
2. Some verbs are followed by infinitives.	We <u>want</u> **to play** soccer. She <u>needs</u> **to call** her boss. I <u>like</u> **to read**. ✓ We **want to leave**. ✗ We <u>want leave</u>.

92 SIMPLE PRESENT: PART 1

10 Put the words in the correct order to make sentences.

1. Saturday / to / work / They / need / on __They need to work on Saturday.__
2. He / have / lunch / wants / at / 1:00 / to _____
3. tonight / to / need / work / until / 7:00 / You _____
4. need / buy / I / to / computer / a / new _____
5. She / play / to / likes / tennis _____
6. want / watch / to / the game / We _____
7. to / He / study / in the library / likes _____
8. need / I / do / my homework / to _____
9. need / I / my / call / mother / to _____
10. ask / to / wants / a / She / question _____

PRACTICE

11 SPEAK.

A Work with a partner. Complete the sentences with information about yourself. Use prepositional phrases, the simple present, and infinitives.

I get up . . .	I like . . . on weekends.
I have breakfast . . .	I need . . . today.
On weekends, I sleep until . . .	I do my homework . . .
I go to bed . . .	I want to . . .

Student A: *I go to bed at midnight.*

Student B: *I do my homework in the morning.*

B Work in a group. Say three sentences about your partner. Use the information from exercise **A**.

Student A: *Sun-hee does her homework in the afternoon.*

Student B: *Walid goes to bed at midnight.*

Student C: *Maria likes to relax on Sundays.*

REAL ENGLISH

Use *on weekends* to talk about activities that happen every weekend or on most weekends.

We relax on weekends.
She doesn't work on weekends.

12 READ, WRITE & SPEAK.

A Read the information about Lia. Then complete the sentences in the chart below with the correct form of the verbs in parentheses and the correct prepositions of time.

> Lia is from Indonesia. She works in Toronto, Canada. This is her first time away from home, and she misses her life in Indonesia. Her life is very different in Canada!

In Indonesia

1. Lia's mother ____cooks____ (cook) breakfast for her.
2. Lia _____ (have) classes _____ 9:30 _____ 12:30 from Monday to Saturday.
3. Lia _____ (go) out with her friends _____ weekends.

In Canada

4. Lia's mother _____ (not cook) breakfast for her.
5. Lia _____ (have) breakfast at a coffee shop _____ about 7:15 _____ the morning.
6. Lia _____ (not have) classes _____ the morning.
7. She _____ (work) _____ 9:00 _____ 5:00 _____ Monday _____ Friday.
8. She also _____ (study) at a business school because she _____ (want to) start a business in Indonesia someday.
9. She _____ (have) a class _____ 6:00 _____ 9:00 _____ night _____ Tuesday and Thursday.
10. Lia _____ (not have) many friends in Toronto.
11. She _____ (not go) out _____ weekends.
12. She _____ (be) lonely.
13. She _____ (miss) her friends in Indonesia.

B Is your life similar to Lia's life, or is it different? Complete the sentences with information about your life.

1. My life is (similar to / different from) Lia's life. In the morning, I _____.
2. During the day, I _____ from _____ to _____.
3. At night, I _____.
4. I _____ friends in _____.
5. On weekends, I _____.
6. I _____ lonely.

C Work with a partner. Share your sentences from exercise **B**.

My life is different from Lia's life. In the morning, I have breakfast at home.

13 EDIT. Read the paragraph. Find and correct six more errors with negatives and prepositions of time.

> Iris is a reporter. She works for a newspaper. She asks questions and writes articles. She ~~don't~~ *doesn't* drive to work. She walks. She don't work in the morning. She works from 2:00 p.m. in 11:00 p.m. She doesn't goes to bed early. She goes to bed on 1:00 a.m. She doesn't work at Saturday and Sunday. She relaxes in weekends.

14 Complete the conversation below. Use words from the box. You can use some words more than once. Then listen and check your answers.

| work | have | from | at | to | in | on |

REAL ENGLISH

Use *How about . . .?* to make suggestions.

A: *Hi. How about coffee this afternoon? I'm free at 4:00.*

B: *Sorry. I work from 9:00 to 5:00. How about Saturday afternoon?*

Ted: Hi, Jana!

Jana: Hey, Ted! How about coffee sometime? (1) I'm free ___in___ the morning ___on___ Thursday.

Ted: (2) I _____ class in the morning. (3) How about _____ 2:00?

Jana: Sorry. I'm not free then. (4) I _____ soccer practice _____ 2:00 _____ 4:00. How about Saturday?

Ted: I'm sorry. (5) I _____ on Saturday _____ 9:00 _____ 5:00. How about Sunday afternoon?

Jana: Sure. That sounds good. (6) How about _____ 2:00?

Ted: Great. See you then!

15 SPEAK. Work with a partner. Partner A, look at the schedule on this page. Partner B, look at the schedule on page **A5**. Do not show each other your schedules. Find a time to meet for coffee. Use the suggestions and answers from the chart below.

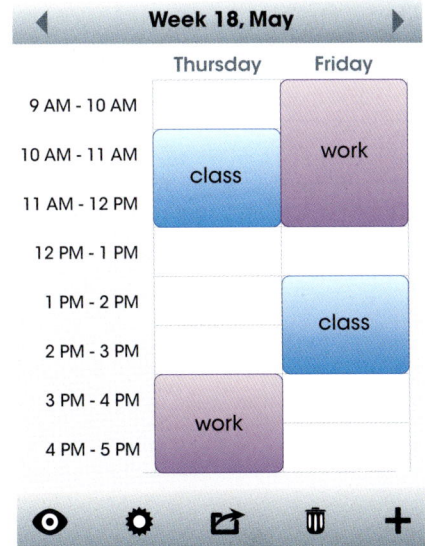

Partner A's Schedule

Week 18, May

	Thursday	Friday
9 AM - 10 AM		
10 AM - 11 AM	class	work
11 AM - 12 PM		
12 PM - 1 PM		
1 PM - 2 PM		class
2 PM - 3 PM		
3 PM - 4 PM	work	
4 PM - 5 PM		

Suggestions	Answers
How about coffee sometime?	Sure. That sounds good.
How about (*time of day*)?	I'm sorry. I have __(class / practice / work / a meeting)__.
How about (*time*)?	
OK. See you then.	Great.

16 LISTEN & SPEAK.

CD1-37

A Listen to the information about workweeks around the world. Check (✓) the workdays for each country in the chart.

	M	T	W	Th	F	Sat	Sun
Canada							
United States							
Thailand							
Austria							
Saudi Arabia							
United Arab Emirates							
Japan							
India							

B Work with a partner. Use the information in your chart from exercise **A** to make true and false statements. Say a statement. Your partner will say "true" or "false" and correct your false statements.

Student A: *People in Canada don't work on Monday.*

Student B: *That's false. People in Canada work on Monday.*

C Tell your partner about the workweek in your country or a country you know about.

People in my country work from Monday to Friday. They don't work on Saturday and Sunday.

17 APPLY.
Write six sentences about the workweeks in different countries. You can write about countries from exercise **16A** or use your own ideas.

People in Canada work from Monday to Friday.
_____
_____
_____
_____
_____
_____

Verbs + Objects   LESSON 3

EXPLORE

 1 READ the conversation about the elephant keepers in Kenya. Notice the words in **bold**.

Elephant Keepers

Bill: Wow! This is an interesting article.

Sue: Oh, baby elephants! Look at **them!** They're so cute! Where are their mothers?

Bill: Hunters killed **them**.

Sue: That's terrible!

Bill: Yeah, it is. These men are elephant keepers. They work at a place for orphan[1] elephants in Kenya. They feed **the baby elephants**, take care of **them**, and even play **soccer** with them.

Sue: Hmmm. Elephant keeper. That's an interesting job.

Bill: Yes, but it isn't easy. The keepers need to feed **the baby elephants** every three hours.

Sue: Really? What about at night?

Bill: They need to feed **them** at night, too. The keepers sleep in buildings with the baby elephants. . . . Listen to this quote from the article. One of the keepers says, "Every three hours you feel **a trunk** reach up and pull **your blankets**[2] off. The elephants are our alarms."

Sue: That's funny. Smart elephants! I want to read **that article**.

[1] An **orphan** is a child or baby animal whose parents are dead.
[2] People use **blankets** in bed at night to stay warm.

▼ Baby elephants and elephant keepers in Nairobi, Kenya

▲ Baby elephants play with their keeper in a wildlife refuge in Nairobi, Kenya.

2 CHECK. Read the false statements about elephant keepers. Then correct each statement to make it true.

    ↓ elephants

1. The keepers feed the ~~baby~~.

2. Hunters killed the baby elephants.

3. The keepers work in Botswana.

4. The keepers sleep in houses with their families.

3 DISCOVER. Complete the exercises to learn about the grammar in this lesson.

A Look at these sentences from the conversation from exercise **1** on page 97. Notice the words in **bold**. Then choose the correct word to complete the statement below.

1. They feed **the baby elephants** . . .

2. I want to read **that article.**

The words in bold in these sentences are _____ .

    a. subjects   b. objects of the verb

B Discuss your answer from exercise **A** with your classmates and teacher.

LEARN

3.7 Verb + Object / Verb + Preposition + Object

Subject	Verb/Verb + Preposition	Object	
I	teach	children.	
He	drives	a bus	every day.
We	listen to	music	a lot.
She	looks at	magazines	in her free time.

1. Many verbs take an object. The object receives the action of the verb. It can be a person or thing.

   Doctors help people.
   We study English.
   She needs a new car.

2. Some verbs are followed by a preposition. Verb + preposition combinations also take an object.

   Many people listen to music.
   I worry about my grades a lot.
   He waits for his sister every day after class.

4 Circle the verb and underline the object in each sentence.

1. He (helps) baby elephants.
2. They play soccer.
3. He likes his job.
4. She writes articles.
5. We visit customers every day.
6. You need a new computer.
7. I ride my bike every day.
8. Makiko loves weekends.

5 Put the words in the correct order to make sentences.

1. has / a / new / job / He   He has a new job.
2. A / cars / mechanic / fixes _____
3. has / huge / office / a / Jasmin _____
4. feed / Zookeepers / animals _____
5. her boss / Deanna / every day / talks to _____
6. beautiful / photographs / takes / Jay _____
7. music / listen to / I / at night _____
8. misses / Katrina / her friends _____

6 WRITE & SPEAK. Complete each sentence with an object. Then share your statements with a partner.

1. I speak _____.
2. I talk to _____ every day.
3. I watch _____ on TV.
4. I listen to _____.
5. I like _____.
6. I love _____.

Student A: *I watch movies on TV.*

Student B: *I love my children.*

3.8 Object Pronouns

Subject Pronouns	Example Sentences
I	I like Tina.
he	He likes Tina.
she	She is nice.
it	It is fun.
we	We know Al and Eva.
you	You are friends with Al and Eva.
they	They are your friends.

Object Pronouns	Example Sentences
me	Tina likes **me**.
him	She likes **him**.
her	I like **her**.
it	We like **it**.
us	They know **us**.
you	They like **you**.
them	You like **them**.

1. Object pronouns replace object nouns.	He rides the bus. → He rides **it** every day. I talk to my parents a lot. → I talk to **them** a lot.
2. Pronouns refer back to an earlier person or thing.	George loves pizza. He eats **it** every night. My sister's son and daughter are cute. I love **them**.

7 Complete the exercises.

A Circle the object pronoun in each pair of sentences.

1. Angel has a new job. He likes (it) a lot.
2. I'm Cory's boss. He works for me.
3. Sally is Joe's employee. She works for him.
4. My sister lives in Australia. I miss her a lot.
5. It's an excellent newspaper. I read it every day.
6. You are in my class. I sit behind you.
7. We go to the park on weekends. Henri sometimes comes with us.
8. Paulina has two dogs. She walks them in the park every morning.

B Work with a partner. Look at each sentence in exercise **A** again. What word or phrase does the object pronoun refer back to? Draw an arrow back to it.

1. Angel has a new job. He likes it a lot.

8 Complete each sentence with the correct object pronoun.

1. Nico's sister is in town this week. I want to meet ____her____.
2. It's my father's birthday today. I need to call _____.
3. She lives near her grandparents. She visits _____ on weekends.
4. Alexa has a difficult job, but she likes _____.
5. Are those students in our class? I don't know _____.
6. The teacher wants to meet with _____. She has a question about your homework.
7. Nadia and Jen want to attend the meeting. Please invite _____.
8. Fumiko is my best friend. She calls _____ every day.
9. Ron and Ella are our neighbors. They live near _____.
10. Spinach is my brother's favorite vegetable. He loves _____!

PRACTICE

9 Complete the exercises.

A Put the words in the correct order to make sentences.

1. thinks / about / He / Linda / every day _He thinks about Linda every day._
2. sometimes / Mr. and Mrs. Lee / visit / We _____
3. my parents / don't call / I / every day _____
4. her sister / Kate / loves _____
5. Fiona and Ken / He / sees / at work _____
6. music / doesn't / listen to / He / every night _____
7. my bike / I / ride / weekends / on _____
8. like / doesn't / his job / He _____

B Look at the sentences in exercise **A**. Replace each object with an object pronoun.

He thinks about ~~Linda~~ her every day.

10 LISTEN, WRITE & SPEAK.

A Listen to the information about three jobs. Match the jobs with the correct names. Write the letter on the line.

> a. pet food taster   b. crocodile hunters   c. golf ball diver

1. Kelly _____   2. Tim _____   3. Max and Jackson _____

B Read each statement. Then listen again. Circle **T** for *true* and **F** for *false*.

1. Kelly likes her job a lot.   T   F
2. The company pays Kelly a lot of money.   T   F
3. Tim sells balls at a golf course.   T   F
4. Tim doesn't wear scuba gear.   T   F
5. An alligator lives in the lake.   T   F
6. Max and Jackson live in South Africa.   T   F
7. Max and Jackson kill crocodiles.   T   F
8. Max and Jackson are very careful.   T   F

▲ Golf ball divers

C All of the statements below are false. Change each statement to make it true. Use a pronoun to replace the words in **bold**.

1. Tim looks for **golf balls** in the ocean.
   He doesn't look for them in the ocean. OR He looks for them in a lake.

2. Tim sells **used golf balls**. _____

3. Tim doesn't like **his job**. _____

4. Tim doesn't watch for **the alligator**. _____

5. Kelly likes **her job**. _____

6. People want **Kelly's job**. _____

7. Kelly eats **animal food**. _____

8. The pet food company doesn't pay **Kelly**. _____

9. An animal park pays **Max and Jackson**. _____

10. Most people don't worry about **crocodiles**. _____

D Work with a partner. Rank the jobs. Write 1, 2, or 3 for each category. (1 is the highest rank, and 3 is the lowest rank.)

	danger	difficulty	excitement	fun
pet food taster				
crocodile hunter				
golf ball diver				

Pet food taster is number 1 for difficulty.

11 READ & SPEAK. Work with a partner. Read about one of the people below. Then close your book. Tell your partner about the person from your paragraph. Use the *-s* form of the simple present and object pronouns.

Student A: *His name is Dan. He loves dogs and they love him.*

Dan
My name is Dan. I love dogs and they love me. I'm a professional dog walker. People pay me, and I take their dogs for walks. Sometimes I take the dogs to the park and run with them. The dogs are very fast, so it's good exercise for me. I have an unusual job, but I love it.

Clara
My name is Clara. I'm a bus driver. I drive a school bus. I take children to school in the morning and take them home in the afternoon. They say hello to me every morning, and sometimes they bring cookies or flowers. I love children, so it's a good job for me.

12 APPLY.

A Write five sentences about your work, your studies, or your family. Use objects and object pronouns.

I am a nurse. I help patients.

_____
_____
_____
_____

B Work with a partner. Share your sentences from exercise **A**.

LESSON 4   Imperatives

EXPLORE

1   READ the advice on how to get a job in game design. Notice the words in **bold**.

How to Get a Job in Game Design

Computer games are very popular. Even orangutans in the zoo enjoy them! A lot of people want to work in game design. Is it difficult to find a job? Lukas Bidelspach is an artist for an online game company. Here is his advice.[1]

- **Don't play** games all the time. Make them! **Use** your time to improve your skills.[2]
- **Don't worry** about a college degree. Experience is more important.
- **Show** your work to other people. **Listen** to their advice.
- **Keep** examples of your work. **Send** them to a game company.
- **Get** experience with a team. **Volunteer**[3] to work at a company.
- **Don't ask for** a lot of money at your first job. **Work** hard.

Good luck!

[1] People give **advice** to help other people.
[2] A **skill** is an ability that helps you do a job well.
[3] A **volunteer** does work for no money.

▼ An orangutan plays computer games in Zoo Atlanta, Atlanta, Georgia, USA.

◀ Young Buddhist monks play video games in Bodhgaya, India.

2 CHECK. Look at each idea in the chart. Does Lukas think it is a good idea or a bad idea? Check (✓) the correct column.

	Ideas	Good Idea	Bad Idea
1.	make games	✓	
2.	play games all the time		
3.	worry about a college degree		
4.	get experience		
5.	ask for a lot of money		

3 DISCOVER. Complete the exercises to learn about the grammar in this unit.

A Find and complete these sentences in the article from exercise **1**. Write the missing words.

1. _____ games all the time. Make them!

2. _____ about a college degree.

3. _____ your work to other people.

4. _____ examples of your work.

5. _____ hard.

B Look at the sentences from exercise **A**. Then circle **T** for *true* or **F** for *false* for each statement below. Discuss your answers with your classsmates and teachers.

1. All the verbs are negative.   **T**   **F**

2. We don't need to write the subjects with these verbs. **T**   **F**

3. The sentences all give advice.   **T**   **F**

UNIT 3 LESSON 4 **105**

LEARN

3.9 Imperatives: Affirmative

Base Form of Verb	
Be	on time for the meeting.
Close	the door.
Open	your books.

1. Use imperatives to give:
   a. commands;
   b. instructions;
   c. directions;
   d. warnings;
   e. advice.
	a. **Sit** down.
	b. **Complete** each sentence.
	c. **Turn** left.
	d. **Be** careful.
	e. **Try** again.

2. Use the base form of the verb for imperatives.	**Write** your name and address. **Do** your homework.
3. *You* is the subject of imperatives, but it is not common to write or say *you*.	**Open** your books. **Call** Margaret.
4. To be polite, use *please* with imperatives.	**Please** take your shoes off. Take your shoes off, **please**.

4 Underline the imperatives.

1. <u>Try</u> to meet people at game companies.
2. Ask people at game companies about their jobs.
3. Please tell me the truth. Do you really like your job?
4. Bob, please call me when you get this message.
5. Read the directions.
6. It's hot in here. Please open the window.
7. Turn right on Elm Street.
8. Please pass your papers to the center of the room.

5 Write an imperative for each situation. Use verbs from the box.

| ask | be | eat | give | go | stay | study | wear |

1. A: I have a test tomorrow. I'm not a good student.   B: _____Study_____ hard.
2. A: I have a big meeting tomorrow. It's midnight now.   B: _____ to sleep.

106 SIMPLE PRESENT: PART 1

3. A: I'm often late to class. I have a test tomorrow.   B: _____ on time.

4. A: I eat junk food every day.   B: _____ healthy food.

5. A: I have a cold. I also need to go shopping.   B: _____ home.

6. A: That old woman doesn't have a seat.   B: Please _____ her your seat.

7. A: Look at all that snow outside.   B: _____ your boots.

8. A: I don't understand the assignment.   B: _____ the teacher.

6 SPEAK. Work in a group. Give instructions. Use verbs from the box and imperatives.

| close | open | say | sit down | stand up | write |

Student A: *Say hello.*

Student B: *Stand up.*

Student C: *Open your book.*

3.10 Imperatives: Negative

Do Not/ Don't	Base Form of Verb	
Do not Don't	open	the windows.

1. To make an imperative negative, put *don't* or *do not* before the base form of the verb.

   Don't drink a lot of coffee.

2. *Do not* is common in formal writing. It is not common in informal writing or conversations.

   Do not park in front of this building.

REAL ENGLISH

In speaking, *Do not* is sometimes used for emphasis.

Do not eat this cake! It's for dessert.
Do not tell Maria about the party! It's a surprise.

7 Underline the imperatives.

1. It's cold. <u>Don't open</u> the window.

2. Don't worry. Everything is OK now.

3. Please don't sit there.

4. Don't stay up late tonight. You have a meeting at 8:00 a.m. tomorrow.

5. I want to read that book. Please don't tell me the ending.

6. Don't forget Eva's birthday. It's tomorrow.

7. Don't be late tomorrow. We have a test.

8. Don't go to that restaurant. The food there is terrible!

8 **SPEAK.** Work with a partner. Change the affirmative imperatives to negative imperatives. Student A reads the affirmative, Student B says the negative. Then change roles.

Student A: *Eat in the library.*

Student B: *Don't eat in the library.*

1. Eat in the library.
2. Be late for work.
3. Sit in that seat.
4. Use the elevator.
5. Call him at midnight.
6. Open the window.
7. Park your car here.
8. Feed the animals.
9. Close your book.
10. Use your phone in class.

PRACTICE

9 **SPEAK & WRITE.** Work with a partner. What do these signs mean? Match each imperative with the correct sign below.

a. ~~Stop.~~
b. Do not use your cell phone.
c. Be careful.
d. Do not feed the animals.
e. Do not eat or drink.
f. Do not enter.
g. Drive slowly.
h. Be quiet.

1. _a_   2. ____   3. ____   4. ____

5. ____   6. ____   7. ____   8. ____

108 SIMPLE PRESENT: PART 1

10 EDIT. Read the advice. Find and correct five more errors with imperatives.

How to Be a Good Employee

1. Be on time. ~~Doesn't~~ *Don't* be late.

2. Be friendly and polite to customers. You say "thank you."

3. Don't rude to coworkers.

4. Don't leaves work early. Stay until five o'clock.

5. Do not you use your cell phone in meetings.

6. Doesn't play computer games at work.

11 Complete the conversations with affirmative or negative imperatives. Use the verbs in the box. You can use each verb more than once.

| call | drink | get | go | quit | save | stay | take |

1. A: I want a job at a computer company, but I also want to take a psychology course.

   B: _____Don't take_____ a psychology course. _____ a course in math or computer science.

2. A: I don't like my job. I want to quit.

   B: _____ your job now. _____ another job first.

3. A: I have a cold. I need to go to a hospital.

   B: _____ to a hospital. Just _____ a doctor or _____ at home and _____ hot tea.

4. A: I'm tired. I need more sleep.

   B: Well, _____ to bed early, and _____ coffee at night.

5. A: I don't have very much money, but I want to go shopping.

   B: _____ shopping. _____ home and _____ your money.

UNIT 3 LESSON 4

12 LISTEN, SPEAK & WRITE.

A Read the list of activities. Then listen to advice on how to be an underwater photographer. Does the speaker think each activity is a good idea or a bad idea? Check (✓) the correct column.

	Good Idea	Bad Idea
1. Swim a lot.		
2. Learn about the ocean.		
3. Try to catch fish.		
4. Choose the right camera.		
5. Practice in a swimming pool.		
6. Jump into the water with your camera.		
7. Leave your camera in the sun.		
8. Have fun.		

▼ A hawksbill turtle

B Compare your answers from exercise **A** with a partner.

C Complete the chart with information from exercise **A**. Use affirmative and negative imperatives.

How to Be an Underwater Photographer: Advice	
Good Ideas	Bad Ideas
Swim a lot.	

13 APPLY.

A Work with a group. Discuss ways to improve your English. Use affirmative and negative imperatives.

Read in English.

Don't miss class.

B Make a chart in your notebook. Organize your ideas from exercise **A** in a chart. Use affirmative and negative imperatives. Use the chart from exercise **12C** as a model.

C As a group, present your advice to the class.

Improve your English! Here is our advice. Read in English. . . .

SIMPLE PRESENT: PART 1

UNIT 3 Review the Grammar

Charts 3.1, 3.4, 3.7, 3.8

1 Change each affirmative statement to a negative statement. Then change each underlined object to an object pronoun.

1. She reads the newspaper every morning. _She doesn't read it every morning._
2. She works with Todd and Oscar. _____
3. My brother has my book. _____
4. She teaches Barbara and me. _____
5. We talk to our friends every day. _____
6. She studies biology. _____
7. He knows my sister. _____
8. He fixes cars. _____

Charts 3.1–3.5

2 Look at the work schedule. Then complete the sentences below. Use the correct prepositions of time and the verbs in parentheses. Use the negative form when necessary.

Name	Days	Times	Break
Petra	MWF	9:00 a.m. – 5:30 p.m.	1:00 – 1:45 p.m.
Ali	M-F	3:00 a.m. – 12:00 p.m.	8:00 – 8:45 a.m.
Nadia	T/Th	11:00 p.m. – 6:00 a.m.	2:30 – 3:00 a.m.
Ken	T/Th	9:00 p.m. – 6:00 a.m.	2:00 – 2:30 a.m.
Cathy	M-F	10:00 a.m. – 6:00 p.m.	2:00 – 2:30 p.m.

1. Petra __works__ (work) from 9:00 a.m. _____ 5:30 p.m.
2. Petra _____ (work) _____ Tuesday or Thursday.
3. Ali _____ (work) _____ 12:00 p.m.
4. Ali _____ (have) a break _____ 8:00 a.m.
5. Nadia _____ (work) _____ the afternoon.
6. Nadia and Ken _____ (work) _____ night.
7. Ken _____ (have) a break _____ 2:00 a.m.
8. Cathy _____ (work) _____ 10:00 a.m. _____ 6:00 p.m.
9. Cathy _____ (work) _____ Saturday and Sunday.
10. Cathy and Petra _____ (have) their breaks _____ the afternoon.

UNIT 3 REVIEW THE GRAMMAR 111

Review the Grammar UNIT 3

3 **EDIT.** Read the paragraph. Find and correct six more errors with verbs and prepositions of time.

Charts 3.1–3.5

>   studies
> Max Kraushaar ~~studys~~ in Seattle. He likes to bake. At Friday and Saturday morning, he bake pies. In night, people call or text Max. They order pies, and Max delivers them. He doesn't drives a car. He rides a bicycle and carries the pies in a basket. He takes orders until 3:00 a.m. Max's company have a funny name. He calls it "Piecycle."

4 Complete the paragraph with the correct form of the verbs in parentheses and prepositions of time. Then listen and check your answers.

CD1-42
Charts 3.1–3.2, 3.10

A Dangerous Job

Chris Hansen (1) _____works_____ (work) in Alaska (2) ____in____ the winter. He (3) _____ (have) a job on a crab boat. He (4) _____ (fish) for crabs (5) _____ October (6) _____ January. Chris and the other fishermen (7) _____ (drop) heavy crab pots in the ocean and (8) _____ (pull) them back onto the boat a day later. Chris (9) _____ (not like) his job. It (10) _____ (be) very dangerous on the ocean. Even in bad weather, the work (11) _____ (not stop). The days (12) _____ (be) very short in the winter. The sun (13) _____ (not rise) (14) _____ about 10:00 a.m., and it (15) _____ (go) down (16) _____ around 4:00 p.m. Chris's mother (17) _____ (worry) about him. She (18) _____ (say), "(19) _____ (be) careful, Chris! (20) _____ (not fall) off the boat!" He (21) _____ (say), "(22) _____ (not worry), Mom!"

◀ Fishermen with a crab pot, Bering Sea, near southwest Alaska, USA

Charts
3.1, 3.2,
3.4–3.7

5 SPEAK & WRITE.

A Look at the activities in the chart. Then write notes about your schedule.

Activity	My Schedule	My Partner's Schedule
wake up	M–F 8:00; Sat, Sun 12:00	M–F 7:00; Sat, Sun 9:00
eat lunch		
work		
go shopping		
see my friends		

B Work with a partner. Discuss your schedules. Take notes about your partner's schedule in the chart in exercise **A**.

From Monday to Friday, I wake up at 7:00 a.m.

C Choose two of the activities from the chart in exercise **A**. Write sentences about your schedule and your partner's schedule.

Marisol wakes up at 7:00 a.m. I wake up at 8:00 a.m.

Charts
3.1, 3.2,
3.4–3.10

CD1-43-46

6 LISTEN, SPEAK & WRITE.

A Listen to information about four problems. Write the number next to each problem when you hear about it.

_____ a test / a party   _____ an important meeting / a headache

__1__ a new job / no car   _____ a bad cold / the emergency room at a hospital

CD1-43-46

B Listen again. Then write two sentences about each problem.

1. Tom has a new job. He doesn't have a car.

2. _____

3. _____

4. _____

C Work with a partner. Write advice for the people from exercises **A** and **B**. Use imperatives.

1. Advice for Tom: Don't miss work! Ask a friend for help.

2. Advice for Sue: _____

3. Advice for Jay and Bill: _____

4. Advice for Ann and Jim: _____

UNIT 3 REVIEW THE GRAMMAR

Connect the Grammar to Writing

1 READ & NOTICE THE GRAMMAR.

A Read the paragraph. What is the writer's advice for new teachers? Discuss with a partner.

My Job as a Teacher

I am a teacher. I work from 8:00 a.m. to 1:30 p.m. I teach four English classes. In class, I write on the board. I ask a lot of questions. I use pictures when I teach vocabulary. I don't arrive late. At home, I plan my lessons. I correct homework and tests. My advice for new teachers—learn your students' names on the first day.

GRAMMAR FOCUS

In the paragraph in exercise **A**, the writer uses the simple present to talk about habits or routines and schedules.

> I **work** from 8:00 a.m. to 1:30 p.m.
> I **don't arrive** late.

B Read the paragraph in exercise **A** again. Underline the verbs in the simple present. Circle the imperative. Then compare your answers with a partner.

C Complete the chart with information from the paragraph in exercise **A**. What does a teacher do in class? At home?

The Job of a Teacher	
In Class	**At Home**
She asks a lot of questions.	
Advice: Learn your students' names.	

114 SIMPLE PRESENT: PART 1

Write about a Job

2 BEFORE YOU WRITE. Complete the chart with information about your job as a student. What do you do in class? At home? What advice do you have for new students? Use the chart from exercise **1C** as a model.

My Job as a Student	
In Class	At Home
Advice:	

3 WRITE a paragraph about your job as a student. Give advice for new students. Use the information from your chart in exercise **2** and the paragraph in exercise **1A** to help you.

> **WRITING FOCUS   Indenting Paragraphs**
>
> Good writers indent the first line of a paragraph. To indent, begin the first line of a paragraph five spaces to the right.
>
>   I am a teacher. I work from 8:00 a.m. to 1:30 p.m. I teach four English classes. In class, I write on the board. I ask a lot of questions.

4 SELF ASSESS. Read your paragraph. Underline the verbs in the simple present. Then use the checklist to assess your work.

- [ ] I did not put *be* in front of other verbs in the simple present. [3.1, 3.3]
- [ ] The verbs in the simple present are spelled correctly. [3.3]
- [ ] I used the base form of the verb for imperatives. [3.9, 3.10]
- [ ] The first line of my paragraph is indented. [WRITING FOCUS]

UNIT 4 Lifestyles

Simple Present: Part 2

▲ Food sellers at a floating market in Damnoen Saduak, Thailand

Lesson 1
page 118

Simple Present:
Yes/No Questions
and Short

Lesson 2
page 125

Frequency
Adverbs and
Expressions

Lesson 3
page 131

Simple Present:
Wh- Questions

Review the Grammar
page 139

Connect the Grammar to Writing

| LESSON 1 | Simple Present: *Yes/No* Questions and Short Answers |

EXPLORE

 1 READ the conversation about the people from the Nicoya Peninsula. Notice the words in **bold**.

The People from the Nicoya Peninsula

Nicoya Peninsula, Costa Rica

Mari: This is an interesting article.

Ben: Really? What's it about?

Mari: It's about the Nicoya Peninsula in Costa Rica. A lot of people there live to be 90 or 100.

Ben: Interesting. What's their secret? **Do they have a healthy diet?**

Mari: **Yes, they do!** They eat a lot of fruit, vegetables, beans, and rice. They also drink a lot of water.

Ben: Well, that sounds healthy. **Do they eat a lot of meat?**

Mari: **No, they don't.** They only eat meat about once a week.

Ben: **Does the article talk about exercise?**

Mari: Hmmm. Let's see. . . **Yes, it does.** It says the people there walk a lot and work outside—even the old people. . . Hey, listen to this—one woman there, Abuela Panchita, is over 100 years old, and she still walks everywhere!

Ben: Wow! That's amazing!

Mari: Yeah, it is. Also, many old people there live with their families. This makes them happy and helps them live longer.

Ben: Hmmm. That makes sense.

▶ A 96-year-old Costa Rican *sabanero* (or cowboy) still works hard.

2 CHECK. Read the statements. Circle **T** for *true* or **F** for *false*.

1. A lot of people from the Nicoya Peninsula live a long time.   (T)   F
2. They eat a lot of meat.   T   F
3. Abuela Panchita doesn't exercise.   T   F
4. A lot of old people from the Nicoya Peninsula live with their families.   T   F

3 DISCOVER. Complete the exercises to learn about the grammar in this lesson.

A Find three questions and answers in the conversation from exercise **1**. Write them in the chart.

Questions	Answers
Do they have a healthy diet?	

B Look at the questions and answers in your chart from exercise **A**. When do we use *Do*? When do we use *Does*? Discuss with your classmates and teacher.

UNIT 4 LESSON 1

LEARN

4.1 Simple Present: *Yes/No* Questions

Do/Does	Subject	Base Form of Verb
Do	I / you / we / you / they	work?
Does	he / she / it	

1. Use the base form of the verb after the subject in *Yes/No* questions in the simple present.
   - ✓ Does she **walk** a lot?
   - ✗ Does she **walks** a lot?

2. Do not use *do* or *does* in *Yes/No* questions with *be*.
   - ✓ Are you healthy?
   - ✗ Do you be healthy?

REAL ENGLISH

When the main verb is *do*, we still use *do* to start *Yes/No* questions.

A: **Do** you **do** your homework in the morning?
B: No, I **do** it in the afternoon.

A: **Does** he **do** the dishes at night?
B: No, he **does** them in the morning.

4 Circle the correct word to complete each question.

1. (Do) / Does people from the Nicoya Peninsula live a long time?
2. Do / Does they drink a lot of water?
3. Do / Does Abuela Panchita exercise?
4. Do / Does she have a healthy diet?
5. Do / Does they live with their families?
6. Do / Does they work outside?
7. Do / Does he eat a lot of vegetables?
8. Do / Does the article talk about exercise?

5 Change each statement to a *Yes/No* question.

1. Abuela Panchita walks every day. _Does Abuela Panchita walk every day?_
2. People from the Nicoya Peninsula eat beans and rice. _____
3. They live in Costa Rica. _____
4. He has a big family. _____
5. We have a healthy lifestyle. _____
6. You live with your grandparents. _____

7. She hikes six miles every day. _____

8. He is healthy and happy. _____

4.2 Simple Present: Short Answers to Yes/No Questions

Yes/No Questions			Short Answers				
Do/Does	Subject	Base Form of Verb	Affirmative			Negative	
Do	I you we you they	work?	Yes,	I you we you they	do.	No,	I you we you they	don't.
Does	he she it			he she it	does.		he she it	doesn't.

6 Complete the short answer for each Yes/No question.

1. A: Do healthy people exercise every day?
   B: Yes, _they do_ .

2. A: Does she live with her family?
   B: Yes, _____ .

3. A: Do they go on vacation every year?
   B: No, _____ .

4. A: Does she have a healthy diet?
   B: No, _____ .

5. A: Does he have a big family?
   B: No, _____ .

6. A: Do you live in a small town?
   B: No, _____ .

7. A: Do Juan and you travel a lot?
   B: Yes, _____ .

8. A: Do I need to eat more vegetables?
   B: Yes, _____ .

7 SPEAK. Work with a partner. Ask and answer the questions in exercise **6**. Use *Do you . . . ?*

Student A: *Do you exercise every day?*   Student B: *No, I don't.*

PRACTICE

8 WRITE, LISTEN & SPEAK.

A Complete the conversation with *Yes/No* questions and short answers. Then listen and check your answers.

Nora: Lucia, hi! How are you? (1) ___Do you like___ (you / like) Miami?

Lucia: (2) ___Yes, I do___. I love the university and the people, but the American lifestyle is so different from my lifestyle at home.

Nora: Really? (3) _____ (you / miss) Italy?

Lucia: (4) _____. I miss my family and friends—and the food.

Nora: (5) _____ (you / like) the food here?

Lucia: (6) _____. American food is terrible!

Nora: Well, I like it. (7) _____ (you / eat) different food in Italy?

Lucia: (8) _____. I don't eat fast food, and I eat fresh vegetables from our garden every day. We have a huge vegetable garden.

Nora: Well, that sounds healthy. (9) _____ (you / help) with the garden?

Lucia: (10) _____. It's a lot of work, but I enjoy it.

Nora: (11) _____ (your parents / speak) English?

Lucia: (12) _____. They only speak Italian and German.

Nora: (13) _____ (you / have) a big family?

Lucia: (14) _____. I have four brothers and three sisters.

Nora: Wow! That *is* a big family! (15) _____ (you all / live) in one house?

Lucia: (16) _____. My grandparents live with us, too. It's noisy, but I love it!

▼ The Dolomites, Val di Fassa, Italian Alps

B Work with a partner. Ask and answer questions (1), (5), (11), and (13) from the conversation in exercise **A**. Use your own answers, not the answers in the book.

Student A: *Do you like _____ (place) _____?*

Student B: *No, I don't. It's very cold. I miss my city.*

9 EDIT. Read the conversations. Find and correct five more errors with *Yes/No* questions and short answers.

1. A: Does Fabian have a big family?
   B: No, he ~~hasn't~~ *doesn't*. He only has one brother.

2. A: Do you work in an office?
   B: Yes, I do.
   A: You live in Toronto?
   B: No, I don't. I live in Montreal.

3. A: Does Richard likes his job?
   B: Yes, he does.

4. A: Does it rain a lot here?
   B: No, it don't. Does it rain a lot in London?
   A: Yes, it does.

5. A: Do you from Italy?
   B: Yes, I am. I live in Rome.

6. A: Do you eat meat?
   B: Yes, I eat.
   A: Do you like fish?
   B: No, I don't.

10 LISTEN & SPEAK.

A Read each statement in the chart. Then listen to Kate and Rena talk about their lifestyles. Is the statement true for Kate, Rena, or both? Put a check (✓) in the correct column(s).

	Kate	Rena
1. She has a job.	✓	✓
2. She cooks every day.		
3. She takes care of her family.		
4. She eats fast food.		
5. She drinks a lot of coffee.		
6. She sleeps every afternoon.		
7. She sleeps 4–5 hours every night.		
8. She needs a vacation.		
9. She has a healthy lifestyle.		
10. She has a stressful lifestyle.		

B Work with a partner. Ask and answer questions about Kate and Rena's lifestyles. Use the information from the chart in exercise **A**.

Student A: *Does Kate have a job?*

Student B: *Yes, she does.*

11 APPLY.

A Write six interview questions in the chart below to ask a classmate about his or her lifestyle.

Lifestyle Survey	Yes, I do.	No, I don't.
1. Do you walk a lot?		
2.		
3.		
4.		
5.		
6.		

B Work with a partner. Ask your questions from exercise **A**. Check your partner's answers.

Student A: *Do you walk a lot?*

Student B: *Yes, I do.*

Frequency Adverbs and Expressions | **LESSON 2**

EXPLORE

1 READ the article about night markets. Notice the words in **bold**.

Night Markets

Most people go to a market in the daytime. They go to buy food, but in some cities in Asia people **often** go to special street markets at night.

These night markets are very busy places. They're also interesting and fun. People **usually** go to night markets with friends. They walk around and look at the things for sale. They **often** buy special snacks[1] at the market. Some night markets are famous for unusual kinds of food. In Taipei (China), stinky[2] tofu is a popular snack. It has a very strong smell and taste. In Beijing, night markets sell fried insects.

Night markets aren't open **every night.** Some night markets are only open on weekends, and some night markets are only open **once a year** at New Year's. Night markets are **always** interesting. They are great places to go for food and entertainment.

[1] **snack:** a small serving of food
[2] **stinky:** an informal way to describe something with a bad smell

▲ A night market in Kaifeng, China

UNIT 4 LESSON 2 125

2 CHECK. Read the statements. Circle **T** for *true* or **F** for *false*.

1. Markets are usually open in the daytime.   (T)   F
2. Night markets are special street markets.   T   F
3. Stinky tofu has a nice smell.   T   F
4. Night markets are open every night.   T   F
5. Night markets are interesting places.   T   F

3 DISCOVER. Complete the exercises to learn about the grammar in this lesson.

A Find these sentences in the article from exercise **1** on page 125. Write the missing words.

1. People _____ go to night markets with friends.
2. They _____ buy special snacks at the market.
3. Night markets are _____ interesting.

B Look at your answers from exercise **A**. What do these words tell us? Choose the correct word(s) to complete the statement below. Then discuss your answer with your classmates and teacher.

These words tell us _____ .

a. where   b. what time   c. how often

▶ A street vendor cooks at a night market in Bangkok, Thailand.

LEARN

4.3 Frequency Adverbs

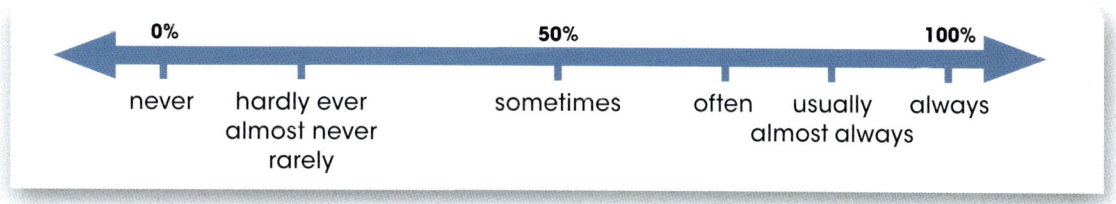

1. Frequency adverbs tell you how often something happens.	She **always** eats eggs for breakfast. I **sometimes** drink coffee at night.
2. Frequency adverbs usually come before other verbs.	✓ They **usually** <u>go</u> to the park. ✗ They <u>go</u> **never** to the park.
3. *Sometimes, often,* and *usually* can also come at the beginning or end of a statement.	**Sometimes** we go to the park. We go to the park **sometimes**.
4. *Rarely, almost never,* and *never* are negative in meaning. Do not use them with *don't* or *doesn't*.	✓ I **never** see Jack. ✗ I <u>don't</u> **never** see Jack.
5. Put frequency adverbs after the verb *be*.	✓ I'm **usually** late. ✗ I <u>usually am</u> late.

4 Put the frequency adverb in the correct place in each sentence.

1. (usually) The night market is ᵘˢᵘᵃˡˡʸ open on weekends.
2. (always) We go to the market with friends.
3. (usually) I buy a snack at the night market.
4. (rarely) The market is open in the morning.
5. (almost always) She goes shopping on Saturday afternoon.
6. (never) He buys groceries.
7. (sometimes) I eat dinner at ten o'clock.
8. (almost never) Marta eats dessert.

5 Put the words in parentheses in the correct order to complete each sentence.

1. I _____usually shop_____ (shop / usually) in the afternoon.
2. The grocery store _____ (always / busy / is).
3. Anna _____ (shops / rarely) at a market.
4. I _____ (am / never / hungry) in the morning.
5. We _____ (buy / always) snacks at the night market.
6. Night markets _____ (open / often / are) late at night.
7. Jim _____ (walks / almost never) to the store.
8. The farmer's market _____ (never / open / is) in the winter.

6 SPEAK. Work with a partner. Use frequency adverbs and the activities from the box to make sentences.

| buy snacks | shop at a grocery store | shop at an outdoor market |

Student A: *I rarely shop at a grocery store.*

Student B: *I usually buy snacks at the movie theater.*

4.4 Frequency Expressions

We go to the market	every day.
	every Monday.
	every week.
	once a week.
	twice a month.
	three times a day.
	four times a year.

1. Frequency expressions tell how often something happens.	We buy bread **twice a week**. He eats meat **every day**.
2. Frequency expressions can come at the beginning or end of a statement.	They go shopping **every Saturday**. **Every Saturday** they go shopping.
3. *once* = one time *twice* = two times *Once* is more common than *one time*.	The market is only open **once a year**. I go to the grocery store **twice** a week.
4. Use a singular noun after *every*. Use a plural noun after *every* + number.	We go there **every** month. We go there **every two** weeks.

7 Circle the correct word(s) to complete each sentence.

1. Mary goes to the market every **Saturdays** / **(Saturday)**.
2. Kara buys flowers **once** / **one** a week.
3. Every **night** / **nights** we eat Italian food.
4. Ben buys clothes **twice** / **two** times a year.
5. Once **week** / **a week** they go to the grocery store.
6. The store has a special sale three **time** / **times** a year.
7. I go to the bakery every **day** / **days**.
8. We usually go to the mall two times **month** / **a month**.
9. My mother buys bread every **day** / **days**.
10. Every three **day** / **days** Carl buys vegetables at the market.

SIMPLE PRESENT: PART 2

8 SPEAK. Work with a partner. Use the activities from the box and different frequency expressions to make sentences.

| exercise | go to a store | go to a restaurant |

Student A: *I exercise every day.*   Student B: *Really? I exercise twice a week.*

PRACTICE

9 LISTEN & WRITE.

A Listen to the information from a travel blog. Write the missing words.

Inside Thailand by Tom Hill

I (1) ___often travel___ for work. I go to Asia about (2) _____ . In Thailand, I (3) _____ to the floating markets. At a floating market, people sell things from their boats. They (4) _____ colorful umbrellas and wear large hats.

The Amphawa floating market is my favorite market, so I (5) _____ there. It's open every weekend from around 4:00 p.m. to about 8:00 p.m. I try a different snack (6) _____ . The Damnoen Saduak floating market is open every day from 7:00 a.m. to 11:00 a.m. I (7) _____ there because (8) _____ very crowded.

▲ The Amphawa floating market in Thailand

B Choose the correct word(s) to complete each sentence. Use the information from Tom Hill's travel blog in exercise **A** to help you.

1. Tom ____ travels for work.   a. almost never   (b.) often
2. ____ he goes to Asia.   a. Sometimes   b. Always
3. He goes there every ____ .   a. week   b. six months
4. He ____ goes to a floating market on his visits to Thailand.   a. usually   b. sometimes
5. Tom ____ goes to the Amphawa market.   a. almost always   b. every time
6. He ____ tries new snacks there.   a. sometimes   b. always
7. He ____ goes to the Damnoen Saduak floating market.   a. rarely   b. never
8. The Damnoen Saduak market is ____ crowded.   a. often   b. rarely

C Write sentences about the floating markets. Use the information from Tom Hill's travel blog in exercise **A** on page 129 and the words below.

1. (always) __People always sell things from their boats__ at the floating markets.
2. (almost always) They _____.
3. (every weekend) The Amphawa market _____.
4. (always) The Damnoen Suduak market _____.
5. (almost always) It _____.

10 **LISTEN** to a phone conversation about Sophie's lifestyle in Canada and France. Complete the notes.

In Canada
Sophie __almost never__ cooks.
She _____ goes to the grocery store.

In France
Sophie walks to the market _____.
She buys bread or pastries _____.
She cooks dinner _____.

11 **APPLY.** Work with a partner. Talk about how often you do each of the activities from the box. Use frequency expressions.

buy clothes on sale	go to a museum
eat candy	shop for clothes
exercise	shop for groceries
get a hair cut	take a bus

Student A: *I shop for food once a week. How about you?*

Student B: *Me, too. / I never shop for food! / I shop for food every day.*

REAL ENGLISH

Use *Me, too* and *Me neither* to show you share a feeling or an experience with someone.

Use *Me, too* after an affirmative statement.

  A: *I like shopping.*
  B: **Me, too.**

Use *Me neither* after a negative statement.

  A: *I don't exercise every day.*
  B: **Me neither.**

SIMPLE PRESENT: PART 2

Simple Present: Wh- Questions — LESSON 3

EXPLORE

1 READ the article about the Amish. Notice the words in **bold**.

The Amish

Who are the Amish and where do they live? Over 250,000 Amish people live in North America. Many live in Pennsylvania and Ohio in the United States. The Amish have a very traditional lifestyle. For example, most Amish people don't own cars or trucks. They own horses and ride in buggies.[1] Many Amish don't have electricity[2] in their houses.

Why do they live this way? The Amish believe in a simple lifestyle. Most Amish people live on farms near small towns. They don't want a lot of contact with the "outside" world.

It is easy to recognize the Amish. The men wear hats, dark pants and jackets, and white shirts. Amish women wear plain[3] dresses and white caps on their heads.

People often ask, "**What do they do for fun? What do they enjoy?**" They sometimes go to restaurants, and young people often play baseball or other games. The Amish enjoy their families, their community, and visits with other Amish families.

[1] **buggy:** a small carriage pulled by a horse
[2] **electricity:** energy used for power
[3] **plain:** simple, not fancy

▼ An Amish family rides in a buggy in Pennsylvania, USA.

131

2 CHECK. Choose the correct information to complete each statement.

1. Many Amish people live in ____.   (a.) North America   b. South America
2. Amish people own ____.   a. cars and trucks   b. horses and buggies
3. Their farms are ____.   a. near cities   b. near small towns
4. Amish women wear ____.   a. plain pants   b. white caps
5. Amish people ____ for fun.   a. visit other families   b. go to the movies

3 DISCOVER. Complete the exercises to learn about the grammar in this lesson.

A Find these questions in the article from exercise **1** on page 131. Write the missing words.

1. _____ do they live?
2. _____ do they live this way?
3. _____ do they do for fun?
4. _____ do they enjoy?

B Look at the questions from exercise **A**. Are the answers to these questions *Yes, No,* or other information? Discuss with your classmates and teacher.

◀ An Amish boy sits on a fence in New Bedford, Ohio, USA.

LEARN

4.5 Simple Present: *Wh-* Questions

Wh- Word	Do/Does	Subject		Answers
Who	do	you	see?	Ted and Amy.
What	do	the women	wear?	Plain dresses.
When	do	they	work?	From Monday to Friday.
Where	do	you	live?	In Berlin.
Why	does	he	live in Miami?	Because he likes the weather.
How	does	she	get to work?	She takes the subway.
How often	does	it	happen?	A lot.

1. Use *Wh-* questions to ask for specific information.

   A: **What** do they do for fun?
   B: They play baseball.

   A: **When** do you get up?
   B: At six-thirty.

2. Notice the difference between questions with *be* and questions with other verbs.

   Be: When **is** your class?

   Other Verbs: When **does** your class **start**?

REAL ENGLISH

Wh- words are often used alone as questions in conversation.

A: *I only sleep four hours a night.*
B: **Why?**
A: *I have two jobs.*

4 Add *do* or *does* to each question.

1. Where ^do^ many Amish people live?
2. How often they visit other families?
3. What an Amish woman wear?
4. Why they live on farms?
5. What an Amish child do for fun?
6. How often they go to big cities?
7. What *cap* mean?
8. When they go to restaurants?

5 Look at each sentence. Write a *Wh-* question about the underlined word or phrase.

1. We live in Ohio.   *Where do you live?*
2. She visits her grandparents.   _____

3. I exercise <u>at the gym</u>. _____

4. He plays baseball <u>because it's fun</u>. _____

5. She teaches <u>Spanish</u>. _____

6. They <u>play soccer</u> in their free time. _____

7. I visit my parents <u>once a week</u>. _____

8. They eat dinner <u>at eight o'clock</u>. _____

4.6 *Who* Questions about a Subject

Who	Verb	
Who	lives	here?
Who	is	our teacher?

1. *Wh-* questions with *Who* are sometimes about a subject.	A: **Who** speaks Spanish? B: <u>Mr. Lopez</u> does.
2. Always use the *-s/-es* form of the verb in *Who* questions about a subject. The answer can be singular or plural.	A: Who **has** my book? B: <u>Rita</u> does. A: Who **knows** the answer? B: <u>We all do</u>!
3. Do not use *do* or *does* + base form of verb when a *Who* question is about a subject.	✓ Who **lives** on that farm? ✗ Who <u>does live</u> on that farm?

6 Put the words in the correct order to make questions.

1. lives / Who / that / farm / on _Who lives on that farm?_

2. has / a traditional lifestyle / Who _____

3. plays / baseball / Who _____

4. wants / Who / coffee _____

5. absent / today / Who / is _____

6. Who / your laundry / does _____

7. speaks / Who / Japanese _____

8. drives / to class / Who _____

7 SPEAK. Work with a partner. Ask and answer questions 5–8 from exercise **6**.

Student A: *Who speaks Japanese?*   Student B: *Takeshi does.*

PRACTICE

8 WRITE, LISTEN & SPEAK.

A Complete the survey. Use *Who, What, When, Where, Why, How,* and *How often.* Then listen and check your answers.

Scott: Hello. Excuse me. Do you have time to answer some questions for a short survey?

Camila: Um . . . Yeah, OK.

Scott: Great! So, here's the first question. (1) ___Where___ do you live?

Camila: Here in Mexico. I'm from Puebla.

Scott: OK, thanks. (2) _____ do you live with?

Camila: My family—my husband and our two daughters. My mother lives with us, too.

Scott: Do you work?

Camila: Yeah, I do. I'm a nurse.

Scott: (3) _____ do you work?

Camila: At the Hospital Betania in Puebla.

Scott: (4) _____ do you get to work?

Camila: Well, I usually drive, but sometimes I take the bus.

Scott: (5) _____ do you start work?

Camila: Early. I usually start work at seven o'clock in the morning.

Scott: Wow! That *is* early! (6) _____ do you do for fun?

Camila: Well, I shop, and I listen to music.

Scott: Really? (7) _____'s your favorite musician?

Camila: Hmmm. Carla Morrison.

Scott: I like her music, too. Next question: (8) _____ do you take a vacation?

Camila: Twice a year.

Scott: Thanks. (9) _____ do you usually go on vacation?

Camila: Well, we usually go to the beach, but this year we want to see the mountains.

Scott: Nice! (10) _____ do you like the beach?

Camila: I love the sun and water! Who doesn't love the beach?

Scott: Well, those are all of my survey questions. Thank you very much!

Camila: No problem. Good luck with your survey!

> **REAL ENGLISH**
>
> *Well* is often used to begin the answer to a question.
>
> A: *When do you usually get up in the morning?*
> B: **Well,** *I usually wake up at 7:00, but on weekends I get up at around 9:00.*
>
> A: *Do you drive to work?*
> B: **Well,** *yes, but sometimes I ride my bike.*

B Work with a partner. Ask and answer questions about Camila.

Student A: *Where does she live?*

Student B: *In Puebla, Mexico.*

UNIT 4 LESSON 3

9 LISTEN and choose the correct answer to each question.

1. (a.) In the morning.   b. At school.
2. a. The Amish.   b. A small hat.
3. a. With her family.   b. In Puebla.
4. a. In France.   b. Marie.
5. a. In September.   b. Because traffic is terrible this morning.
6. a. Every day for lunch.   b. With Nancy.
7. a. At the coffee shop.   b. A sandwich.
8. a. I walk.   b. At 7:00 a.m.

10 READ, WRITE & SPEAK.

A Read the story about Jeremy Stubbs. Underline the verbs in each sentence.

52 Hikes a Year!

Jeremy Stubbs <u>lives</u> in Tacoma, Washington. He teaches math at a high school. On weekends, he likes to go on hikes. In fact, he goes on a hike every weekend, 52 times a year!

In the winter, Jeremy sometimes climbs a mountain trail in snowshoes[1] and carries his skis[2]. Then he has a fast trip back down the mountain on the skis!

Jeremy sometimes goes on hikes alone, but other teachers and students usually go with him. Sometimes he writes and posts photos on his blog, "52 Hikes 52 Weekends."

[1] People use **snowshoes** to walk on top of deep snow.
[2] People use **skis** to move quickly across snow, especially downhill.

▼ Mount Rainier National Park, Washington, USA

B Complete the questions about the story from exercise **A**.

1. Where __does Jeremy__ live?
2. What _____ at a high school?
3. When _____ to go on hikes?
4. How often _____ on hikes?
5. What _____ sometimes _____ in the winter?
6. Why _____ his skis?
7. Who usually _____ with him?
8. What _____ sometimes __ _____ alone?

C Work with a partner. Ask and answer the questions from exercise **B**.

Student A: *Where does Jeremy live?*
Student B: *In Tacoma, Washington.*

> **REAL ENGLISH**
>
> In conversation, the answers to *Wh-* questions are often not complete sentences.
>
> A: *Where does he live?*
> B: *In Moscow.*
>
> A: *Why do you hike all the time?*
> B: *Because I like it!*

11 EDIT. Read the conversations. Find and correct four more errors with *Wh-* questions.

1. A: Where he does live?
   B: In Tacoma, Washington.

2. A: When he goes on hikes?
   B: He goes on weekends.

3. A: When have a vacation?
   B: In the summer.

4. A: How often does he go on hikes?
   B: Almost every weekend.

5. A: Who does goes on hikes with him?
   B: His students and other teachers.

6. A: Where he teaches?
   B: At a high school.

12 LISTEN, WRITE & SPEAK.

A These people have very different lifestyles. Listen and take notes about their daily activities.

Sara and Max

exercise in the morning
_____
_____
_____
_____
_____

Kai

_____
_____
_____
_____
_____
_____

Julie

_____
_____
_____
_____
_____

B How many questions can you write about the people from exercise **A**? Use *Who, Where, When, What,* and *How often*.

Who has a job in a store?

C Work with a partner. Ask and answer your questions from exercise **B**.

Student A: *Who has a job in a store?*   Student B: *Kai does.*

13 APPLY.

A Write three *Wh-* questions for a classmate about his or her lifestyle.

What do you do in your free time?

B Work with a partner. Ask your questions from exercise **A**.

UNIT 4 Review the Grammar

Charts 4.1, 4.2, 4.4–4.6

1 Complete the exercises.

A Complete each conversation with the correct question word(s).

1. A: ____What____ does he do? B: He's a professor.
2. A: _____ Mateus live in Costa Rica? B: No, he doesn't.
3. A: _____ do you live? B: I live on Livingston.
4. A: _____ do you travel to China? B: Twice a year.
5. A: _____ do the night market open? B: At 9:00 p.m.
6. A: _____ you miss your family? B: Yes, I do.
7. A: _____ does he usually buy at the market? B: Special snacks.
8. A: _____ wants a snack? B: I do!
9. A: _____ do you get to work? B: I take the subway.
10. A: _____ do you live in a small town? B: Because I like the peace and quiet.

B Work with a partner. Practice the conversations from exercise **A**.

2 LISTEN and choose the correct answer for each question.

Charts 4.1, 4.2, 4.4–4.6

1. a. Yes, I do. (b.) Twice a week.
2. a. Because it's fun. b. No, I don't.
3. a. Yes, it does. b. It means *very big*.
4. a. Because it's good exercise. b. Every day.
5. a. They live in Italy. b. No, she doesn't.
6. a. Dora and I do. b. Never.
7. a. To the beach. b. Twice a year.
8. a. On Saturday. b. At the market.
9. a. At 9:00 a.m. b. She takes a bus.
10. a. My sister. b. In an apartment.

Review the Grammar UNIT 4

Charts 4.1–4.6

3 EDIT & SPEAK.

A Read the conversations. Find and correct six more errors with simple present questions and answers and frequency adverbs and expressions.

1. A: Who's that?

   B: That's my sister Katie.

   A: Does she ~~visits~~ visit you often?

   B: No, she doesn't. She comes rarely to California.

2. A: How often do you travel for your job?

   B: Once a month.

   A: Wow, that's a lot. You do like it?

   B: Yes, I like, but sometimes it's difficult. I miss my family.

3. A: Where you do live?

   B: I live on River Road.

   A: How you get to class?

   B: I usually take the subway.

4. A: Do you exercise every day?

   B: Yes, I go to the gym every days.

B Work with a partner. Ask and answer the questions from conversations 3 and 4 from exercise **A**. Use your own answers, not the answers in the book.

Student A: *Do you exercise every day?*   Student B: *Yes, I do.*

Charts 4.1–4.6

4 LISTEN & SPEAK.

CD1-60

A Look at the Internet activities in the chart. Ask your teacher about any words or activities you don't know. Then listen to the conversation. Check (✓) the Internet activities you hear.

Internet Activity	How Often
✓ Sends or reads e-mail	Three times a week
☐ Watches videos online	
☐ Uses a social networking site	
☐ Banks online	
☐ Plays online games	
☐ Shops online	
☐ Reads the news online	

140 SIMPLE PRESENT: PART 2

B Look at the Internet activities you checked in exercise **A**. Listen again. How often does Lena do each activity? Take notes in the chart.

C Work with a partner. Ask and answer questions about how often Lena does the Internet activities in exercise **A**.

Student A: *How often does Lena read or send e-mail?*   Student B: *Three times a week.*

Charts 4.1–4.6

5 WRITE & SPEAK.

A Write five interview questions in the chart for a classmate about his or her Internet activities. Write *Yes/No* and *Wh-* questions.

Interview Questions	Answers
Do you watch videos online?	

B Work with a partner. Ask your questions from exercise **A**. Take notes on your partner's answers in your chart.

C In your notebook, write five sentences about your partner's Internet activities.

Juliana watches videos online every day.

Connect the Grammar to Writing

1 READ & NOTICE THE GRAMMAR.

A Read the paragraph. Is Pradit's daily life similar to your life? Discuss with a partner.

▶ Bangkok, Thailand

Pradit's Daily Life

Pradit lives in Bangkok, Thailand. He works in a trading company. He often travels because of his job. Every night he goes out with his friends. They usually go to a restaurant. Sometimes they go to the movies. On weekends, he usually visits his parents or goes to the beach. He enjoys his life in Bangkok.

GRAMMAR FOCUS

In the paragraph in exercise **A**, the writer uses frequency adverbs and frequency expressions to talk about how often certain activities happen.

He **often** travels because of his job.
Every night he goes out with his friends.

B Read the paragraph in exercise **A** again. Underline the frequency adverbs and fequency expressions. Then work with a partner and compare answers.

C Complete the chart with questions and answers about Pradit's lifestyle.

Information about Pradit		
	Questions	Answers
Where	Where does Pradit live?	In Bangkok.
What		
Why		
How often		
Who		
Yes/No		

142 SIMPLE PRESENT: PART 2

Write about Someone's Daily Life

2 BEFORE YOU WRITE.

A Write questions in the chart below to ask someone about his or her daily life. Use the chart from exercise **1C** as a model.

Information about _____		
	Questions	Answers
Where		
What		
Why		
How often		
Who		
Yes/No		

B Choose a person to interview. Ask him or her your interview questions from exercise **A**. Take notes in your chart.

3 WRITE a paragraph. Use the information from your chart from exercise **2A** and the model paragraph in exercise **1A** to help you.

> **WRITING FOCUS   Subject-Verb Agreement**
>
> Subject-verb agreement is important for good writing. Subject-verb agreement means the verb agrees with the subject.
>
> **Remember:** In the simple present, add *-s* to the verb for *he, she, it*, and subjects that are the name of a person or a singular noun.
>
> Pradit **lives** in Bangkok, Thailand.
> He **works** in a trading company.
> He **enjoys** his life in Bangkok.

4 SELF ASSESS. Read your paragraph. Underline the adverbs of frequency and expressions of frequency. Then use the checklist to assess your work.

- ☐ I put the frequency adverbs in the correct place. [4.3]
- ☐ I put the frequency expressions in the correct place. [4.4]
- ☐ I used a singular noun after *every*. [4.4]
- ☐ The forms of the verbs agree with the subjects. [WRITING FOCUS]

UNIT 5 Food and Hospitality

Count and Non-Count Nouns

▶ Weaverbirds stand on a lunch table in Queen Elizabeth National Park, Uganda.

Lesson 1
page 146

Count and Non-Count Nouns; Articles

Lesson 2
page 154

Measurement Words; *Some, Any*

Lesson 3
page 163

Much, Many, A Lot Of; A Few, A Little

Review the Grammar
page 171

Connect the Grammar to Writing
page 174

LESSON 1 Count and Non-Count Nouns; Articles

EXPLORE

1 READ the conversation. Notice the words in **bold**.

At the Grand Hotel

Front Desk Clerk: Good afternoon, sir. Welcome to **the Grand Hotel**. Do you have **a reservation**?

Mike Martin: Yes, my **last name**'s Martin.

Front Desk Clerk: Yes, Mr. Martin. I see **the reservation**. It's for **a double room** for **two nights**.

Mike Martin: That's right.

Front Desk Clerk: All right. Just **a minute**, please. . . . OK, here's **information** about **the fitness center,**[1] and here's **the key** for your **room**. Do you need any **help** with **luggage**?

Mike Martin: No, thanks. I only have **one bag**.

Front Desk Clerk: All right. **The coffee shop** is on this **floor**. It's open every **morning** from six-thirty to ten-thirty for **breakfast**. We also have **vending machines**[2] near **the elevators** on each **floor**.

Mike Martin: OK, thank you. Are there any good **restaurants** nearby?

Front Desk Clerk: Oh, yes! There's **an** excellent Italian **restaurant** just around **the corner**. It's called Little Venice, and **the food** there is very good.

Mike Martin: Great. Thanks.

[1] **fitness center:** a gym
[2] **vending machine:** a machine that give snacks or drinks after money is put in it

2 CHECK. Look at the statements and questions from the conversation in exercise **1**. Who says each? Put a check (✓) in the correct column.

	Front Desk Clerk	Mike Martin
1. Do you have a reservation?	✓	☐
2. Just a minute, please.	☐	☐
3. Do you need any help with luggage?	☐	☐
4. I only have one bag.	☐	☐
5. Are there any good restaurants nearby?	☐	☐

3 DISCOVER. Look at the question and statement from the conversation. Notice the words in **bold**. Why do we say *one bag* but not *one luggage*? Discuss with your classmates and teacher.

1. Do you need any help with **luggage**?

2. No, thanks. I only have **one bag**.

▼ Negril Beach, Jamaica, West Indies

LEARN

5.1 Count and Non-Count Nouns

1. Count nouns are things we can count. They have a singular and plural form.	I eat an **apple** every morning. Andrea eats two **apples** every day.
2. Non-count nouns are things we cannot count.	**Sugar** is sweet. A: *Do we have **homework** tonight?* B: *Yes, we have two grammar exercises.*
3. Non-count nouns do not have a plural form.	✓ This **information** is important. ✗ These <u>informations are</u> important.

Some Common Non-Count Nouns

Foods	Liquids	Activities	Category Nouns	Abstract Nouns
bread	coffee	baseball	clothing (dresses, pants, shoes)	advice
butter	gasoline	basketball	furniture (chairs, tables)	fun
cheese	milk	golf	fruit (apples, oranges)	help
chicken	oil	hockey	homework (assignments, exercises)	information
fish	soup	soccer	jewelry (earrings, necklaces, rings)	love
flour	tea	tennis	luggage (backpacks, bags, suitcases)	work
meat	water	yoga	money (coins, dollars)	
pasta			time (hours, minutes)	
rice			traffic (buses, cars)	
salad			weather (hurricanes, showers, storms)	
salt				
sugar				
yogurt				

REAL ENGLISH

Some nouns can be count and non-count.

I like **pizza**. (non-count noun)
We need five **pizzas** for the party. (count noun)

4 Look at the underlined noun in each sentence. Is it a count noun or a non-count noun? Put a check (✓) in the correct column.

	Count Noun	Non-Count Noun
1. I don't need any help with <u>luggage</u>.	☐	✓
2. I only have a small <u>bag</u>.	☐	☐
3. I need a <u>room</u> with a double bed.	☐	☐
4. She has two <u>suitcases</u>.	☐	☐
5. He needs some <u>information</u> about restaurants.	☐	☐
6. That restaurant has very good <u>pasta</u>.	☐	☐
7. Let's get some <u>coffee</u> at the coffee shop.	☐	☐
8. I need <u>coins</u> for the vending machine.	☐	☐
9. Our hotel room has two <u>beds</u>.	☐	☐
10. I don't need <u>help</u> with anything.	☐	☐

5 Complete each sentence with the correct category from the box.

clothing	furniture	jewelry	money	~~traffic~~
fruit	homework	luggage	time	weather

1. Cars and buses are examples of _____traffic_____.
2. A grammar exercise is an example of _____.
3. Minutes and hours are examples of _____.
4. A suitcase is an example of _____.
5. Rings and watches are examples of _____.
6. Beds and chairs are examples of _____.
7. Dollars and cents are examples of _____.
8. A storm is an example of _____.
9. Oranges and bananas are examples of _____.
10. A shirt is an example of _____.

5.2 Using *A/An* with Count Nouns

1. **Remember:** Use *a* or *an* before singular count nouns or before an adjective + singular count noun.	**Singular** **Plural** **a** suitcase suitcases **an** old suitcase **an** orange oranges **a** big orange
Don't use *a* or *an* with plural nouns.	✓ That store sells suitcases. ✗ That store sells <u>a</u> suitcases.
2. Do not use *a* or *an* with non-count nouns.	✓ Look online for information. ✗ Look online for <u>an</u> information.
3. **Remember:** Use *a* before a consonant sound. Use *an* before a vowel sound.	He usually has **a sandwich** and **an apple** for lunch. It is **a hard exercise**. He's **an honest man**.

6 Complete each sentence with *a*, *an*, or Ø for no article.

1. He works for __a__ hotel.
2. This is ____ excellent restaurant.
3. Cindy needs ____ new suitcase for her trip.
4. That vending machine doesn't take ____ coins.
5. That store sells ____ luggage.
6. It's ____ old hotel.
7. The gift shop sells ____ jewelry.
8. Do we have ____ time for breakfast?

7 Write *a*, *an*, or Ø for no article.

1. _Ø_ sugar
2. ____ sandwich
3. ____ jacket
4. ____ information
5. ____ minute
6. ____ people
7. ____ egg
8. ____ old furniture
9. ____ hour
10. ____ difficult exercise
11. ____ traffic
12. ____ earring
13. ____ help
14. ____ assignment
15. ____ rain

8 SPEAK. Work with a partner. Look around the classroom and in your bags. Which things are count nouns? Which things are non-count nouns? Write each noun in the correct column of the chart.

Count Nouns	Non-Count Nouns
a desk	money

5.3 A/An vs. The

1. *A* and *an* are indefinite articles. Use *a* or *an* when the person, place, or thing is not specific. **Remember:** Do not use *a* or *an* before plural nouns.	I usually have **a** sandwich and **an** apple for lunch.
2. *The* is the definite article. Use *the* before count and non-count nouns when: a. there is only one of something; b. the person, place, or thing is specific and something both the speaker and listener know about; c. you refer to a person, place, or thing a second time.	a. **The** earth is round. b. Do you have **the** suitcases? (The speaker and listener are on a trip together.) c. I always stay at a hotel downtown. **The** hotel is very nice.

9 Circle the correct article to complete each statement or question.

1. What's **a** / **(the)** number of our hotel room?
2. My room's on **a** / **the** sixth floor.
3. Do you need **Ø** / **the** help with your luggage?
4. Do you have **the** / **Ø** key to our hotel room?

5. Do you have **a / Ø** reservation, sir?

6. Do you know **an / the** address of our hotel?

7. **Ø / The** restaurant in the hotel is very good.

8. Do you like **a / Ø** pasta? **A / The** pasta at that restaurant is excellent.

9. What time does **a / the** fitness center close?

10. **A / The** people in this hotel are very friendly.

11. Our hotel room has **a / the** great view of **a / the** city.

12. Wow! Look at **a / the** moon! It's beautiful.

PRACTICE

10 Write *a, an, the,* or *Ø* for no article to complete each conversation.

1. A: Hello. Welcome to *the* Pacific Hotel.

   B: Hi. I have _____ reservation. My name is Sims.

2. A: Excuse me. Is there _____ fitness center in the hotel?

   B: Yes. It's on _____ second floor next to _____ elevators.

3. A: Do you have _____ restaurant here in the hotel?

   B: Yes, we do. It's on _____ first floor.

4. A: I'm hungry. Let's look for _____ restaurant.

   B: OK. I like _____ restaurant at the hotel. Do you want to go there?

5. A: We need to buy _____ fruit.

   B: Right. We need _____ apples, oranges, and bananas.

6. A: OK, we have all _____ food for the party. Let's go buy _____ flowers.

   B: Good idea. Let's go to Vinny's Farm. _____ flowers there are always very pretty.

7. A: It's really nice today. _____ sky is very blue.

   B: It really is! _____ weather is perfect. Let's have a picnic.

8. A: I have _____ question about _____ homework.

   B: Ask _____ teacher.

> **REAL ENGLISH**
>
> Use *Let's* + verb to make suggestions. *Let's* includes you and your listener(s).
>
> A: **Let's have** lunch.
>
> B: *Good idea. I'm hungry.*
>
> A: **Let's not go** to the deli. *The food there isn't very good.*
>
> B: *OK.*

11 EDIT. Read the paragraph. Put five more articles in the correct place.

> ### Barney's
>
> We have ^a big hotel in our city. name of hotel is Barney's. It's expensive, but many people like to stay there. It has pool. It also has restaurant with very good food. restaurant's name is Martindale by the Sea. Sometimes my family goes there for special celebrations.

12 SPEAK. Work with a partner. Discuss these questions.

1. Does your city have a famous hotel? What is special about it?
2. Do you know any good restaurants? Why do you like it / them?

▶ Customers enjoy the view at a popular village restaurant, Oia, Santorini, Greece.

13 LISTEN.

A Listen to the conversations. Write the number of the conversation next to the word(s) you hear in each conversation.

a. _____ radio   b. __1__ front desk   c. _____ job   d. _____ train

B Read the questions about the conversations from exercise **A**. Then listen again and choose the correct answer for each question.

1. What does the caller in Conversation 1 need?
   a. a new computer   b. help with the TV   c. information

2. What does the traveler in Conversation 2 ask for?
   a. a map   b. information   c. a ticket

3. What is the problem in Conversation 3?

   a. traffic   b. cars at the airport   c. the news

4. What advice does the worker's friend give in Conversation 4?

   a. Work late.   b. Get a new job.   c. Have some dinner.

C Work with a partner. Read the sentences from the conversations. Complete the sentences with the words you remember. Then listen again and write any missing words.

Conversation 1

Hotel Clerk: Hello. Front desk. May I help you?

Guest: Yes, I need _____ . I have ____ problem with _____ in my room.

Hotel Clerk: I'm sorry to hear that.

Conversation 2

Woman: Good afternoon. Welcome to the Philadelphia airport. Would you like _____ of _____ ?

Traveler: Yes, I would. Thanks. I'd also like _____ about _____ into the city.

Woman: Sure. No problem. It's really easy to take _____ downtown.

Conversation 3

Mike: Do you drive to _____ ? Well, don't get stuck in _____ !

Mary: Right now _____ is very slow on all of our _____ .

Conversation 4

Karen: Hey, sorry. I'm still at _____ . I have about _____ of _____ here.

Berta: I think you need _____ !

> **REAL ENGLISH**
>
> *Would like* means *want*, but *would like* is more polite.
>
> A: **Would you like** coffee or tea?
>
> B: **I'd like** tea. Thanks.
>
> In a short answer, do not use the contraction.
>
> A: **Would you like** a cup of coffee?
>
> B: Yes, **I would**.

14 APPLY.

A Work with a partner. Write a short conversation. Use at least two of the words in the box.

assignment	information	restaurant	test
exercise	jewelry	rice	watch
food	job	ring	weather
help	necklace	snow	wind
homework	rain	soup	work

B Role-play your conversation for your classmates.

LESSON 2 Measurement Words; *Some, Any*

EXPLORE

 1 READ the blog entry. Notice the words in **bold**.

Budapest, Hungary

ERIK'S FOOD BLOG
WELCOME FOOD LOVERS!
Enjoy! Share your recipes.

SUNDAY, JANUARY 28

Every summer I travel home to Budapest. My grandmother lives downtown. When I arrive, she always gives me **some** coffee and **a piece of** honey[1] cake. She's a wonderful cook!

Unfortunately, my grandmother doesn't have **any** recipes[2] on paper. She never writes them down, and she doesn't have **any** cookbooks. She doesn't need them. "How do you make goulash,[3] Grandma?" I asked. "Oh, that's simple," she answered. "You need **some** meat, onions, oil, flour, paprika, salt, and a green pepper. Then cook everything for two to three hours."

That *is* an easy recipe, but my first goulash was *not* very successful. I need exact directions, so now I watch her in her kitchen and write down every step and every ingredient[4] in her goulash recipe. She cooks, and I write down the ingredients: **2 pounds of** meat, 2 onions, **1/2 cup of** flour, **1 teaspoon of** paprika, 1 green pepper, and **2 teaspoons of** salt.

For the full recipe, click below and enjoy!

GOULASH RECIPE
OTHER HUNGARIAN FOOD

[1] **honey:** a sweet, sticky food made by bees
[2] **recipe:** a set of directions that tells you how to make something to eat
[3] **goulash:** a favorite Hungarian dish
[4] **ingredient:** one of the things you use to make a particular food

POSTED BY ERIK AT 10:56 PM
2 COMMENTS:

Nick Burke said . . .
Great goulash recipe. Thank you!
February 5, 5:21 PM

POST A COMMENT

2 CHECK. Match each measurement or number in the box with the ingredient from the goulash recipe in exercise **1**. Write the letter.

| a. 1 | b. 1/2 cup | c. 2 pounds | d. 1 teaspoon | e. 2 teaspoons | f. 2 |

1. _c_ meat 2. ____ onions 3. ____ flour 4. ____ paprika 5. ____ green pepper 6. ____ salt

3 DISCOVER. Complete the exercises to learn about the grammar in this lesson.

A Find these sentences in the blog entry from exercise **1**. Write the missing words.

1. When I arrive, she always gives me __some__ coffee and a piece of honey cake.
2. Unfortunately, my grandmother doesn't have _____ recipes on paper.
3. She never writes them down, and she doesn't have _____ cookbooks.
4. "You need _____ meat, onions, oil . . ."

B Look at the sentences in exercise **A**. When do we use *any*? When do we use *some*? Discuss with your classmates and teacher.

▼ A view of the Hungarian Parliament Building, Budapest, Hungary

LEARN

5.4 Measurement Words

1. Use measurement words + *of* to talk about specific quantities.	We need a **bag of** rice. Please get a **pound of** meat at the market. Would you like a **cup of** coffee?
2. **Be careful!** Make a count noun plural after a measurement word + *of*.	✓ We need a carton of egg**s**. ✗ We need a carton of <u>egg</u>.

Some Common Measurement Words

Containers	Portions	Specific Measurements	Other
a **bag** of rice	a **bowl** of soup	a **cup** of sugar	a **bar** of soap
a **bottle** of shampoo	a **cup** of coffee	a **gallon** of gasoline	a **bunch** of bananas
a **box** of cookies	a **glass** of juice	a **liter** of water	a **head** of lettuce
a **carton** of eggs	a **piece** of fruit	a **pound** of meat	a **loaf** of bread
a **can** of soup	a **slice** of bread	a **tablespoon** of honey	a **sheet** of paper
a **carton** of milk		a **teaspoon** of salt	a **stick** of butter
a **jar** of honey			a **tube** of toothpaste

4 Complete each sentence with the correct measurement word from the box.

bowl	cup	jar	piece
~~carton~~	glass	loaf	stick

1. Please get a ___carton___ of milk at the grocery store.
2. We need a _____ of butter for the recipe.
3. She drinks a _____ of orange juice every morning.
4. Would you like a _____ of pizza?
5. She usually has a _____ of soup and a sandwich for lunch.
6. He always has a _____ of tea after dinner.
7. We need a _____ of jam. How about strawberry?
8. I buy a _____ of bread at that bakery every morning.

5 Choose the correct word to complete each sentence.

1. I'd like a glass of _____, please.
   a. flour   (b.) water   c. honey

2. I'd like a bunch of _____ and three apples, please.
   a. lettuce   b. bananas   c. bread

156   COUNT AND NON-COUNT NOUNS

3. My family drinks a gallon of _____ each week.
   a. meat　　　b. bread　　　c. milk

4. Would you like a cup of _____?
   a. pizza　　　b. coffee　　　c. cereal

5. Please buy a box of _____ at the grocery store.
   a. cookies　　b. bread　　　c. eggs

6. We need a teaspoon of _____ for the recipe.
   a. sugar　　　b. eggs　　　c. bread

7. I always order a bowl of _____ here. It's delicious!
   a. cake　　　b. soup　　　c. juice

8. I buy two pounds of _____ every week.
   a. juice　　　b. gasoline　　c. meat

6 **WRITE & SPEAK.** Complete the sentences. Include measurement words. Then share your sentences with a partner.

I drink ___six glasses of water___ every day.

I have _____ in the morning.

I usually buy _____ every week.

Student A: *I drink six glasses of water every day.*

Student B: *I have a bowl of cereal in the morning.*

5.5 *Some, Any*

	Non-Count Nouns	Plural Count Nouns
Affirmative Statements	I have **some** food at home.	I have **some** onions.
Questions	Do you have **any** paper? Do you have **some** paper?	Do we need **any** cups? Do we have **some** cups?
Negative Statements	We don't have **any** homework.	We don't need **any** onions.

1. Use *some* in affirmative statements.
2. Use *any* in negative statements.
3. Use *some* and *any* in questions.

REAL ENGLISH

Some is often used to make offers.

Would you like **some** coffee?
Do you need **some** help?

UNIT 5　LESSON 2

7 Circle *some* or *any* to complete each sentence.

1. I don't have **some** / **any** green peppers for the recipe.
2. We need **some** / **any** orange juice.
3. She doesn't eat **some** / **any** meat.
4. Add **some** / **any** water to the soup.
5. We don't have **some** / **any** bread.
6. My aunt knows **some** / **any** great recipes.
7. She doesn't use **some** / **any** salt in her cooking.
8. Adam doesn't want **some** / **any** soup.
9. I need **some** / **any** money for groceries.
10. He doesn't need **some** / **any** help.

8 **WRITE & SPEAK.** Complete the sentences. Then share your sentences with a partner.

I usually eat some _____rice_____ every day.

I don't eat any _____ .

I'd like _____ right now.

I want some _____ .

I usually eat some rice every day.

PRACTICE

9 Complete the conversations. Use the words from the box. You can use some words more than once. Then listen and check your answers.

| any | bowl | box | glass | jar | pieces | slice | some |

1. **Server:** Are you ready to order?
   Customer: Yes, I'd like a (1) ____glass____ of lemonade.
   Server: I'm sorry. We don't have (2) _____ lemonade. Would you like (3) _____ iced tea or juice?
   Customer: Hm. No, thank you. I'd just like a (4) _____ of water.
   Server: Would you like something to eat?
   Customer: Yes, I'd like a (5) _____ of tomato soup.

2. **Dalia:** You look great, Mila. What's your secret?

   Mila: Thanks. I just eat healthy food. I don't eat (6) _____ meat, and I eat a lot of vegetables. I also have about six (7) _____ of fruit each day.

   Dalia: Wow! Do you eat (8) _____ bread or sweets?

   Mila: I don't eat sweets, but every morning I have a (9) _____ of bread with (10) _____ butter on it! I love butter!

3. **Andy:** Do you have (11) _____ easy recipes for dinner?

   Tasha: Sure. I have a very easy recipe for spaghetti. For four people, you need a (12) _____ of pasta, a (13) _____ of pasta sauce, and (14) _____ cheese.

   Andy: Great! Thank you!

> **REAL ENGLISH**
>
> *Or* is often used to talk about choices.
>
> A: *Would you like soup **or** salad?*
> B: *Soup, please.*
>
> *Also* is often used to show an addition.
>
> *I'd **also** like some salad.*

10 EDIT. Find and correct five more errors with *some*, *any*, and measurement words.

Fried Rice

This is an easy recipe for fried rice. You need two or three eggs, four cup~s~ of rice, any green onions, and some oil. Any people also use some small piece of chicken or shrimp. First, chop the onions and mix the eggs. Then, cook the eggs in two tablespoon of oil, and add some salt. Next, fry the rice in some oil. Add the eggs and onions. This is also delicious with a cup of vegetable such as peas.

A woman prepares a meal in a kitchen in Pematangsiantar, Sumatra, Indonesia.

11 LISTEN, SPEAK & WRITE.

A Listen to the conversation about a recipe. Circle the ingredients the speakers have at home.

	Some	A carton	2 tablespoons	A large bag	2 cups	1
(Potatoes)				✓		
Eggs						
Onions						
Flour						
Oil						
Salt						

▲ Potato pancakes

B Listen again. In the chart in exercise **A**, check the amount you hear for each ingredient.

C Work with a partner. Ask and answer *Yes/No* questions about the conversation from exercises **A** and **B**. Use the information from the chart in exercise **A** to help you.

Student A: *Do they have any potatoes?*   Student B: *Yes, they do.*

D **WRITE** affirmative and negative statements about the conversation from exercises **A** and **B**. Use the information from the chart to help you.

1. They have a large bag of potatoes.
2. _____
3. _____
4. _____
5. _____
6. _____

12 READ, SPEAK & WRITE.

A Work with a partner. Read the recipe. Notice the underlined verbs. Which verbs do you know? Ask your teacher about any verbs you do not know.

Spaghetti Sauce Recipe

Directions

<u>Chop</u> the onion and the green pepper.
<u>Slice</u> the garlic.
<u>Heat</u> two tablespoons of olive oil in a sauce pan.
<u>Fry</u> the onion and the green pepper in the olive oil for 5-10 minutes.
<u>Stir</u> the onion and green pepper every one to two minutes.
<u>Add</u> the garlic, ground beef, salt, and Italian seasoning.
<u>Mix</u> the tomato sauce, tomatoes, and tomato paste and add them to the pot.
<u>Add</u> the sugar.
<u>Boil</u> water in a large pot.
<u>Add</u> the spaghetti to the water and <u>cook</u> it for 12-15 minutes.
<u>Heat</u> a loaf of garlic bread in the oven.
<u>Serve</u> the spaghetti with garlic bread and some salad.

B Work with a partner. Partner A, look at this page. Partner B, look at page A6.

Partner A, look at the ingredients in the recipe. Ask your partner questions about the ingredients. Put a check (✓) next to the food you have. Write the amount of each ingredient you need to buy.

Partner A: *Do we have* **one and a half pounds of ground beef**?

Partner B: *No, we don't. We have* **one pound**.

Spaghetti Sauce

Ingredients

- 1½ pounds of ground beef
- 2 tablespoons of olive oil
- 1 large onion
- 1 green pepper
- 2 tablespoons of garlic
- 2 cans of tomato paste
- 1 can of tomato sauce
- 1 large can of cooked tomatoes
- 1 tablespoon of Italian seasoning
- 1 teaspoon of salt
- 2 tablespoons of sugar

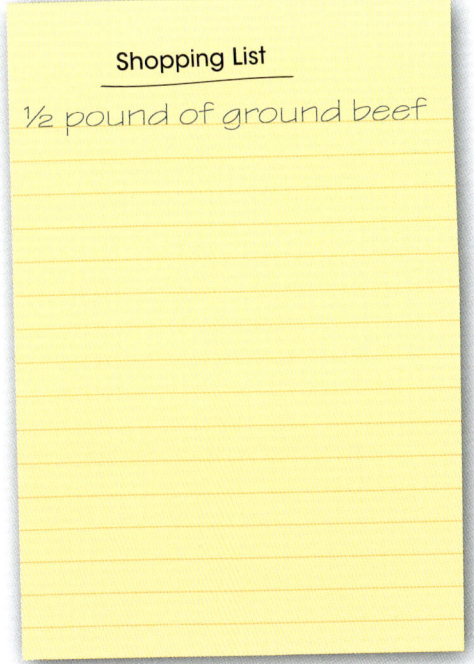

Shopping List

½ pound of ground beef

C Compare your shopping list with your partner's. Are your shopping lists the same?

13 APPLY. Complete the exercises.

A Do you know any easy recipes? What ingredients do you need? Write the name of the ingredients and the amount you need of each. Use the recipe below as a model.

Hot Chocolate Recipe

Ingredients
- 1 cup of milk
- 2 tablespoons of sugar
- 1 tablespoon of cocoa

Directions

Heat the milk in a pan, and slowly add the sugar and cocoa. Stir well, and then pour the hot chocolate into your favorite mug.

_____
(name of your dish)

Ingredients
-
-
-
-
-
-

Directions
-
-
-
-

B Work with a partner. Talk about how to make your recipes. Use the verbs in the box to help you. Then write the directions for your recipe in exercise **A**.

add	chop	mix
bake	fry	slice
boil	heat	stir

C Discuss these questions.

1. Are you a good cook?

2. What do you usually make?

Much, Many, A Lot Of; A Few, A Little — LESSON 3

EXPLORE

 1 READ the article about the Hadza people. Notice the words in **bold**.

The Hadza People

The Hadza people live in northern Tanzania around Lake Eyasi. **Many** Hadza people are hunters and gatherers. In other words, they move from place to place to find food. They don't live in towns or cities, and they don't have permanent[1] homes. Instead, they build small, simple shelters.[2] This usually takes just **a few** hours.

The Hadza people don't buy their food. The women gather food from plants and trees. The Hadza eat **a lot of** berries. They also eat **a lot of** fruit from a tree called the *baobab*. Baobab fruit has **a lot of** vitamins, so it's an important part of the Hadza diet. The men hunt animals, but the Hadza people don't eat **much** meat. Most of their diet comes from plants. Honey is also an important part of the Hadza diet. It's sweet and delicious, and just **a little** honey has **a lot of** calories.[3]

The Hadza people have a very interesting, traditional lifestyle.

For more information about the Hadza's traditional lifestyle, look at the links below.

How many Hadza people live in Tanzania today?

How much land do the Hadza people own?

What language do the Hadza people speak?

Facts about Lake Eyasi

[1] **permanent:** lasting for a long time or forever
[2] **shelter:** a building or covering that gives protection
[3] **calorie:** a unit used to measure the amount of energy in food

▲ Hadza hunters, Lake Eyasi, Tanzania

UNIT 5 LESSON 3 163

2 CHECK. Read each statement about the Hadza people. Then circle **T** for *true* or **F** for *false*.

1. The Hadza people don't eat a lot of berries. T (F)
2. They eat a lot of fruit from the baobab tree. T F
3. Baobab fruit doesn't have a lot of vitamins. T F
4. The Hadza people don't eat a lot of meat. T F
5. Honey doesn't have a lot of calories. T F

3 DISCOVER. Complete the exercises to learn about the grammar in this lesson.

A Find and complete these sentences in the article from exercise **1** on page 163.

1. _____ Hadza people are hunters and gatherers.
2. They also eat _____ fruit from a tree called the *baobab*.
3. Baobab fruit has _____ vitamins, so it's an important part of the Hadza diet.
4. The Hadza people don't eat _____ meat.

B Look at the sentences in exercise **A**. Then circle **T** for *true* or **F** for *false* for each statement below. Discuss your answers with your classmates and teacher.

1. We use *many* with non-count nouns. T F
2. We use *a lot of* with non-count nouns. T F
3. We use *a lot of* with plural count nouns. T F
4. We use *much* in negative statements with non-count nouns. T F

▶ Baobab trees in Morondava, Madagascar

LEARN

5.6 Much, Many, A Lot Of

	Non-Count Nouns	Plural Count Nouns
Affirmative Statements	I eat **a lot of** honey.	We eat **a lot of** vegetables. **Many** people drink tea in the morning.
Negative Statements	They don't eat **much** meat. She doesn't drink **a lot of** coffee.	They don't grow **many** vegetables. We don't eat **a lot of** potatoes.
Questions	Does he drink **much** coffee? Do they grow **a lot of** fruit?	Do you eat **many** snacks? Does the menu have **a lot of** choices?

1. Use *much*, *many*, or *a lot of* to talk about large quantities.
2. Use *much* with non-count nouns in negative statements and questions.
3. Use *many* with plural count nouns in affirmative statements, negative statements, and questions.
4. Use *a lot of* with plural count nouns or non-count nouns in affirmative and negative statements and questions.

4 Look at the underlined noun in each sentence. Then circle the correct word(s) to complete each statement or question.

1. The Hadza people eat **much** / (**a lot of**) fruit.
2. They don't drink **many** / **much** milk.
3. The women collect **a lot of** / **much** berries.
4. Does honey have **many** / **much** calories?
5. The article has **a lot of** / **many** interesting information about the Hadza people.
6. We have **a lot of** / **much** questions about the article.
7. I read **a lot of** / **much** articles about food and healthy lifestyles.
8. **Many** / **Much** people in my country eat cereal for breakfast.
9. Do people in your country drink **many** / **much** coffee?
10. Do people in your country eat **much** / **many** potatoes?
11. Are **much** / **many** people in your country vegetarians?
12. Do you eat **many** / **much** junk food?

> **REAL ENGLISH**
>
> In informal situations, some people use *lots of* instead of *a lot of*.
>
> A: *We have **lots of** homework tonight.*
>
> B: *Yeah, we do.*

5 SPEAK. Work with a partner. Ask and answer questions 9–12 from exercise **4**.

Student A: *Do people in your country drink much coffee?*

Student B: *Yes, the coffee in my country is delicious!*

5.7 A Few, A Little

1. Use *a few* and *a little* to talk about small quantities.	I drink **a few** cups of tea every day. I usually put **a little** milk in my tea.
2. Use *a few* with plural count nouns.	I have **a few** pencils in my bag. She has **a few** questions.
3. Use *a little* with non-count nouns.	He drinks **a little** orange juice every morning. We have **a little** time before class.

6 Complete each sentence with *a few* or *a little*.

1. She drinks _____*a few*_____ cups of tea every day.
2. I'm not a vegetarian. I usually have _____ meat for dinner.
3. A healthy diet includes _____ pieces of fruit every day.
4. People in my country eat _____ junk food, but not a lot.
5. I always buy _____ bananas when I go to the market.
6. I like _____ sugar in my coffee.
7. _____ students in our class are vegetarians.
8. The article has _____ new words.
9. I need _____ help with my homework.
10. We only have _____ minutes before class.

5.8 Questions with *How Much* and *How Many*

Questions			Answers
How Much/ How Many	Non-Count Noun		
How much	time homework	do we have?	A lot. Not much. A little.
	Plural Count Noun		
How many	oranges chairs	do we need?	A lot. Not many. A few.

REAL ENGLISH

The noun after *how much* or *how many* is not necessary when the listener knows what the speaker is referring to.

A: *We need some oranges.*
B: **How many** *do we need?*
A: *Six.*
B: **How much** *do they cost?*
A: *Seventy-five cents each.*

1. Use *how much* and *how many* for questions about quantity.	**How much** milk is in the refrigerator? **How many** bottles of water do we need?
2. Use *how much* with non-count nouns.	✓ **How much** money does it cost? ✗ How <u>much</u> dollars does it cost?
3. Use *how many* with plural count nouns.	✓ **How many** bags do you have? ✗ How <u>many</u> luggage do you have?

7 Use the words in parentheses to write questions with *How much/How many*.

1. (cups of coffee / you / drink / every day)

   How many cups of coffee do you drink every day?

2. (meat / you / eat / every day)

3. (meals / you / have / every day)

4. (junk food / you / eat)

5. (money / you / spend / on food / every week)

6. (free time / you / have / every day)

7. (hours / you / sleep / every night)

8. (brothers / you / have)

9. (homework / our teacher / give)

10. (hours / you / spend on homework / every day)

11. (English / you / know)

12. (languages / you / speak)

8 SPEAK. Work with a partner. Ask and answer the questions from exercise **7**.

Student A: *How many cups of coffee do you drink every day?*
Student B: *Two.* OR *I don't drink coffee.*

PRACTICE

9 Circle the correct word(s) to complete each statement. Then write a *How much/How many* question about the underlined noun in each statement.

1. She puts (**a lot of**) / **much** / **many** <u>honey</u> in her tea.

    How much honey does she put in her tea?

2. Yogurt doesn't have **many** / **a few** / **much** <u>calories</u>. It's a healthy food.

    _____

3. She eats **much** / **a few** / **a little** <u>pieces</u> of fruit every day.

    _____

4. I don't use **much** / **a little** / **a few** <u>sugar</u>. I don't like my coffee very sweet.

    _____

5. Samir doesn't use **much** / **many** / **a few** <u>salt</u>.

    _____

6. We don't need **many** / **much** / **a little** <u>flour</u> for the recipe.

    _____

7. My daughter drinks **a lot of** / **much** / **a few** <u>milk</u>. It's her favorite drink.

    _____

8. Hilda has **a lot of** / **a little** / **a few** <u>homework</u>. She has seven assignments for tomorrow.

    _____

9. **A few** / **A little** / **Much** <u>students</u> are absent today.

    _____

10. Marco speaks **a little** / **a few** / **much** <u>languages</u>. He speaks French, Italian, and Arabic.

    _____

11. Pedro knows **much** / **many** / **a lot of** <u>English</u>. He lives in Toronto.

    _____

12. I'm new here. I don't know **much** / **many** / **a few** <u>people</u> in this city.

    _____

13. I don't have **a little** / **a lot of** / **a few** <u>time</u> these days. I'm very busy at work.

    _____

14. These flowers cost **many** / **much** / **a lot of** <u>money</u>. They're very expensive!

    _____

10 EDIT. Read the information about the Mediterranean Diet Food Pyramid. Find and correct six more errors with *much, many, a lot of, a few,* and *a little*. There is more than one way to correct some errors.

The Mediterranean Diet Food Pyramid

This food pyramid shows the Mediterranean diet. In general, Mediterranean people eat ~~many~~ *a lot of* brown rice and pasta. They eat much vegetables. They eat a lot of fruit and nuts. They eat a few cheese and yogurt. They also eat fish a little times every week, but they don't eat many meat. They also don't eat much sweets. They usually have fresh fruit for dessert. They drink a lot of water—six to eight glasses a day.

The Mediterranean lifestyle is also very healthy. Mediterranean people get a lot of exercise, and they spend much time with their families. This is the Mediterranean secret to a long and happy life!

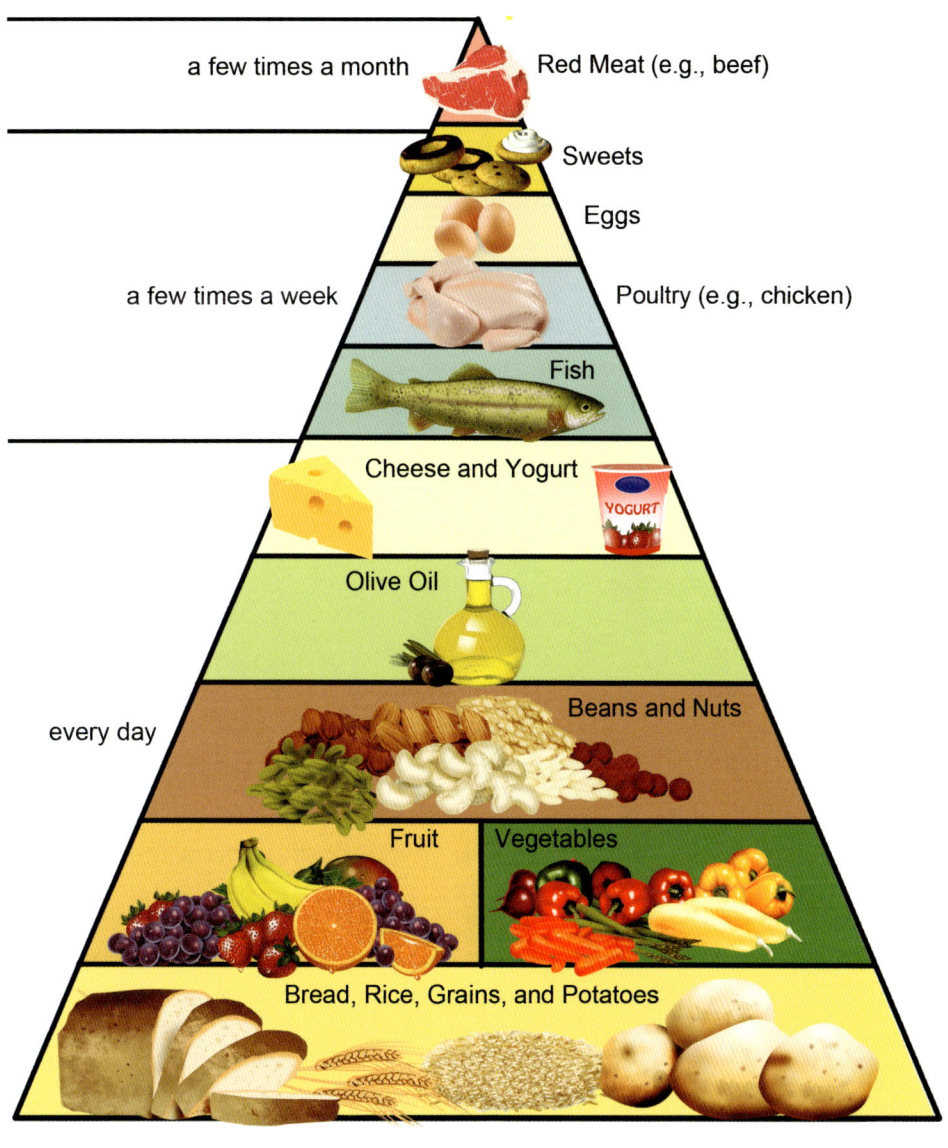

11 LISTEN & SPEAK.

A Read each statement in the chart. Then listen to Sunil and Henry talk about their diets. Is the statement true for Sunil, Henry, or both? Put a check (✓) in the correct column(s).

	Sunil	Henry
1. He's from India.	✓	
2. He eats a lot of rice.		
3. He eats a lot of beef.		
4. He eats a lot of fruit.		
5. He eats a lot of vegetables.		
6. He eats a little fruit.		
7. He doesn't eat any beef.		
8. He eats a lot of potatoes.		
9. He eats a lot of ice cream.		
10. He only eats a few sweets.		
11. He follows the Mediterranean diet.		
12. He follows the Mediterranean lifestyle.		

B Work with a partner. Ask and answer questions about Sunil and Henry's diets. Use the information from exercise **A**.

Student A: *Does Henry eat much rice?*   Student B: *No, he doesn't.*

12 APPLY.

A Work with a partner. What do you eat? Ask and answer *How much/How many* questions about the food in the box below. Add three of your own ideas. Use *much, many, a lot of, a few,* or *a little*. Put a check (✓) next to the things your partner eats a lot of. Put **X** next to the things your partner only eats a little of.

Student A: *How much rice do you eat?*   Student B: *A lot. How about you?*

1. rice _____
2. fruit _____
3. cheese _____
4. eggs _____
5. meat _____
6. fish _____
7. vegetables _____
8. ice cream _____
9. sweets _____
10. bread _____
11. potatoes _____
12. yogurt _____
13. (your idea) _____
14. (your idea) _____
15. (your idea) _____

B Discuss your answers. Do you or your partner follow the Mediterranean diet? Report to your classmates.

C Now write a paragraph about your partner. Does he or she follow the Mediterranean diet? Use your information from the chart in exercise **A**.

Barbara doesn't follow the Mediterranean diet. She eats a lot of ice cream and sweets. She doesn't eat many vegetables. She doesn't eat a lot of fruit . . .

UNIT 5 Review the Grammar

Charts 5.1–5.3, 5.5–5.7

1 Circle the correct words to complete the paragraph.

Potluck Dinners

Do you have (1) **a** / **an** /**Ø**/ **the** potluck dinners in your country? (2) **Many** / **Much** people have this kind of dinner in the United States. At a potluck dinner, everyone brings (3) **some** / **any** food to share. At many potluck dinners, (4) **a** / **an** / **Ø** people usually bring (5) **a** / **an** / **Ø** / **the** dish for eight to twelve people. (6) **Some** / **Any** people bring (7) **a lot of** / **a few** / **much** food. Other people don't bring (8) **some** / **much**. (9) **A** / **An** / **Ø** / **The** potluck dinners are always (10) **a lot of** / **a few** fun.

Charts 5.1, 5.4–5.8

2 LISTEN, WRITE & SPEAK.

A Listen and circle the correct word(s) to complete each sentence.

1. This story is about a **coffee** / **tea** ceremony in **England** / **Ethiopia**.

2. The ceremony takes a few **minutes** / **hours**.

3. **Many** / **A few** people come in the open door of the house.

4. People sometimes have **a lot of** / **a few** salty snacks.

5. The ceremony takes **a little** / **a lot of** time.

▲ An Ethiopian woman pours coffee.

B Use the words in parentheses to write *How much/How many* questions about the Ethiopian coffee ceremony.

1. (time / people / usually / spend) <u>How much time do people usually spend</u> with their morning coffee?

2. (time / the coffee ceremony / take) _____ in Ethiopia?

3. (neighbors / come) _____ in the open door?

4. (minutes / she / boil / the coffee) _____ with the water?

5. (cups of coffee / they / usually / have) _____ ?

C Work with a partner. Ask and answer the questions from exercise **B**.

UNIT 5 REVIEW THE GRAMMAR 171

Review the Grammar — UNIT 5

D Do you have any customs such as the coffee ceremony in Ethiopia? Discuss with your classmates and teacher.

In Argentina, we drink yerba mate. We drink it with friends or family members. The first person drinks and then gives the mate to the next person. We often drink mate in the park. It's not a ceremony, but it's a very nice custom.

▲ Typical gourds used for yerba mate, San Telmo District, Buenos Aires, Argentina

Charts 5.1–5.3, 5.5

3 EDIT. Read the information about barbecues. Add the missing articles in the correct places. There are five more errors.

Barbecues

The definition of *barbecue* is "to cook meat or other food over ^an open fire, usually outside."
It's common all over world. In many countries, people barbecue on grill. Other people use a spit. spit turns to cook the meat. It's great idea for party!

Charts 5.1, 5.2, 5.5

4 LISTEN & SPEAK.

CD2-13

A Listen to the conversation about a barbecue dinner. What do the speakers plan to serve? Write the correct word for each category.

1. Main dish: _____
2. Vegetable: _____
3. Dessert: _____

172 COUNT AND NON-COUNT NOUNS

B Listen again. Check the items on their shopping list.

Shopping List
- ☐ steak
- ☑ hamburger meat
- ☐ tomatoes
- ☐ onions
- ☐ broccoli
- ☐ green beans
- ☐ corn
- ☐ apple pie
- ☐ vanilla ice cream
- ☐ hamburger rolls

C Work with a partner. Look at the items on the shopping list in exercise **B**. What amount of each item do you think they need for eight hungry people? Ask each other questions and discuss.

Student A: *How much hamburger meat do they need?*   Student B: *Two pounds.*

Charts 5.1–5.8

5 SPEAK & WRITE.

A Plan a picnic for your class. What food do you like? What food is good for a picnic? Look at and discuss the items in the box and discuss them with your group.

Student A: *I like apples. I don't like broccoli.*

Student B: *Me neither, and broccoli isn't good for a picnic.*

apples	chicken	juice	pears	soda
bananas	coffee	lemonade	peppers	soup
beans	cookies	milk	pie	steak
beef	cucumbers	noodles	pizza	strawberries
bread/rolls	eggs	nuts	potatoes	tea
broccoli	fish	olives	rice	tomatoes
cake	grapes	onions	salad	water
carrots	hamburgers	oranges	sandwiches	
cheese	ice cream	pasta	shrimp	

B Decide on the menu for your picnic. Choose a main dish, a vegetable, a dessert, drinks, and other items. Then make a shopping list.

Student A: *Let's have hamburgers.*

Student B: *I don't like hamburgers. How about sandwiches?*

Student C: *Good idea. How much bread do we need?*

Connect the Grammar to Writing

1 READ & NOTICE THE GRAMMAR.

A Read the paragraph. What kind of event is it? Discuss with a partner.

How to Plan a Potluck Dinner

It's very easy to plan a potluck dinner. Here are some things you need to do. First, choose the date and the time. Next, invite some friends. Prepare or buy some food. Put some plates and glasses on a table. Leave some space on the table for a lot of other dishes. Last, put on some music. Have a great party!

◀ A potluck dinner

GRAMMAR FOCUS

In the paragraph in exercise **A**, the writer uses *a*, *the*, *a lot of*, and *some* before count and non-count nouns.

Remember: Use *a* before count nouns that begin with a consonant sound. Use *an* before count nouns that begin with a vowel sound. Use *the* before specific nouns when there is only one of something or when you want to refer to a person, place, or thing for a second time.

It's very easy to plan **a** potluck party.
First, choose **the** date and **the** time.

B Read the paragraph in exercise **A** again. Underline the nouns and circle the articles. Why does the writer use *a* and *the*? Discuss your answers with a partner.

C Complete the chart with information from the paragraph in exercise **A**. How many steps does the writer list? Write them in the chart.

How to Plan a Potluck
1. Choose the date and the time.

174 COUNT AND NON-COUNT NOUNS

Write about an Event

2 BEFORE YOU WRITE. Think of an event; for example, a party, a wedding, or a trip. What do you need to do to prepare for this event? Write the steps in the chart. Use the chart in exercise **1C** as a model.

How to Plan a _____

3 WRITE a paragraph about how to plan your event. Use the information in your chart from exercise **2** and the paragraph in exercise **1A** to help you.

> **WRITING FOCUS**   Using Transition Words
>
> Writers use transition words to explain the steps in a process. Use transition words at the beginning of a sentence. These transition words are often used to explain a process: *first, second, then, next, after that, last,* and *finally.*
>
> **First,** choose the date and the time.
> **Next,** invite some friends.
> **Last,** put on some music.

4 SELF ASSESS. Read your paragraph. Underline the articles *a, an,* and *the.* Then use the checklist to assess your work.

☐ I used an article before each singular count noun. [5.1–5.3]

☐ I used a plural ending at the end of each plural count noun. [5.1, 5.4–5.7]

☐ I used singular verbs with non-count nouns. [5.1]

☐ I used transition words at the beginning of sentences. [WRITING FOCUS]

UNIT 6 Homes and Communities

There Is/There Are

▶ The town of Uummannaq, Greenland

Lesson **1**
page 178
There Is/There Are

Lesson **2**
page 187
Too Much/Too Many; Enough/ Not Enough

Lesson **3**
page 193
Indefinite Pronouns

Review the Grammar
page 201

Connect the Grammar to Writing
page 204

LESSON 1   *There Is/There Are*

EXPLORE

 1 READ the online forum about side trips from Shanghai, China. Notice the words in **bold**.

Side Trips from Shanghai

VIAJERO
Madrid, Spain

I have three free days during a business trip to Shanghai. Any ideas for side trips[1]? I'm interested in historic places. Thanks.

CHEN C
Qingdao, China

There are a lot of interesting places near Shanghai. Suzhou is on the Grand Canal. It's famous for its gardens. Near Suzhou, **there are** a lot of ancient water towns. Tongli is my favorite. It has 15 canals, and **there are** 49 bridges. It's beautiful.

VIAJERO
Madrid, Spain

Thanks. **Is there** a bus from Shanghai to Tongli? And how much time do I need to see the city? **Are there** many tourists there?

VIET
Da Nang, Vietnam

There's no bus, but **there's** a train to Suzhou and a bus from Suzhou to Tongli. One day is enough time to see Tongli. Go early in the day when **there aren't** a lot of tourists.

VIAJERO
Madrid, Spain
Thanks, everyone!

[1] **side trip:** a short trip during a longer visit

2 **CHECK.** Read the false statements. Then correct each statement to make it true.

1. There are ~~not~~ a lot of places to visit near Shanghai.
2. There are 25 canals in Tongli.
3. There are 49 roads in Tongli.
4. There is no train from Shanghai to Suzhou.
5. There are a lot of tourists in Tongli early in the day.

3 **DISCOVER.** Complete the exercises to learn about the grammar in this lesson.

A Find these sentences in the online forum from exercise **1**. Write the missing words.

1. _____ a lot of interesting places near Shanghai.
2. It has 15 canals, and _____ 49 bridges.
3. _____ bus, but _____ a train to Suzhou and a bus from Suzhou to Tongli.
4. Go early in the day when _____ a lot of tourists.

B Look at the sentences in exercise **A**. Then choose the correct words to complete each statement below. Discuss your answers with your classmates and teacher.

1. We use **there is / there are** with singular nouns.
2. We use **there is / there are** with plural nouns.

▼ A water town near Suzhou, China

LEARN

6.1 There Is/There Are: Statements

Affirmative			
There	Be	Subject	
There	is / 's	a hospital / a lot of traffic	on Main Street.
	are	two elevators	in this building.

Negative			
There	Be + Not	Subject	
There	is not / isn't	a hospital / a lot of traffic	on Elm Street.
	are not / aren't	any classes	at night

1. Use *There is/There are* to refer to things or people for the first time and to emphasize that they exist. Sometimes we include additional information about when or where these things or people exist.	**There are** two students from Peru in my class. **There is** a post office near my house. **There's** a class from 9:30–12:30 on Monday.
2. Use *There is*, *There's*, and *There isn't* with a singular count noun or a non-count noun*.	**There is** a lamp on the table. **There isn't** a lot of noise on my street.
3. Use *There are*, *There are not*, and *There aren't* with plural count nouns*.	**There are** a few students in the hallway. **There aren't** any classes tomorrow.
4. These contractions are used in conversation or informal writing: *There's*, *There isn't*, and *There aren't*. *There're* is used in conversation, but it is not common in writing.	A: **There's** a test on Monday. B: Really? I need to study this weekend! **There aren't** any students absent today.
5. When *There is/are* is followed by two or more nouns, the verb usually agrees with the first noun.	**There's** a book and a pen on my desk. **There's** coffee and tea. **There are** some cookies, milk, and juice in the kitchen.
6. *There is no* and *there are no* are often used in negative statements. They mean the same as *There isn't any* and *There aren't any*.	**There is no** homework tonight. **There are no** classes on Sunday.

*See 5.1 in Unit 5 for more information on count and non-count nouns.

REAL ENGLISH

There can also mean "in that place" or "to that place."

There's a beautiful park **there**.
We go **there** almost every day.

4 Complete each sentence with *There is* or *There are*.

1. ___There are___ 49 bridges in Tongli.
2. _____ a bus to the town.
3. _____ some beautiful gardens in the city.
4. _____ two trains every morning.
5. _____ a lot of tourists in the summer.
6. _____ three buses and a train in the afternoon.
7. _____ a coffee shop and two restaurants in the train station.
8. _____ a lot of water towns in China.

9. _____ a park near my apartment.

10. _____ no museums in my city.

11. _____ a bus stop on my street.

12. _____ a lot of traffic in the morning.

5 SPEAK. Work with a partner. Make sentences with *There is/isn't, There are/aren't,* or *There is/are no.* Use the words in the box.

| in our classroom | in this building | in this city | in my family |

There's a cafeteria in this building.

There aren't any vending machines in this building.

6.2 *There Is/There Are*: Yes/No Questions and Short Answers

Yes/No Questions				Short Answers	
Be	There	Subject		Affirmative	Negative
Is	there	an entrance	on Main Street?	Yes, **there is.**	No, **there isn't.**
		a lot of traffic			
Are		two elevators	in this building?	Yes, **there are.**	No, **there aren't.**

Be comes before *there* in Yes/No questions.

✓ **Is there** a bus stop on Park Street?
✗ There is a bus stop on Park Street?

6 Underline the verb in each statement. Then change the statement to a *Yes/No* question.

Statements   ***Yes/No* Question**

1. There <u>aren't</u> a lot of tourists in the summer.   __Are there__ a lot of tourists in the summer?

2. There isn't much traffic.   _____ much traffic?

3. There's no parking.   _____ any parking?

4. There's a coffee shop near here.   _____ a coffee shop near here?

5. There aren't any more cookies.   _____ any more cookies?

6. There are no students absent today.   _____ any students absent today?

7. There's a lot of homework.   _____ a lot of homework?

8. There's a test today.   _____ a test today?

7 SPEAK. Work with a partner. Ask and answer *Yes/No* questions with *Is there* and *Are there*. Use a word or phrase from each column.

a/an any	bus stop subway station Indian restaurant coffee shops post office parking student(s) from Japan / Germany / Brazil, etc.	near here in this class

Student A: *Is there a bus stop near here?*
Student B: *Yes, there's one on the next block.*
Student A: *Thanks!*

> **REAL ENGLISH**
>
> *There's one* is often used in answers to *Yes/No* questions with *Is there/Are there*.
>
> A: *Is there a post office near here?*
> B: *Yes, **there's one** across the street.*
>   (one = a post office)

6.3 How Much... Is There? / How Many... Are There?

How Much/ How Many	Subject	Be	There		Answers
How much	homework	is	there	tonight?	There's a little. A little. A lot. Not much.
How many	computers	are		in the library?	There are six. Six. A lot. A few. Not many.

1. **Remember:** Use *How much* and *How many* for questions about quantity.	**How much** time **is there**? **How many** Brazilian students **are there** in our class?
2. **Remember:** Use *How much* with non-count* nouns.	✓ **How much** space **is there**? ✗ How <u>much</u> windows **are there**?
3. **Remember:** Use *How many* with plural count* nouns.	✓ **How many** windows **are there**? ✗ How <u>many</u> space **is there**?

*See 5.1 in Unit 5 for more information on count and non-count nouns.

8 Complete each question with *much* or *many* and the correct form of *be*.

1. How __many__ buses __are__ there in the morning?
2. How _____ traffic _____ there at 5:00 p.m.?
3. How _____ tourists _____ there every summer?
4. How _____ information _____ there on the website?
5. How _____ universities _____ there in your city?
6. How _____ classrooms _____ there in this building?
7. How _____ teachers _____ there in this program?
8. How _____ snow _____ there in the winter?
9. How _____ desks _____ there in his room?
10. How _____ questions _____ there in this exercise?

PRACTICE

9 WRITE & SPEAK.

A Use the words in parentheses to write questions with *How much . . . is there?* and *How many . . . are there?*

1. (students / in this class) __How many students are there in this class?__
2. (tables / in this room) _____
3. (floors / in this building) _____
4. (windows / in our classroom) _____
5. (homework / tonight) _____
6. (money / in your wallet) _____
7. (train stations / in your city) _____
8. (furniture / in your home) _____

B Work with a partner. Ask and answer the questions from exercise **A**.

Student A: *How many students are there in this class?*
Student B: *There are sixteen. / Sixteen.*

C Ask your partner other questions with *How much . . . is there?* and *How many . . . are there?* Use your own ideas.

Student A: *How many people are there in your family?*
Student B: *Three. / There are three. / Just one.*

10 EDIT.
Read the conversation between two people on an airplane. Find and correct five more errors with *there is/there are*.

Al: Wow! Look at the islands. They're incredible.

Dan: They sure are. That's Santa Cruz Island over there.

Al: It looks like there is [are] some boats down there.

Dan: They're probably tour boats. There is a lot of tourists at this time of year.

Al: Is this your first time in the Galápagos Islands?

Dan: No. I'm actually from here. I live on San Cristóbal. It's that island over there.

Al: Really? Have there a town on the island?

Dan: Yes, there are a small town and a few thousand people on the island. They live there.

Al: How about hotels? There are any hotels on the island?

Dan: Yes, a few small ones, but there haven't any big hotels on the island.

Al: Do people live on all of the islands?

Dan: No, only on four of them.

Al: Interesting.

11 READ, WRITE & SPEAK.

A Read about the Galápagos Islands.

The Galápagos Islands: Not Just Home to Animals

The Galápagos Islands belong to Ecuador and are about 600 miles (1000 kilometers) off the coast of South America. They are home to many different kinds of unusual animals, such as giant tortoises[1] and land iguanas. The islands are also home to over 25,000 people. There are permanent[2] residents on four of the islands. There are airports on two of the islands, Santa Cruz and San Cristóbal.

The island of Santa Cruz has the largest population. Many of the people there live in Puerto Ayora, a busy town with hotels, restaurants, banks, shops, scuba diving schools, and one of the Galápagos' two airports. It's an important tourist stop, so there are a lot of tourists in the town. The island has beautiful beaches, and, of course, a lot of interesting wildlife. The Charles Darwin Research Center is also on this island.

[1] **tortoise:** a land turtle
[2] **permanent:** lasting a long time

▶ Puerto Ayora harbor, Galápagos Islands

B Rewrite each false statement to make it true.

1. There aren't any unusual animals on the Galápagos Islands.
   <u>There are many unusual animals on the Galápagos Islands.</u>
2. There aren't any giant tortoises on the islands. _____
3. There are about 10,000 people on the islands. _____
4. There are four airports. _____
5. There isn't an airport on Santa Cruz. _____
6. There aren't any hotels in Puerto Ayora. _____
7. There aren't many tourists on Santa Cruz. _____
8. There's no wildlife on Santa Cruz. _____

C Write five or six quiz questions to find out how much a classmate remembers about the article from exercise **A**. Begin your questions with *Is there, Are there, How much,* and *How many.*

<u>Are there any unusual animals on the Galápagos Islands?</u>

_____

D Work with a partner. Ask and answer your quiz questions from exercise **C**.

Student A: *Are there any unusual animals on the Galápagos Islands?*

Student B: *Yes, there are.*

◀ A giant tortoise, Isabela Island, Galápagos Islands

12 LISTEN & SPEAK.

A Listen to a man talk about Vancouver, Canada. Check (✓) the topics you hear.

✓	fun activities	☐	water
☐	clubs and restaurants	☐	scenery
☐	cost of activities	☐	rain
☐	movies	☐	snow
☐	open space	☐	canals
☐	parks	☐	highway
☐	mountains	☐	bridges
☐	fishing	☐	traffic

> **REAL ENGLISH**
>
> *There* sounds the same as *they're* and *their*. Be careful about the spelling when you write these.
>
> **There** is a man in the boat.
> I see Ted and Amy. **They're** in the park.
> **Their** house is on Pine Street.

B The speaker does not like some things about Vancouver. Listen again and circle the things in exercise **A** he doesn't like.

C Work with a partner. What does the speaker like about Vancouver? What doesn't he like about it? Use the topics from exercise **A** to help you.

There are a lot of things to do. They're expensive.

13 APPLY.

A Think of a city or town. Do you like it? Why or why not? Complete the chart with your ideas.

Things I like about _____	Things I don't like about _____
There are a lot of good restaurants.	There is a lot of traffic.

B Work with a partner. Tell your partner about your city or town. Talk about the things you like and do not like about it. Use the information from your chart in exercise **A**. Use affirmative and negative forms of *There is* and *There are*.

Student A: *My city is Lisbon in Portugal. There are a lot of good restaurants. Are there good restaurants in your city?*

Student B: *No. I'm from a small town. There aren't many restaurants. There are a lot of beautiful parks. Are there many parks in Lisbon?*

Too Much/Too Many; Enough/Not Enough — LESSON 2

EXPLORE

1 READ the advertisement about home design. Notice the words in **bold**.

▼ A living room with straight lines, basic colors, and lots of empty space

What color are the walls? How much furniture do we need? Do we need a sofa? Where do we put it? Is there **enough art** on the walls? Do we have **too many things** on the tables? These are some common question about home design. There are many different ideas and opinions!

Some people like a very simple design. They like straight lines and basic colors such as white or black. In their opinions, most people have **too much furniture** in their homes. They like empty space. For them, "the right amount" of furniture is one or two pieces.

Other people prefer round edges and soft colors such as blue and beige. They like comfortable furniture, and they like to have **enough furniture** so that people can sit close together and talk. They like **enough tables** and **shelves** for their books, lamps, and photographs.

How about you? What do you like? What questions about home design do you have? Ask us! We're experts[1] in home design. Contact us today!

[1] **expert:** a person who knows a lot about a particular subject

2 CHECK. People have different ideas about home design. Write these words from the advertisement from exercise **1** on page 187 in the correct column of the chart.

| basic colors | empty space | ~~simple design~~ | straight lines |
| comfortable furniture | ~~round edges~~ | soft colors | |

Some people like . . .	Other people like . . .
simple design	round edges

3 DISCOVER. Complete the exercises to learn about the grammar in this lesson.

A Find these sentences in the reading from exercise **1** on page 187. Write the missing words.

1. Do we have **too many** _____ on the tables?

2. In their opinions, most people have **too much** _____ in their homes.

B Look at the sentences in exercise **A**. Then choose the correct answer to complete each statement below. Discuss your answers with your classmates and teacher.

1. *Too much* and *too many* have a ____ meaning.
    a. positive
    b. negative

2. We use *too much* with ____ .
    a. plural count nouns
    b. non-count nouns

3. We use *too many* with ____ .
    a. plural count nouns
    b. non-count nouns

◀ A living room with soft colors and comfortable furniture

LEARN

6.4 Too Much/Too Many + Noun

	Too Much	Non-Count Noun
We have		homework.
There is	too much	traffic.
He drinks		coffee.

	Too Many	Plural Count Noun
We have		chairs.
There are	too many	tourists.
He eats		sweets.

1. *Too much* and *too many* mean "more than necessary." They have a negative meaning.	There is **too much** noise. (We aren't happy about the noise.) There are **too many** people here. (We aren't happy about it.)
2. Use *too much* with non-count nouns.	✓ There is **too much** traffic. ✗ There are <u>too much</u> cars.
3. Use *too many* with plural count nouns.	✓ We have **too many** chairs. ✗ We have <u>too many</u> furniture.

4 Complete each sentence with *too much* or *too many*.

1. I don't like Marco's apartment. There's ___too much___ space with nothing in it.
2. There are _____ lamps in this room. Let's put one in the bedroom.
3. I don't like that wallpaper. It has _____ different colors.
4. Jill prefers a simple style. In her opinion, my house has _____ furniture.
5. My sister spends _____ money on furniture. She needs to save more money.
6. It's always difficult to find my keys. I have _____ things in my bag.
7. I don't like Seattle in the winter. It gets _____ rain.
8. There's no place to park. There are _____ cars here today.
9. I drink _____ soda. I need to stop.
10. _____ coffee keeps me awake at night.

5 **WRITE & SPEAK.** Complete the sentences. Then share your ideas with a partner.

1. There's too much ___furniture___ in my home.
2. There are too many _____ in my home.
3. I eat too much _____ .
4. I eat too many _____ .

6.5 Enough/Not Enough + Noun

	Enough	Non-Count Noun
We have	enough	time.
We don't have		information.
There's		furniture.
There isn't		space.

	Enough	Plural Count Noun
We have	enough	desks.
We don't have		chairs.
There are		cups.
There aren't		plates.

1. *Enough* means "the necessary amount."	There is **enough** furniture. We don't need more furniture.
2. *Not enough* means "less than the necessary amount."	There are **not enough** chairs. We need more chairs.
3. Do not use *enough* with singular count nouns.	✓ We have **enough** chairs in our classroom. ✗ We have **enough** teacher in our classroom.

6 LISTEN.

A Listen to each sentence. Is the amount *enough* or *not enough*? Put a check (✓) in the correct column.

	Enough	Not Enough		Enough	Not Enough
1.	☐	✓	5.	☐	☐
2.	☐	☐	6.	☐	☐
3.	☐	☐	7.	☐	☐
4.	☐	☐	8.	☐	☐

B Listen again. Complete the sentences from exercise **A**.

1. _There isn't enough_ furniture in the room.
2. _____ empty space.
3. _____ chairs.
4. _____ books for everyone.
5. We _____ money.
6. _____ time.
7. We _____ food for dinner.
8. _____ light in the kitchen.

PRACTICE

7 Read the statements. Then complete the sentence(s). Use *enough, not enough, too much,* and *too many.*

1. My apartment is very small. There are two sofas, three tables, and ten chairs in it.
   I have <u>too much furniture. There isn't enough space.</u>

2. I need more shelves in my office. I have a lot of books. There isn't a place for all of them.
   I have _____. My office doesn't have
   _____.

3. I like my apartment. It has one bedroom, a living room, and a kitchen. It's perfect for me.
   My apartment has _____.

4. The sofa costs $600. I have $600. It's perfect.
   I have _____.

5. This classroom has 15 chairs. There are 18 students.
   This is a big problem. We don't have _____.

6. We have 25 books and 15 students.
   We have _____.

7. I don't want to drive to Ed's house. There are a lot of cars and buses on the roads today.
   There _____. Let's take the subway.

8. The apartment building has 12 parking spaces, and 20 people have cars.
   It's a big problem. There _____.

8 LISTEN & SPEAK.

A Listen to the conversation. Then choose the correct answer to complete each sentence.

1. They are talking about ____ .
   a. some friends' apartment   b. a hotel   c. their home

2. The two speakers are ____ .
   a. coworkers   b. a married couple   c. a mother and her son

B Listen again. Are the man and woman's opinions positive or negative? Write **P** for *positive* and **N** for *negative*.

	Man	Woman
Neighborhood	N	P
Stairs		
Windows		
Size		
Decor		

C What are the problems with their friends' neighborhood and apartment? Use *too many/much* or *enough* with the words in the box.

| flowers | nightclubs | parking | stairs | windows |
| light in the room | noise | space | things on tables | |

There are too many nightclubs in the neighborhood.

9 WRITE sentences in your notebook about the photograph below. Use the words in parentheses and *too much/many* or *enough*.

1. (He / work)
   He has too much work.
2. (He / space on his desk to work)
3. (He / things on his desk)
4. (He / space for his coffee cup)
5. (There / papers in his office)
6. (He / furniture)
7. (His office / space)
8. (He / time to clean his office)

▲ A busy author and filmmaker at work in his messy office

10 APPLY.

A Think about the positive and negative things about your own room, office, or home. In the chart, put a check (✓) to show your opinion about each item.

	Too Much	Too Many	Enough	Not Enough
Space	☐	☐	☐	☐
Bookshelves	☐	☐	☐	☐
Furniture	☐	☐	☐	☐
Places for papers, books, furniture, windows, etc.	☐	☐	☐	☐
Your idea _____	☐	☐	☐	☐

B Work with a partner. Talk about your room, office, or home. Use the information from your chart in exercise **A**.

My room is similar to the room in the photograph. I don't have enough space for . . .

Indefinite Pronouns — LESSON 3

EXPLORE

1 READ the online forum about dune shacks. Notice the words in **bold**.

Dune Shacks

Li592 Does **anyone** know **anything** about dune shacks[1] on the beach on Cape Cod, Massachusetts?

BW Yes. Don't stay in one! They are very, very small, and they don't have any water or electricity.[2] There's **nothing** to do there. **Someone** told me about them, so we stayed in one last summer. Big mistake.

BeachBunny That's the best thing about them. There isn't **anything** to do! Actually, that's not true. There's always **something** to do—walk on the beach, swim in the ocean, and enjoy nature. I love the dune shacks.

Traveler212 These little houses are very special, but they're not for **everyone**. Take warm clothes and **something** to read. Don't take **anything** that uses electricity. They're a great place to go and just relax!

Birdy The dune shacks are fine in warm, sunny weather. On a rainy day, **no one** wants to stay out there. Believe me. I know! I love the beach, but now I stay in town at a hotel. There's always **something** to do in town, even when it rains.

[1] **dune shack:** a small house on the sand dunes of a beach
[2] **electricity:** energy used for heat or light, or to power machines

▶ A dune shack, Cape Cod, Massachusetts, USA

2 CHECK. Are the writers' opinions from the online forum on page 193 positive or negative? Write **P** for *positive* and **N** for *negative*.

	Opinion
1. BW	N
2. BeachBunny	
3. Traveler212	
4. Birdy	

3 DISCOVER. Complete the exercises to learn about the grammar in this lesson.

A Find these sentences from the online forum in exercise **1** on page 193. Write the missing words.

1. _____ told me about them, so we stayed in one last summer.

2. That's the best thing about them. There isn't _____ to do.

3. There's always _____ to do.

4. Take warm clothes and _____ to read.

5. Don't take _____ that uses electricity.

B Look at the sentences in exercise **A**. Then choose the correct word to complete each statement below. Discuss your answers with your classmates and teacher.

1. We use *anything* and *something* for ____ .
   a. people   b. things

2. We use *anyone* and *someone* for ____ .
   a. people   b. things

3. We use ____ for negative statements.
   a. *something*   b. *anything*

▼ A beach cottage in Truro, Cape Cod, Massachusetts, USA

LEARN

6.6 Indefinite Pronouns: *Nothing, Anything, Something, Everything*

Affirmative Statements

Indefinite Pronoun	
Something Nothing Everything	is on your desk.

Negative Statements

	Indefinite Pronoun	
There isn't	anything	in the kitchen.
I don't need		from the store.

Yes/No Questions

Do you want **anything** from the store?
Is there **something** wrong?
Do we have **everything**?

1. Use the indefinite pronouns *nothing*, *anything*, *something*, and *everything* to refer to things that are not specific or are not known.	There's **nothing** in the box. **Everything** in that store is expensive.
2. *Nothing* has a negative meaning. Use it with an affirmative verb form, not a negative verb.	✓ He <u>knows</u> **nothing** about Cape Cod. ✗ He <u>doesn't know</u> **nothing** about Cape Cod.
3. Use *anything* in negative statements.	I don't see **anything** under the table. There isn't **anything** for homework tonight.
4. Use *anything*, *something*, and *everything* in questions.	Is there **anything** in that bag? Would you like **something** to drink? Is **everything** ready?
5. Use the singular form of the verb when an indefinite pronoun is the subject.	✓ **Nothing** <u>is</u> wrong with my computer. ✗ **Nothing** <u>are</u> wrong with my computer.

REAL ENGLISH

Indefinite pronouns are often used with infinitives.

*There's always **something** <u>to do</u> on Cape Cod.*
*I want **something** <u>to eat</u>.*
*There's **nothing** <u>to do</u> there.*

4 Choose the correct word to complete each sentence.

1. I don't know _____ about dune shacks.   a. nothing   (b.) anything
2. I love Cape Cod. There's always _____ to do there.   a. something   b. anything
3. Don't stay in a dune shack. There's _____ to do!   a. nothing   b. anything
4. Do you know _____ about Cape Cod?   a. nothing   b. anything
5. This is a very boring town. There's _____ to do here!   a. nothing   b. anything
6. Take _____ warm to wear. It gets cold at night.   a. something   b. nothing

7. I don't have _____ warm to wear.   a. anything   b. nothing

8. The hotel is very nice. _____ is perfect.   a. Everything   b. Anything

9. I'm hungry. Let's get _____ to eat.   a. something   b. nothing

10. I'm not thirsty. I don't want _____ to drink.   a. nothing   b. anything

5 Complete the sentences with *nothing, anything, something,* or *everything*. For some sentences, more than one answer is possible.

1. I don't know __anything__ about Boston, Massachusetts. I want to learn about it.

2. Boston is an interesting city. There's always _____ to do there.

3. Let's get up early and walk around town. I want to see _____.

4. The city has _____ : interesting museums, great restaurants, shops, and beautiful parks.

5. Does Jackie know _____ about buses from Boston to Cape Cod?

6. I know _____ about the history of Boston. I want to learn about it.

7. Do you know _____ about Boston or Cape Cod?

8. Tell me _____ about your hometown.

▼ Boston, Massachusetts, USA

6.7 Indefinite Pronouns: *No One, Nobody, Anyone, Anybody, Someone, Somebody, Everyone, Everybody*

Affirmative Statements	
Indefinite Pronoun	
No one/Nobody	is absent today.
Someone/Somebody	
Everyone/Everybody	knows the answer.

Negative Statements		
	Indefinite Pronoun	
There isn't	anyone/anybody	in the kitchen.
I don't know		in your class.

Yes/No Questions
Is **anyone/anybody** home?
Does **everyone/everybody** understand the problem?
Is there **someone/somebody** at the door?

1. The indefinite pronouns *no one, nobody, someone, somebody, everyone,* and *everybody* are used to refer to people that are not specific or are not known.	**Nobody** lives in that house. There's **someone** in the office.
2. *No one* and *nobody* have a negative meaning. Use them with affirmative verb forms, not negative verb forms.	✓ I <u>know</u> **nobody** from Spain. ✗ I <u>don't know **nobody**</u> from Spain.
3. Use *anyone* and *anybody* in negative statements.	I don't know **anyone** from Spain. There isn't **anybody** from Norway in our class.
4. Use *anyone, anybody, someone, somebody, everyone,* and *everybody* in questions.	Does **anybody** live in that house? Is there **someone** at the door? Is **everybody** ready?
5. **Remember:** Indefinite pronouns are always singular, not plural. They take the same form of the verb as *he, she,* and *it*. However, we often use a plural pronoun to refer back to *everyone*.	✓ **Everybody loves** ice cream. ✗ **Everybody** <u>love</u> ice cream. A: Where **is everyone**? B: **They're** all in the coffee shop.

6 Choose the correct indefinite pronoun to complete each sentence.

1. Do you know **no one** / **anyone** from Cape Cod?
2. Is **someone** / **everyone** ready to go? We're late!
3. I work with **someone** / **anyone** from Boston.
4. I see **somebody** / **anybody** in the yard. Who is it?
5. **Anyone** / **Everyone** likes the beach. Let's go there on Saturday.
6. **Anyone** / **Someone** in our building plays loud music every night.
7. I don't know **anybody** / **nobody** from Thailand.
8. **Anyone** / **No one** is in the office. Let's come back later.

7 Complete each sentence with *no one*, *anyone*, *someone*, or *everyone*. For some sentences, more than one answer is possible.

1. It's rainy today. _____No one_____ is on the beach.
2. Listen! _____ is at the door.
3. Does _____ speak Italian?
4. I don't know _____ from Iceland.
5. _____ knows Alice. She has a lot of friends.
6. Our classroom is empty. Where is _____?
7. Does _____ have an extra pencil? I need one for the test.
8. _____ is absent. We're all here.

PRACTICE

8 Complete each conversation with the correct indefinite pronouns. In some sentences, more than one answer is possible.

1. A: Let's do ___something___ different on vacation this winter. How about camping?

   B: What? Are you serious? _____ goes camping in the winter!

2. A: Is _____ wrong?

   B: No, _____ is wrong. I'm fine.

3. A: Knock on the door again. There's always _____ home.

   B: Well, there's _____ there now.

4. A: Do we need more chairs?

   B: No, we have enough for _____ .

5. A: There's _____ wrong with my camera.

   B: I'd like to help you, but I don't know _____ about cameras.

9 LISTEN & SPEAK.

A Read each statement. Then listen to a conversation about camping and glamping (a new form of camping). Circle **T** for *true* or **F** for *false*.

1. Someone wants to go camping. (T) F
2. Everyone likes to go camping. T F
3. Camping is a relaxing vacation. T F
4. Everyone gets enough sleep. T F
5. Glamping is a lot of work. T F
6. In glamping, someone else gets wood for the fire. T F
7. In glamping, someone cooks for you. T F
8. No one likes the idea of glamping. T F

> **REAL ENGLISH**
>
> *Someone else* means another person or a different person.
>
> *Jack doesn't know anything about cameras. Let's ask **someone else**.*
>
> A: *Who's at the door? Is it Lucy?*
>
> B: *No, it's **someone else**.*

B Listen again. Complete the sentences from the conversation with the correct indefinite pronouns. Then listen again and check your answers.

1. What does ___*everyone*___ want to do for vacation?
2. Does _____ want to go camping?
3. On vacation, I don't want to do _____ .
4. I want to relax and do _____ .
5. You don't do any work or _____ .

▲ A luxury tent

6. _____ else does _____ for you.

7. _____ else gets the wood for the fire.

8. _____ good is ever free, right?

C Work with a partner. Discuss these questions.

1. Is camping a relaxing vacation? Why or why not?

2. Do you want to try glamping? Why or why not?

10 Complete the conversation with *everyone, everything, no one, nothing, anyone,* or *anything.* Then listen and check your answers.

Alex: Hey, (1) ___*everyone*___! Let's talk about our camping trip.

First, (2) _____ needs to bring a sleeping bag.

Matt: Right. We also need a tent or (3) _____ to put over our sleeping bags. Does (4) _____ have one?

Jim: I have a tent.

Alex: Great. Next, it gets cold at night. Does (5) _____ have warm clothes?

Matt: No. I don't have (6) _____ warm to wear. Does (7) _____ have an extra jacket or something?

Jim: Yeah, I do. Now, how about food? We need eggs or (8) _____ for breakfast. How about pancakes? They're easy to make.

Alex: Sure. That's fine. There's a store near the campground. It sells (9) _____: food, maps, bug spray . . .

Jim: Great. Let's go there tomorrow.

> **REAL ENGLISH**
>
> We often use *or something* in speaking to add another possibility.
>
> A: *Where's Pamela?*
> B: *I don't know. Maybe her bus is late **or something.***

11 APPLY. Work in a small group. Follow the directions below.

A Decide on a type of trip to take (e.g., an overnight camping trip, a visit to a city with an overnight stay in a hotel, or a tour, etc.). Decide on a place to go (e.g., Paris, the Galápagos Islands, a national park, etc.). Write three sentences about the reasons for your decision.

There's always something to do there. Someone makes all the arrangements. No one needs to . . .

B Make a list of things you need to do to prepare for the trip. Then write a conversation about your plans. Use the conversation from exercise **10** as a model. Use indefinite pronouns.

Everyone needs to bring something warm to wear.

C Role-play your conversation for your classmates.

UNIT 6 Review the Grammar

Charts 6.1–6.7

1 LISTEN. Complete the conversation about a beach house. Use the words in the box. You can use some words more than once. Then listen and check your answers.

anyone	there's	is there	enough
anything	there isn't	are there	much
nobody	there are		too much
something	there aren't		

Luisa: I'm so excited about our little beach house. Let's go this weekend and figure out the furniture.

Carmen: We don't need (1) ___much___ furniture. (2) _____ much space.

Rosa: True. We don't want to have (3) _____ furniture. What do we need?

Luisa: Well, we need (4) _____ to sit on, so we need some chairs.

Rosa: (5) _____ a few chairs in my garage. Let's use those.

Carmen: OK, good. Does (6) _____ have a small table?

Luisa: I do. (7) _____ one in my bedroom at home.

Rosa: Great! (8) _____ space for a sofa?

Luisa: Yes, (9) _____ space for a small one.

Carmen: How about the kitchen?

Rosa: It's really small. It doesn't have (10) _____ space. (11) _____ many cabinets or shelves.

Luisa: That's OK. Do you want to cook on vacation? I don't!

Carmen: Me neither. (12) _____ wants to cook on vacation.

Rosa: True! After all, it is a vacation house.

▼ A small cottage near the ocean in Wellfleet, Cape Cod, Massachusetts, USA

Review the Grammar UNIT 6

Charts 6.1–6.3

2 EDIT. Find and correct six more errors with *There is/There are*, *Yes/No* questions, and questions with *How much/How many . . . is/are there*.

Reporter: Welcome back to *WZCZ News*. Listen to this everyone! ~~There's~~ *There are* great white sharks near the beach in Cape Cod, Massachusetts. We're on the phone now with Tom Hardy. He's in our traffic helicopter over the beach. Tom, tell us, how much sharks are there? There is any danger?

Tom: Yes! There are a shark right below me. I see a lot more nearby. I'm glad I'm in a helicopter!

Reporter: Right. Are there many people in the water?

Tom: No, there isn't. There's a shark warning, and everyone knows about the danger.

Reporter: OK, Tom. Thanks. How many traffic is there today?

Tom: Usually, there aren't a lot of traffic out here, but today there are a lot of cars on the roads. Everyone wants to see the sharks!

Charts 6.1–6.7

3 LISTEN, SPEAK & WRITE.

A Listen to the conversation about an apartment. What does the apartment have? Check (✓) the items on the list below.

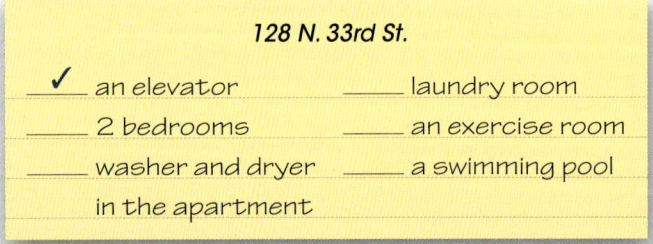

128 N. 33rd St.
- ✓ an elevator
- ___ 2 bedrooms
- ___ washer and dryer in the apartment
- ___ laundry room
- ___ an exercise room
- ___ a swimming pool

B Write questions about the apartment.

1. (How many / bedrooms)
   How many bedrooms are there?

2. (a washer and dryer)
   _____

3. (enough / laundry rooms)
   _____

4. (How many / units)
   _____

5. (How many / buildings)
   _____

6. (an exercise room)
   _____

7. (have / a swimming pool)
   _____

8. (anyone / in the apartment / now)
   _____

C Work with a partner. Use your questions from exercise **B** to practice the conversation about an apartment.

Charts 6.1–6.7

4 SPEAK. Partner A, look at the picture. Partner B, look at the picture on page A6. Ask and answer questions to find eight differences between the two pictures.

How many sofas does it have?   *Is there a table?*   *Is there anything on the table?*

5 SPEAK. Work with a partner. Discuss the room in the photo. Ask and answer questions with *enough, too many,* and *too much.*

Student A: *Do you like the room design?*

Student B: *No, I don't. There's too much empty space.*

Connect the Grammar to Writing

1 READ & NOTICE THE GRAMMAR.

A Read the paragraph. Does the writer like the college? Discuss with a partner.

My College

I like my college. It has a beautiful campus. There are about 1500 students. Everyone is very friendly. There is always someone to talk to. The classes are small. There are no large lectures, and the professors know all of their students' names. In my opinion, there is only one problem. There is too much homework!

Unfortunately, the college is in a very small town. There is only one restaurant. There are only two small stores. There are no movie theaters, and there is nothing to do on weekends. After college, I want to live in a big city.

GRAMMAR FOCUS

In the paragraph in exercise **A**, the writer uses affirmative and negative forms of *there is/there are* to express her opinion about a place.

. . . **there is** nothing to do on weekends.
There is too much homework!

B Read the paragraph in exercise **A** again. Underline the sentences with *There is* and *There are* (affirmative and negative). Then work with a partner and compare answers.

C Complete the chart with information from the paragraph in exercise **A**. What does the writer like about her college? What doesn't she like about it?

My College	
Positive Things	Negative Things
It has a beautiful campus.	

Write Your Opinion about a Place

2 BEFORE YOU WRITE. Think of a place or a community. What do you like about it? What don't you like about it? Write notes in the chart. Use the chart from exercise **1C** as a model.

_____ (your place or community)	
Positive Things	Negative Things

3 WRITE a paragraph about your place or community. Use the information from your chart in exercise **2** and the paragraph in exercise **1A** to help you.

> **WRITING FOCUS   Expressing Opinions**
>
> An opinion is how someone feels about something. It can be positive or negative. These introductory phrases are commonly used to introduce an opinion: *fortunately, unfortunately, in my opinion, personally,* and so on.
>
> **In my opinion**, there is only one problem.
> **Unfortunately**, the college is in a very small town.

4 SELF ASSESS. Read your paragraph. Underline *there is* and *there are* (negative and affirmative). Then use the checklist to assess your work.

- [ ] I used a singular count noun or non-count noun after *there is*. [6.1]
- [ ] I used a plural count noun after *there are*. [6.1]
- [ ] I used a non-count noun after *too much*. [6.4]
- [ ] I used a plural count noun after *too many*. [6.4]
- [ ] I used introductory phrases to introduce the opinions in my paragraph. [WRITING FOCUS]

UNIT 7 Extremes
Present Progressive

▲ A climber in an ice cave, Myrdalsjokull Glacier, Iceland

Lesson 1
page 208

Present Progressive: Statements

Lesson 2
page 218

Present Progressive: Questions

Lesson 3
page 228

Simple Present vs. Present Progressive; Non-Action Verbs

Review the Grammar
page 235

Connect the Grammar to Writing
page 238

LESSON 1 — Present Progressive: Statements

EXPLORE

 1 READ the conversation about highliners. Notice the words in **bold**.

Highliners

Angie: Hey, Cary. What are you doing?

Cary: Oh, hi, Angie. **I'm looking** at photos of extreme sports.[1] Look at this one!

Angie: Oh, wow. That's scary! How high are they?

Cary: 3600 feet. The article says they**'re walking** toward Troll Wall. It's the highest cliff in Europe. It's in Norway.

Angie: That's really extreme—it's incredible!

Cary: Yeah, it's called "highlining." See. They**'re balancing**[2] on lines. They**'re not wearing** shoes. I guess that helps them balance. It says they're tied to the lines. They**'re wearing** belts[3] or something for safety.

Angie: That's good, but I'm glad **I'm not doing** that. I don't like heights.[4]

Cary: Me neither. Listen. Here's a quote from the photographer. His name's Branislav Beliancin. He**'s standing** really close to the edge[5] of the mountain. He says, "You need to be careful because you are directly on the mountain's edge. One bad step and bye-bye."

Angie: He**'s not joking**. That's true for the highliners, too!

[1] **extreme sport:** a sport that is physically dangerous such as bungee jumping
[2] **balance:** the ability to stand, walk, etc., without falling down
[3] **belt:** a piece of leather, plastic, etc., worn around the waist
[4] **heights:** high places
[5] **edge:** the place or line where something ends

2 CHECK. Read each statement about the highliners. Then circle **T** for *true* or **F** for *false*.

1. The highliners are in Norway.   (T)   F
2. The highliners are wearing shoes.   T   F
3. Angie wants to try highlining.   T   F
4. Cary doesn't like heights.   T   F
5. Beliancin is walking on a highline in this photo.   T   F

3 DISCOVER. Complete the exercises to learn about the grammar in this lesson.

A Find these sentences in the conversation from exercise **1**. Write the missing words.

1. I _____ at photos of extreme sports.
2. The article says they _____ toward Troll Wall.
3. They _____ shoes.
4. He _____ very close to the edge of the mountain.

B Look at the sentences in exercise **A**. Notice the verbs. Then choose the correct answer to complete the statement below. Discuss your answer with your classmates and teacher.

The verb after *be* _____ .   a. ends with an -s
　　　　　　　　　　　　　　 b. is the base form
　　　　　　　　　　　　　　 c. has -*ing* at the end

◀ Highliners Alexander Lauterbach and Julien Miller walk on lines of nylon webbing in the mountains of Norway.

UNIT 7 LESSON 1 **209**

LEARN

7.1 Present Progressive: Affirmative Statements

Subject	Be	Verb + -ing
I	am / 'm	writing.
You	are / 're	teaching.
He / She / It	is / 's	working.
We / You / They	are / 're	reading.

1. Use the present progressive* to talk about actions that are in progress now. The actions are not completed.	A: Are you busy? B: Yes, I'm reading this book for homework.
2. Use the present progressive to talk about actions that are in progress at the present time but maybe not at this moment.	She's taking three classes this semester. He's teaching in Japan this year.
3. When the subject is doing two actions, do not repeat the subject and the verb be.	✓ I'm studying and living in Chicago. ✗ I'm studying and am living in Chicago.
4. Remember: Contractions are usually used in conversation and informal writing.	A: My brother's studying in Italy this semester. B: Interesting! A: Are you busy right now? B: Yes. I'm doing my homework.

*The *present progressive* is sometimes called the *present continuous*.

4 Underline the present progressive in each sentence.

1. They're walking on lines above a valley.
2. They're wearing safety belts.
3. The photographer is standing on the cliff.
4. He's taking photos.
5. He's watching the highliners.
6. They're doing this in Norway.
7. We're talking about extreme sports.
8. She's looking at the photo and asking about the highliners.

◀ A mountain climber in her tent on Tahir Tower, Karakoram, Pakistan

5 Look at the photo of the mountain climber above. Then complete each sentence with the present progressive form of the verb in parentheses.

1. The mountain climber ____is relaxing____ (relax) in her tent.
2. She _____ (climb) a mountain in Pakistan.
3. She _____ (wear) warm clothing.
4. She _____ (check) her e-mail.
5. Her tent _____ (hang) from the cliff.
6. The photographer _____ (look) at her through his camera.
7. He _____ (think) about the photo.
8. The other climbers _____ (camp) on the mountain.
9. They _____ (rest) in their tents.
10. Everyone _____ (wait) to continue the climb the next day.

6 SPEAK. Work with a partner. Make three more sentences about the photo at the top of the page. Use the present progressive and the verbs from the box.

| hang | read | wear |

She's wearing a red jacket.

UNIT 7   LESSON 1   **211**

7.2 Present Progressive: Negative Statements

Subject	Be Not	Verb + -ing
I	am not 'm not	writing.
You	are not 're not aren't	teaching.
He She It	is not 's not isn't	working.
We You They	are not 're not aren't	reading.

REAL ENGLISH

When the subject is a noun that ends in an -s, -z, -ch, -sh, or soft -g sound, use the contraction with the verb. Do not use the contraction with the noun.

✓ Marge isn't watching TV. She's studying.
✗ Marge's not watching TV. She's studying.

To make a negative statement in the present progressive, put *not* after *be*.	He*'s not studying.* He's watching TV.

7 Change each affirmative statement to a negative statement.

1. We're doing an exercise right now. _We're not doing an exercise right now._
2. I'm changing the sentences to questions. _____
3. She's taking a test. _____
4. Our teacher is wearing a jacket. _____
5. We're eating lunch. _____
6. He's checking his e-mail. _____
7. Tom's reading a book in class. _____
8. My parents are working right now. _____
9. You're teaching math. _____
10. They're taking Greek this semester. _____

8 SPEAK. Work with a partner. Say two things you are doing. Say two things you are not doing. Use the present progressive of the verbs in the box or your own ideas.

| sit | speak | stand | study | talk | wear |

I'm speaking English.

We're not studying Spanish.

7.3 Spelling Rules: -ing Forms

1. Add -ing to the base form of most verbs.	talk-talk**ing**	study-study**ing**
2. Verbs that end in a consonant and silent e: drop the -e and add -ing.	hike-hik**ing**	make-mak**ing**
3. One-syllable verbs that end in CVC*: double the final consonant and add -ing.	shop-sho**pping**	sit-si**tting**
4. Two-syllable verbs that end in CVC and have the stress on the first syllable: add -ing, but do not double the final consonant.	enter-enter**ing**	listen-listen**ing**
5. Two-syllable verbs that end in CVC and have the stress on the second syllable: double the final consonant and add -ing.	begin-be**ginning**	
6. Verbs that end in -w, -x, or -y: add -ing, but do not double the final consonant.	grow-grow**ing**	fix-fix**ing** play-play**ing**
7. Verbs ending in –ie: change the ie to y and add -ing.	tie-t**ying**	die-d**ying**

*consonant + vowel + consonant

9 Write the -ing form of each verb.

1. play _____
2. plan _____
3. try _____
4. make _____
5. practice _____
6. hit _____
7. exercise _____
8. climb _____
9. show _____
10. enter _____

10 LISTEN and complete the sentences. (CD2-26)

1. The ice climber ___is using___ special equipment.
2. She _____ special boots.

▼ A female ice climber in British Columbia, Canada

3. The kiteboarder _____ in the air.
4. He _____ on his kiteboard.
5. The skier _____ to win the race.
6. She _____ very fast.
7. The hang glider _____ over the valley.
8. He _____ at the camera.
9. These people _____ interesting things.
10. They _____ fun.

▲ A professional kiteboarder

▲ A skier in a race

▲ A hang glider

PRACTICE

11 Complete the e-mail with the present progressive form of the verbs in parentheses. Use contractions where possible.

Greetings from Austria! (1) <u>I'm not spending</u> (I / not spending) this semester on campus. (2) _____ (I / study) here in Austria. (3) _____ (I / not live) in a dormitory. (4) _____ (I / stay) with a family in Salzburg. They're very nice. (5) _____ (They / help) me with my German. (6) _____ (I / do) a lot of interesting things here. (7) _____ (I / take) a hang gliding class on Saturdays. It's a little scary, but I like it! My class has four people, and our teacher is great. (8) _____ (We / learn) a lot. Right now (9) _____ (I / sit) outside and (10) _____ (enjoy) the scenery. (11) Some _____ (children / play) games and (12) _____ (have) a lot of fun. I miss you. Write soon!

Amanda

12 Put the words in the correct order to make sentences about the photo on this page. Use the present progressive form of the verbs in bold.

1. this / **climb** / not / Andy / photo / in   Andy is not climbing in this photo.
2. He / dangerous / **do** / very / something _____
3. **jump** / from a cliff / He / to a rock _____
4. rope / a / **carry** / He _____
5. safety / belt / He / **wear** / a / not _____
6. He / right now / in the air / **fly** _____
7. The / **watch** / photographer / him _____
8. photos / He / great / **take** / some _____

◀ Andy Marquardt is a rock climber in Sedona, Arizona in the United States.

13 EDIT. Read the text message. Find and correct six more errors with the present progressive form and spelling.

> I'm
> I texting you from Arizona. I'm visitting my sister Carol. Right now I'm siting near a huge cliff. I enjoying the scenery. Carol is takeing lessons. She's climbing the cliff with her teacher today. I waiting for her. They no are climbing very high, but it's dangerous!

14 SPEAK & WRITE. Complete the exercises.

A Work with a partner. Look at the words in the chart. Check (✓) the words you know. Ask your teacher about any words you do not know.

Nouns	Verbs
bathing suit	feel scared/happy
belt	fly (in the air)
board	hold (onto)
father	kiteboard
hat	ride
kite	teach
ocean	learn
son	smile
water	stand

B Look at the photos. Say a sentence in the present progressive about one of the photos. Use the words in exercise **14A** and your own ideas. Your partner says, "Photo A" or "Photo B."

Student A: *The father is wearing a hat.*   Student B: *Photo A.*

▲ A father and son kiteboard together in Nags Head, North Carolina, USA.

▲ A father teaches his six-year-old son to kiteboard in Nags Head, North Carolina, USA.

C Work with a partner. Complete the Venn diagram with information about the photos from exercise **B**. Use the words from exercise **A** and your own ideas. Use the present progressive.

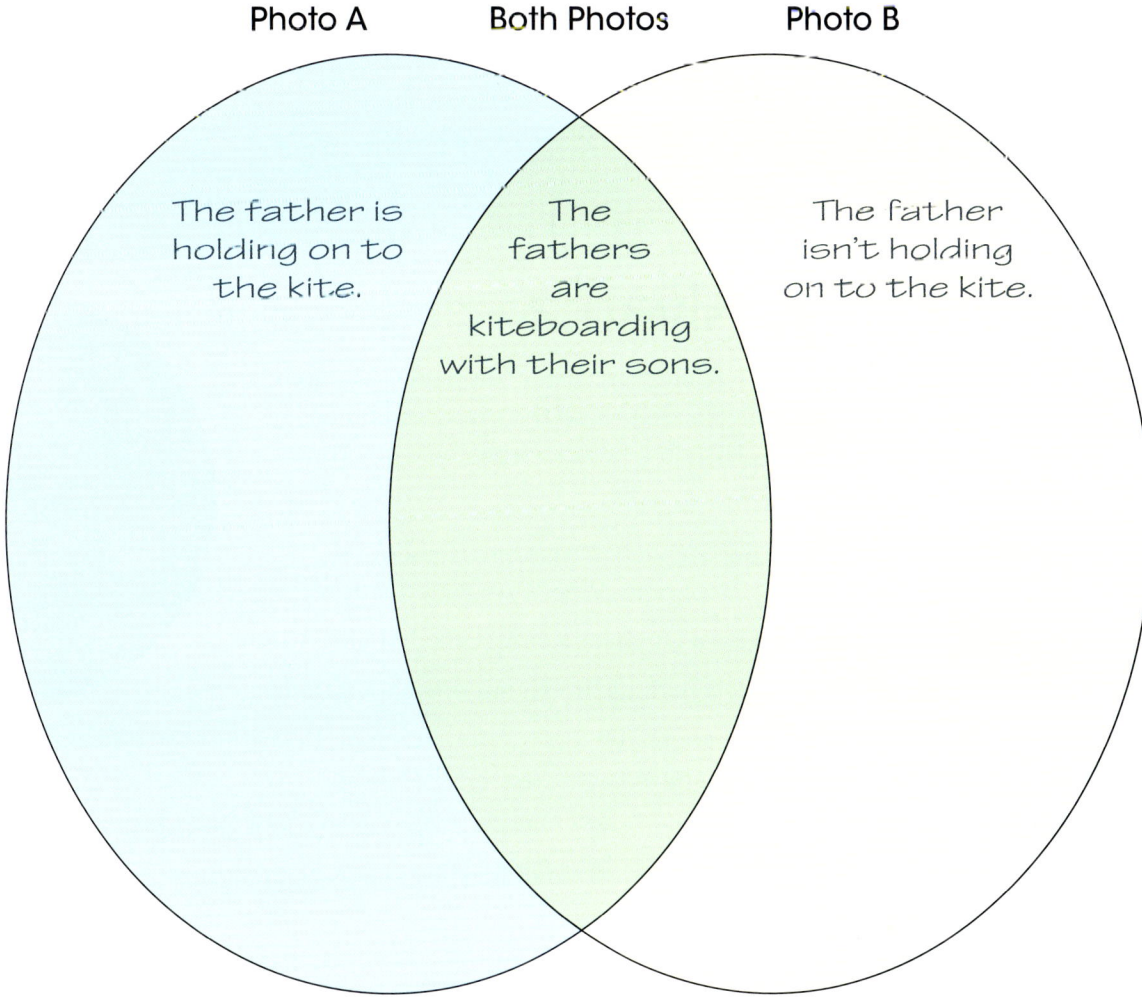

D Form a group with another pair of students. Compare your Venn diagrams from exercise **C**.

15 APPLY. Work with a partner. Describe a classmate to your partner. Use affirmative and negative statements in the present progressive. Who is it?

Student A: *This student is wearing a white shirt. This student isn't talking right now.*

Student B: *Is it Layla?*

Student A: *Yes, it is. / No, it isn't.*

LESSON 2 | Present Progressive: Questions

EXPLORE

1 READ the interview with a National Geographic photographer. Notice the words in **bold**.

An Interview with Stephen Alvarez

Stephen Alvarez is a photographer for National Geographic. He travels to interesting places around the world and takes amazing photographs. His job is very exciting, but sometimes it's dangerous, too.

Interviewer: So, Stephen, please tell us about this photograph. Where are you exactly?

Stephen Alvarez: I'm in Oman at a cave¹ called Majlis al Jinn.

Interviewer: How high up are you in this photograph?

Stephen Alvarez: I'm about 700 feet off the cave floor. Below me, the rock opens up into one of the largest cave rooms in the world.

Interviewer: Are you afraid of heights? Do you ever look down?

Stephen Alvarez: No, I'm not afraid of heights, and it's a good thing. I have to look down to see where I am!

Interviewer: Are you hanging from ropes? Oh, yes, I see you are. What are the ropes attached to?

Stephen Alvarez: They're attached to steel² anchors.³ I drilled the anchors into the rock.

Interviewer: **What are you taking a photograph of?**

Stephen Alvarez: I'm taking a photograph of Dr. Louise Hose. She's a geologist.⁴

Interviewer: **What's she doing?**

Stephen Alvarez: She's climbing out of the cave.

Interviewer: **Who's taking the photograph of you?**

Stephen Alvarez: My assistant, Ben.

Interviewer: Were you afraid?

Stephen Alvarez: No, I wasn't afraid. When I take photographs, I don't think about anything except the photograph.

Interviewer: How often do you do things like this? Is this kind of risk normal in your job?

Stephen Alvarez: I do things like this all the time. It's part of my job.

¹ **cave:** a large space or hole under the ground or in a mountain
² **steel:** a hard metal
³ **anchor:** a device to keep something in place
⁴ **geologist:** a person who studies the earth

2 CHECK. Choose the correct answer for each question about the interview from exercise **1**.

1. What is Stephen Alvarez's job?   a. He's a geologist.   b. He's a photographer.
2. Where is he?   a. At a cave.   b. On a mountain.
3. Is he afraid of heights?   a. Yes.   b. No.
4. What is Dr. Hose's job?   a. She's a climber.   b. She's a geologist.
5. How often does Alvarez do things like this? a. Rarely.   b. All the time.

3 DISCOVER. Complete these exercises to learn about the grammar in this lesson.

A Look at the sentences from the interview in exercise **1**. Notice the words in **bold**. Then choose the correct word to complete the rule below.

1. What **are you taking** a photograph of?
2. What**'s she doing**?

Rule: The subject usually comes **before / after** the verb *be* in questions.

B Discuss your answer from exercise **A** with your classmates and teacher.

▶ Stephen Alvarez and Dr. Louise Hose at the top of Majlis al Jinn in Oman

LEARN

7.4 Present Progressive: *Yes/No* Questions and Short Answers

Yes/No Questions

Be	Subject	Verb + -ing
Am	I	
Are	you	
Is	he / she / it	working?
Are	we / you / they	

Short Answers

	Affirmative			Negative	
Yes,	you	are.	No,	you're	not.
	I	am.		I'm	
	he / she / it	is.		he's / she's / it's	
	you / we / they	are.		you're / we're / they're	

1. The verb *be* goes before the subject in a *Yes/No* question.	Statement: Sam **is taking** the photograph. Question: **Is** Sam **taking** the photograph?
2. Use the verb *be* in short answers to *Yes/No* questions. Do not use *do* or *does*.	A: **Is** she **sleeping**? ✓ B: Yes, she **is**. ✗ B: Yes, she <u>does</u>.
3. **Remember:** There are two forms of contractions for negative short answers with *is* and *are*.	A: Is it working? B: No, it**'s not**. B: No, it **isn't**. A: Are they climbing? B: No, they **aren't**. B: No, **they're** not.
4. **Remember:** Do not use contractions in affirmative short answers.	A: Is she checking her e-mail? ✓ B: Yes, she **is**. ✗ B: Yes, <u>she's</u>.

4 Read each question. Then choose the correct answer.

1. Is Stephen taking a photograph?   a. Yes, he is.   b. Yes, they are.
2. Is Dr. Hose climbing out of the cave?   a. Yes, she is.   b. Yes, she does.
3. Are they sitting in a tent?   a. No, they don't.   b. No, they aren't.
4. Are they working?   a. Yes, they're.   b. Yes, they are.
5. Is Stephen wearing a jacket?   a. No, he isn't.   b. No, he doesn't.
6. Is the interviewer asking questions?   a. Yes, she is.   b. Yes, they are.
7. Is Stephen answering the questions?   a. Yes, he's.   b. Yes, he is.
8. Are you looking at the photograph?   a. Yes, I'm.   b. Yes, I am.
9. Are they listening to the interview?   a. No, they're not.   b. No, we're not.
10. Are we studying English?   a. Yes, we are.   b. Yes, we do.

5 Look at the photo and read the information. Then use the words in parentheses to write Yes/No questions in the present progressive.

> The scientist in this photo is studying sharks. He's putting tags on them. The tags help him find the same sharks later and collect information about them. In this photo, he's standing inside a shark cage in the Bahamas. There's a boat above him.

1. _Is the scientist studying_ (the scientist / study) sharks?
2. _____ (he / work) in the Bahamas now?
3. _____ (he / stand) in a shark cage?
4. _____ (the shark / swim) near the cage?
5. _____ (the shark / look) at him?
6. _____ (the scientist / do) something dangerous?
7. _____ (he / put) a tag on the shark?
8. _____ (he / wear) special clothing?
9. _____ (the people in the boat / help) him?
10. _____ (they / watch) him?

6 SPEAK. Work with a partner. Ask and answer the questions from exercise **5**.

Student A: *Is the scientist studying sharks?*   Student B: *Yes, he is.*

7.5 Present Progressive: Wh- Questions

Wh- Word	Be	Subject	Verb + -ing
Who	are	you	calling?
What	is	she	studying?
Where	are	they	going?
Why	are	you	running?
Why	aren't	you	eating?

Answers
I'm calling Alma.
She's studying Spanish.
They're going to the market.
We're late. Because we're late.
I'm not hungry. Because I'm not hungry.

1. **Remember:** Wh- questions ask for specific information.	A: **What** are you reading? B: An article about sharks.
2. *Why* is often used with negative questions.	A: **Why** aren't you playing in the game? B: Because I have a cold.
3. The contracted form of the verb *be* is usually used in negative questions.	Common: Why isn't she coming? Not Common: Why is she not coming?

7 Look at each sentence. Write a Wh- question about the underlined word or phrase.

1. I'm calling <u>Ned</u>. _What are you doing?_

2. I'm crying <u>because this story is very sad</u>. _____

3. She's calling <u>her daughter</u>. _____

4. They're living <u>in Hong Kong (China)</u>. _____

5. We're watching <u>a movie about sharks</u>. _____

6. He's working <u>at his father's company</u>. _____

7. She's teaching <u>English 101</u> this semester. _____

8. I'm not working today <u>because it's a holiday</u>. _____

REAL ENGLISH

In informal conversation, many common questions are in the present progressive.

How are you doing? (How're you doing?)
How is it going? (How's it going?)

These questions are often used as greetings, and the speaker does not expect a specific answer.

A: *How's it going?*
B: *Oh, hey, Bob. How're you doing?*

8 SPEAK. Work with a partner. Ask and answer Wh- questions in the present progressive. Use the verbs in the box or your own ideas.

| do | live | sit | study | wear |

Student A: *Why are you wearing your jacket in class?*
Student B: *Because I'm cold.*

7.6 Wh- Questions with Who

Questions about a Subject		
Who	Be	Verb + -ing
Who	is	calling?

Answers
Hector.
Hector is.
Hector is calling.

Questions about an Object			
Who	Be	Subject	Verb + -ing
Who	is	he	calling?

Answers
Kayla.
He's calling Kayla.

1. Wh- questions with *Who* can be about a subject or an object. In very formal English, *Whom* is used in questions about an object.

    Who is talking? (*Who* = subject)
    Who are you talking to? (*Who* = object of "to")
    Whom are you talking to?

2. **Remember:** In *Who* questions about a subject, use the singular form of the verb even if the answer is plural.

    A: *Who is studying French?*
    B: *I am. / She is. / They are.*

9 Read each question. Is it about a subject or an object? Check (✓) the correct column.

	Subject	Object
1. Who is helping them?	✓	☐
2. Who is taking the photograph?	☐	☐
3. Who is he talking to?	☐	☐
4. Who are you working with?	☐	☐
5. Who is talking?	☐	☐
6. Who are they waiting for?	☐	☐
7. Who is sitting next to Julio?	☐	☐
8. Who is she calling?	☐	☐
9. Who is he teaching?	☐	☐
10. Who is teaching?	☐	☐

10 Read the answer to each question. Then complete the question. Use the present progressive form of the verb in parentheses.

1. A: Who __are you studying__ (study) with?
   B: I'm studying with Fran and Taylor.

2. A: Who _____ (give) the lessons?
   B: Nick Stone. He's an excellent teacher.

3. A: Who _____ (stand) in the hallway?

   B: Alice and Tina.

4. A: Who _____ (sit) behind?

   B: He's sitting behind Anna.

5. A: Who _____ (write) on the board?

   B: Efren and Henri are.

6. A: Who _____ (live) with?

   B: She's living with her parents.

7. A: Who _____ (wait) for?

   B: We're waiting for Professor Carter.

8. A: Who _____ (teach) the class?

   B: Professor Lang is.

11 SPEAK. Work with a partner. Ask and answer questions with *Who*. Use the words in parentheses. Use short or long answers.

1. (Who / you / sit next to)

2. (Who / sit / in front of you)

3. (Who / wear / jeans today)

4. (Who / I / look at)

Student A: *Who are you sitting next to?*   Student B: *Martin.* OR *I'm sitting next to Martin.*

PRACTICE

12 LISTEN and choose the correct answer for each question.

1. a. Yes, they are.   b. In the ocean.   (c.) Studying sharks.

2. a. Yes, he is.   b. Stephen is.   c. On the mountain.

3. a. No, they aren't.   b. In Thailand.   c. They're trying.

4. a. Yes, he is.   b. Michael.   c. Yes, he does.

5. a. Yes, I am.   b. With my brother.   c. I don't like scary movies.

6. a. Yes, I am.   b. English.   c. In London.

7. a. No, she isn't.   b. In Taipei (China). c. Her parents.

8. a. No, she's reading.   b. Yes, they are.   c. Because she's tired.

13 WRITE & SPEAK.

A Look at the photos and read the captions. Then use the words in parentheses to complete each *Wh-* or *Yes/No* question. Use the present progressive.

▲ Rescue workers in Sedona, Arizona

▲ A firefighter at work in a forest

Photo A

1. (What / those men / do) __What are those men doing__ ?
2. (Who / stand) _____ on the cliff?
3. (Where / those men / work) _____ ?
4. (they / work / at night in this photo) _____ ?

Photo B

5. (What / the firefighter / do) _____ ?
6. (Why / the firefighter / do) this _____ ?
7. (the firefighter / wear) special clothing _____ ?
8. (the firefighter / sit) down _____ ?

B Work with a partner. Match each question in exercise **A** with the correct answer below. Then take turns asking and answering the questions.

a. ____ A rescue worker.
b. _1_ They're rescuing someone.
c. ____ In Arizona.
d. ____ He's fighting a fire.
e. ____ Yes, they are.
f. ____ Because it's his job.
g. ____ Yes, he is.
h. ____ No, he isn't.

Student A: *What are those men doing?*   Student B: *They're rescuing someone.*

▲ A technician on a wind turbine

14 LISTEN, WRITE & SPEAK.

A Listen to the conversation. Match each activity to the correct person.

1. Tay _____   a. He climbs wind turbines in his job.
2. Evan _____   b. He wants to climb in Logan Canyon.
3. Jake _____   c. He is working on a project.

B Write the correct question for each answer. Use the words in parentheses and the present progressive of each verb.

1. A: Who _____ (call)?   B: Jake is.
2. A: What _____ (Tay / do)?   B: He's working on a project right now.
3. A: _____ (Evan / live) at home?   B: No, he's not.
4. A: What _____ (do)?   B: He's working on wind turbines.
5. A: (make) _____ much money?   B: Yes, he's making a lot of money.
6. A: Where _____ (Evan / travel)?   B: All over the world.
7. A: _____ (Tay / joke)?   B: No, he's serious.
8. A: Where _____ (Evan / work) now? B: In Greece.

226 PRESENT PROGRESSIVE

C Work with a partner. Look at the photo on page 226. Then write interview questions for the worker in the photo. Use the words in the box to help you.

Nouns		Verbs	
helmet	sun	blow	look at
rope(s)	wind	climb	look down
safety belt	wind turbine	hang	shine
		hold on	turn
			wear

What are you doing?

Is the turbine turning?

_____

_____

_____

_____

_____

15 APPLY.

A Work with a partner. Write questions for other classmates. Use the present progressive. Use the verbs in the box or your own ideas.

| do | live | sit | study | take | write | wear | text | look |

Who . . . ?	_Who's sitting next to you?_
Who . . . ?	
What . . . ?	
Where . . . ?	
Why . . . ?	
Are . . . ?	

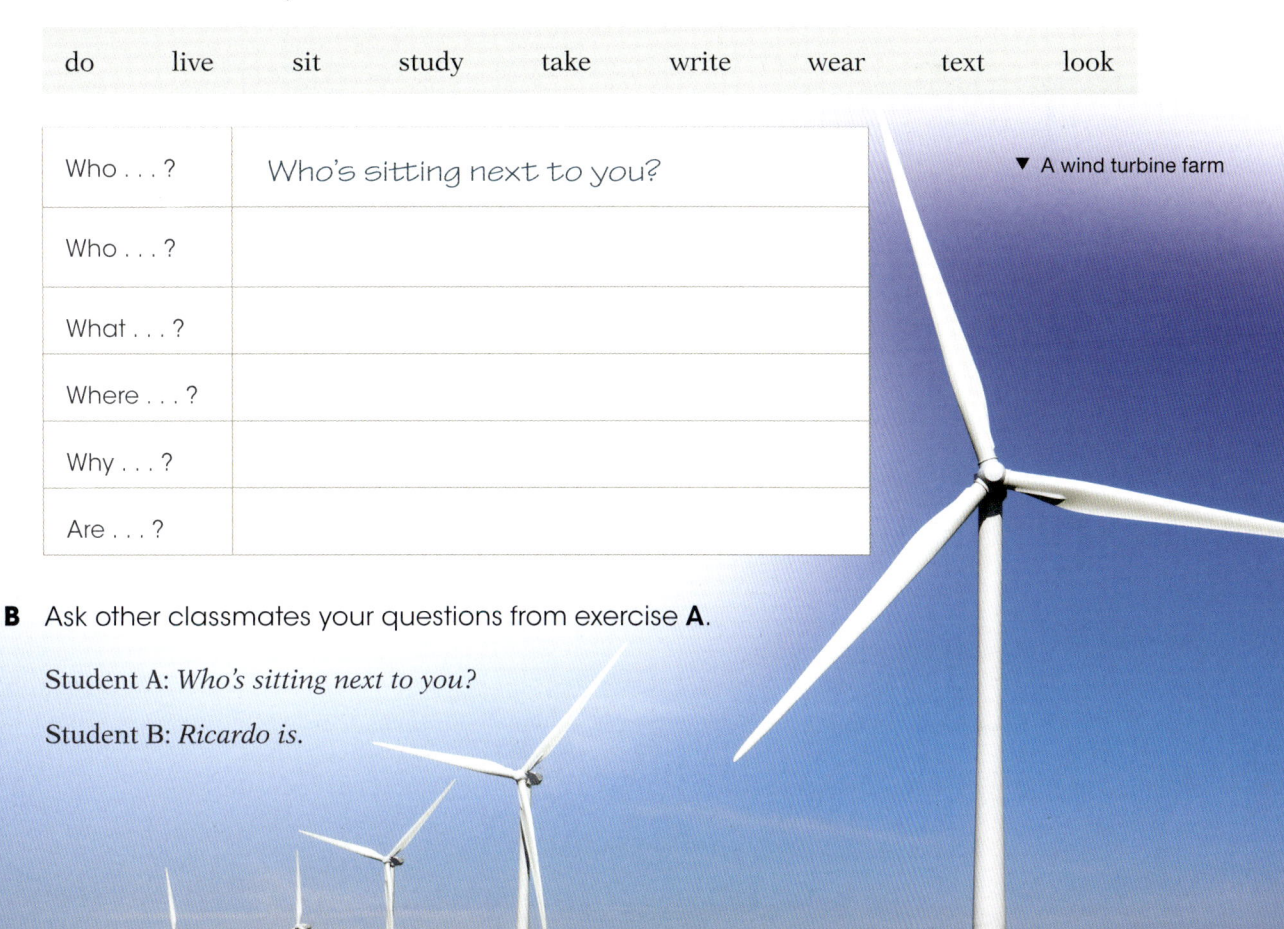

▼ A wind turbine farm

B Ask other classmates your questions from exercise **A**.

Student A: *Who's sitting next to you?*

Student B: *Ricardo is.*

LESSON 3 — Simple Present vs. Present Progressive

EXPLORE

1 READ the article about tornadoes and storm chasers. Notice the verbs in **bold**.

Tornado!

Rex Geyer **is standing** near the window in his house. He**'s watching** a storm in the distance. The sky **is getting** dark. In the dark clouds, he **sees** a tornado. It**'s moving** directly toward him. He **needs** to get out of the storm's path.[1] It's time to leave his house and drive away.

While Rex **is driving** away from the storm, another car **is driving** toward it. A storm chaser **is driving** this car. Most people **run** away from tornadoes. Storm chasers **chase**[2] them. When storm chasers **hear** about tornadoes, they **try** to get near them. Some storm chasers **do** this as a hobby. Others **do** it because they are scientists and engineers. It's part of their research. They **use** weather probes to study tornadoes. Weather probes **measure** the wind and **give** scientists important information about storms. Tornadoes are extremely powerful storms, so storm chasers **have** very dangerous jobs.

[1] **path:** the direction that something or someone moves in
[2] **chase:** follow something or someone quickly

2 CHECK. Read each statement about tornadoes and storm chasers. Then circle **T** for *true* or **F** for *false*.

1. Rex is watching the storm on TV.   T   (F)
2. The storm is moving closer.   T   F
3. Storm chasers run away from tornadoes.   T   F
4. Some storm chasers are scientists.   T   F

3 DISCOVER. Complete the exercises to learn about the grammar in this lesson.

A Find these sentences in the article from exercise **1**. Write the missing words.

1. Rex Geyer _____ near the window in his house.

2. The sky _____ dark.

3. Most people _____ away from tornadoes.

4. When storm chasers _____ about tornadoes, they _____ to get near them.

228 PRESENT PROGRESSIVE

B Look at the sentences from exercise **A**. Then answer the questions below. Discuss your answers with your classmates and teacher.

1. Which sentences have verbs in the simple present? _____

2. Which sentences have verbs in the present progressive? _____

3. Which verb form talks about general information, not an action in progress?

   a. simple present   b. present progressive

▶ A tornado in Campo, Colorado, USA.

LEARN

7.7 Simple Present vs. Present Progressive

Simple Present	Present Progressive
I **study** every day.	I'**m studying** right now.
She **calls** her sister once a week.	She'**s calling** her sister right now.
We usually **eat** dinner at 7:00.	We'**re not eating** dinner now.
It **gets** dark early in winter.	It'**s getting** dark outside.

1. **Remember:** Use the simple present to talk about habits or routines, schedules, and facts.	Habit or Routine: I **walk** to work every day. Schedule: He **leaves** work at 6:00 p.m. Fact: It **doesn't snow** a lot in Rome.
2. **Remember:** Use the present progressive to talk about actions that are in progress now or are in progress at the present time, but maybe not at this moment.	Look out the window! It'**s snowing**! Max **is taking** Greek this semester. He'**s not studying** right now.
3. Frequency adverbs and frequency expressions are often used with the simple present.	I <u>always</u> **walk** to work. She **visits** her parents <u>once a month</u>.
4. The present time expressions *now, right now, at the moment, today, this week, this moment, this month,* and *this year* are often used with the present progressive.	A: What **are** you **doing** <u>right now</u>? B: I'**m cooking** dinner. John'**s visiting** his sister <u>this week</u>.

4 Circle the correct form of the verb to complete each sentence.

1. Rex **watches** / (**is watching**) a tornado right now.
2. Storm chasers have dangerous jobs. They **study** / **are studying** tornadoes.
3. Right now, **he listens to** / **he's listening to** a tornado report.
4. Take your umbrella. **It rains!** / **It's raining!**
5. Quebec City **gets** / **is getting** a lot of snow in the winter.
6. We **learn** / **'re learning** about storms in class this week.
7. She **gives** / **is giving** the weather report every morning.
8. The weather is perfect today. It's warm, and the sun **shines** / **is shining**.
9. I **read** / **'m reading** a book about tornadoes. It's very interesting.
10. They **watch** / **'re watching** the weather report every night.

5 Complete each sentence with the simple present or present progressive form of the verb in parentheses.

1. We ____are having____ (have) a thunderstorm right now.
2. Look! The tornado _____ (move) toward us!
3. Florida _____ (get) a lot of hurricanes.
4. It _____ (rain). Let's go inside.
5. Tom never _____ (listen) to the weather report.
6. It _____ (rain) almost every afternoon in August here.
7. The wind _____ (blow) very hard today.
8. She _____ (check) the weather online every morning.
9. I always _____ (wear) a hat when it's hot and sunny.
10. They _____ (not hike) today because it's very hot.

7.8 Non-Action Verbs

1. Some verbs do not show actions. These *non-action* verbs are not common in the progressive. For example: *hear, know, like, own, see, want, be,* and *need*.	I **know** the answer. He **wants** some coffee. I **don't own** a car.
2. Non-action verbs do not describe actions. They describe things such as: a. emotions b. thoughts c. possessions d. states of being e. senses	 a. She **loves** her children. b. Kim **knows** the answer. c. He **owns** a car. d. We **are** happy. e. I **see** Tanya.
3. Some verbs have both an action meaning and a non-action meaning.	He's **having** lunch right now. *(action)* He **has** a car. *(non-action)*

REAL ENGLISH

The verbs *see* and *hear* are *non-action verbs* because we see and we hear automatically; we do not control these actions. The verbs *look (at), watch,* and *listen (to)* are action verbs because we choose to do these actions.

> I **see** the train.
> I'**m watching** a movie with my sister.

> I **hear** a strange noise.
> We'**re listening to** the teacher.

6 Read each sentence. Is the underlined verb used as an action verb or a non-action verb? Put a check (✓) in the correct column.

	Action	Non-Action
1. Scientists <u>study</u> tornadoes.	✓	☐
2. The tornado <u>is coming</u> towards his house.	☐	☐
3. Storm chasers <u>have</u> a dangerous job.	☐	☐
4. We're <u>listening to</u> the weather report right now.	☐	☐
5. I <u>hear</u> thunder.	☐	☐
6. He <u>knows</u> a lot about tornadoes.	☐	☐
7. Hurricanes <u>are</u> very dangerous.	☐	☐
8. Tornadoes often <u>destroy</u> houses.	☐	☐
9. I <u>don't like</u> storms.	☐	☐
10. She <u>reads</u> a lot of books about extreme weather.	☐	☐
11. I <u>see</u> dark clouds in the distance.	☐	☐
12. My dog <u>is</u> afraid of thunderstorms.	☐	☐
13. It's <u>snowing</u> very hard.	☐	☐
14. They usually <u>watch</u> the news at 10:00 p.m.	☐	☐

7 Complete each sentence with the simple present or present progressive form of the verb in parentheses.

1. Toronto ____gets____ (get) a lot of snow in the winter.
2. Please be quiet. I _____ (listen) to the weather report.
3. The reporter _____ (talk) about the storm right now.
4. They _____ (not like) snow storms.
5. She _____ (not own) a raincoat.
6. I _____ (hear) the wind. It's blowing very hard.
7. The weather in Chicago _____ (be) terrible today.
8. That umbrella _____ (belong) to Lisa.
9. I _____ (look) at the thermometer. It's 32 degrees.
10. I _____ (see) a lot of clouds, but it's not raining.
11. The hurricane _____ (not move) toward Miami.
12. We _____ (check) the weather report online right now.

PRACTICE

8 Choose the correct form of the verb to complete each sentence.

Climate Change

The earth's climate (1) **changes** / **is changing**. The biggest change is in the Arctic. The Arctic (2) **gets** / **is getting** warmer. The ice there (3) **melts** / **is melting**. In the oceans, the water level (4) **rises** / **is rising**. Scientists also often (5) **use** / **are using** the Maldive Islands in the Indian Ocean as an example. The ocean (6) **rises** / **is rising** and (7) **starts** / **is starting** to cover parts of these islands. Scientists (8) **know** / **are knowing** the causes of climate change. Governments (9) **need** / **are needing** to do something, but it is a difficult problem.

▶ A Maldivian island

9 Complete each sentence with the correct form of the verb in parentheses.

Weather around the World

Every night we (1) _____ (listen) to the news. We often (2) _____ (hear) reports about bad weather. Some places around the world never (3) _____ (get) enough rain. In other places, it (4) _____ (rain) too much. This often (5) _____ (cause) floods.

Today we (6) _____ (listen) to all the weather reports because they (7) _____ (talk) about a huge snow storm. We almost never (8) _____ (get) snow in this part of the country, but this storm (9) _____ (move) in our direction.

I (10) _____ (need) to get ready for the storm now. I (11) _____ (not like) to drive in the snow at all, so I (12) _____ (want) to go to the supermarket and buy groceries.

10 **EDIT.** Read the paragraph. Find and correct five more errors with action and non-action verbs.

>   I am looking
> Right now I ~~look~~ out the window of my house. I see a lot of dark clouds. A storm comes. The sky gets dark. Now I am hearing the wind. It's raining hard now. I am not liking storms. I'm being afraid of them!

11 **LISTEN & SPEAK.**

🎧 CD2-31

A Listen to the conversation. Choose the correct answer for each question.

1. Who is talking?   a. News reporters.   b. Weather reporters.
2. What are they talking about?   a. A tsunami.   b. A hurricane.
3. What do they see?   a. Police.   b. Smoke.

B Match the items in Columns A and B to make sentences. Then complete each sentence with the simple present or present progressive form of the verb in parentheses.

Column A

1. Maria Lopez __is reporting__ (report) __b__
2. The storm _____ (cause) _____
3. Alvaro _____ (see) _____
4. He _____ (hear) _____
5. Some people _____ (want) _____
6. The police _____ (ask) _____
7. Houses _____ (burn) _____
8. Maria _____ (feel) _____

Column B

a. a lot of damage.
b. ~~from the coast.~~
c. in the fire.
d. people to leave their homes.
e. safe.
f. the waves.
g. the wind.
h. to stay in their homes.

12 **APPLY.**

A Work with a partner. Plan a news report about an extreme weather event (for example: a bad storm, or very hot or cold weather). Answer the questions in the chart with the information about your news report.

What's the weather event?	A hurricane
What's happening right now?	
What are people doing?	

B Practice your weather report from exercise **A**. Partner A is the news reporter at the station. Partner B is the reporter outside. Then role-play your weather report for your classmates.

UNIT 7 Review the Grammar

Charts 7.1–7.8

1 LISTEN. Listen to each question. Choose the correct answer.

1. a. Yes, I am.   b. Stephen is.
2. a. I'm studying.   b. I study.
3. a. Greg.   b. To the park.
4. a. Because they like it there.   b. In Oklahoma.
5. a. They're watching the waves.   b. Jen and Makiko.
6. a. I'm not feeling well.   b. With Carol.
7. a. An article.   b. Because it's interesting.
8. a. Yes, we are.   b. Yes, they are.

Charts 7.1–7.8

2 EDIT. Read the conversation. Find and correct six more errors with the present progressive and simple present.

Tony: Wow. Look at this photo. This man ~~competes~~ *is competing* in a marathon. He runs in the Sahara.

Kay: Why are people wanting to run in the desert?

Tony: They are liking the challenge. That marathon is very, very difficult. It lasts for five or six days. Are you seeing his backpack? He's having all his food in there.

Kay: Do the runners stop at night to sleep?

Tony: That's a good question. I'm not knowing the answer.

◀ A competitor climbs a dune during the Marathon des Sables in the Sahara.

Review the Grammar | UNIT 7

3 WRITE & LISTEN. Complete the interview with the words in parentheses. Use the present progressive or simple present. Then listen and check your answers.

Charts 7.1–7.8
CD2-33

Alex: Hello, everyone. Our visitor today is Isabel Lee. Isabel,
(1) _how are you doing_ (how / you / do)?

Isabel: (2) _____ (I / do) great, Alex.

Alex: So, (3) _____ (you / train) for a new event now?

Isabel: Yes, (4) _____ (I / train) for a triathlon competition.

Alex: Really? Wow. What (5) _____ (you / like) about triathlons?

Isabel: (6) _____ (I / enjoy) the challenge. Triathlons are very difficult! Also, triathlons include three sports: biking, swimming, and running, and (7) _____ (I / like) all of them a lot!

Alex: Interesting. How many bicycles (8) _____ (you / own)?

Isabel: (9) _____ (I / have) three. (10) _____ (I / need) all of them because (11) _____ (bicycles / often / break).

Alex: Well, good luck in your next triathlon!

Isabel: Thank you.

Charts 7.1–7.8
CD2-34

4 SPEAK, WRITE & LISTEN.

A Listen to the conversation about the photo. Check (✓) the words you hear.

1. a. ____ in the Arctic
   b. ✓ in Norway

2. a. ____ from a mountain
   b. ____ from an airplane

3. a. ____ at the scenery
   b. ____ for a place on the ground to land

4. a. ____ a parachute
   b. ____ a tent

▲ A parachutist on an expedition, Spitsbergen Island, Svalbard, Norway

236 PRESENT PROGRESSIVE

B Write three *Wh-* questions and one *Yes/No* question about the photo on page 236. Use the present progressive.

1. _What is he doing?_
2. _____
3. _____
4. _____
5. _____

C Work with a partner. Ask and answer your questions from exercise **B**. Use the words in exercise **A** to help you.

Student A: *What's he doing?*

Student B: *He's hanging from a plane.*

Charts 7.1–7.8

5 SPEAK & WRITE.

A Choose one of the photos in this unit and write five questions about it. Use the present progressive or simple present. Use the verbs in the box to help you.

| carry | do | feel | happen | have | hold | look at | see | wear |

I'm looking at the photo on page _____.	
What . . . ?	What is she wearing?
Is / Are . . . ?	
Who . . . ?	
Where . . . ?	
Why . . . ?	

B Work with a partner. Ask and answer your questions from exercise **A**.

Student A: *What is she wearing?*

Student B: *She's wearing a red jacket and . . .*

Connect the Grammar to Writing

1 READ & NOTICE THE GRAMMAR.

A Read the e-mail. Where is the writer, and what is he doing? Discuss with a partner.

Hi everyone,

I'm writing to you from London. Right now I'm sitting in the university library. Some people are studying, but I don't have any homework yet. Most people are walking around and chatting. It's not quiet at all.

I'm not spending all my time in the library. I'm also playing tennis and singing in the school choir. I already know a lot of people. I like it here a lot, but I miss you!

Please write to me soon!

David

GRAMMAR FOCUS

In the e-mail in exercise **A**, the writer uses the present progressive to describe activities that are happening at the present time.

I**'m writing** to you from London.
Right now I**'m sitting** in the university library.

B Read the e-mail in exercise **A** again. Underline the present progressive. Then work with a partner and compare answers.

C Complete the chart with information from the e-mail in exercise **A**. What activities is he doing right now? What activities is he doing, but not right now?

David's Life in London	
Right Now	Not Right Now
writing	

238 PRESENT PROGRESSIVE

Write about the Activities in Your Life

2 **BEFORE YOU WRITE.** Think about the activities in your life. What are you doing right now? What activities are you doing, but not right now? Write your notes in the chart. Use the chart from exercise **1C** as a model.

My Life in _____	
Right Now	Not Right Now

3 **WRITE** an e-mail to a friend or family member. Describe where you are and what you are doing. Use the information from your chart in exercise **2** and the e-mail in exercise **1A** to help you.

> **WRITING FOCUS** — Using *And* to Join Two Verbs
>
> *And* is a conjunction. It joins two similar parts of speech. For example, it joins two nouns or two verbs. Using *and* to join similar activities or activities that are in progress at the same time helps make the writing flow more smoothly and sound more natural.
>
> Two sentences: *People are walking around. They are chatting.*
> One sentence with *and*: *People are walking around **and** chatting.*
>
> **Remember:** Do not repeat the subject and the verb *be* when the subject is doing two actions.
>
> Most people <u>are walking</u> around **and** <u>chatting</u>.
> I'm also <u>playing</u> tennis **and** <u>singing</u> in the school choir.

4 **SELF ASSESS.** Read your e-mail. Underline the present progressive. Circle *and*. Then use the checklist to assess your work.

- ☐ I used the present progressive for activities I am doing now. [7.1, 7.2]
- ☐ I used the simple present for non-action verbs. [7.8]
- ☐ I spelled the verb + *-ing* forms correctly. [7.3]
- ☐ I did not repeat the subject and the verb *be* in sentences with two activities in progress at the same time. [7.1]
- ☐ I used *and* to join two similar activities in progress at the same time. [WRITING FOCUS]

APPENDICES

1 Spelling Rules for Regular Plural Nouns

Rule	Examples
1. Add -s to most nouns.	student-student**s** teacher-teacher**s** pen-pen**s**
2. Add -es to nouns that end in -ch, -s, -sh, and -x.	watch-watch**es** class-class**es** dish-dish**es** box-box**es**
3. Add -s to nouns that end in a vowel + -y.	boy-boy**s** day-day**s**
4. Change the -y to -i and add -es to nouns that end in a consonant + -y.	city-cit**ies** country-countr**ies**
5. Add -s to nouns that end in a vowel + -o.	video-video**s** radio-radio**s**
6. Add -es to nouns that end in a consonant + -o. Exceptions: photo → photo**s** piano → piano**s**	potato-potato**es** tornado-tornado**es**

2 Common Irregular Noun Plurals

Singular	Plural	Explanation
man woman tooth foot goose	men women teeth feet geese	Vowel change
sheep fish deer	sheep fish deer	No change
child person mouse	children people mice	Different word forms
No singular form	belongings clothes groceries glasses jeans pajamas pants scissors shorts	

3 Simple Present Spelling Rules: -s and -es Endings

1. Add -s to most verbs.	like-like**s** sit-sit**s**
2. Add -es to verbs that end in -ch, -s, -sh, -x, or -z.	catch-catch**es** miss-miss**es** wash-wash**es** mix-mix**es** buzz-buzz**es**
3. Change the -y to -i and add -es when the base form of the verb ends in a consonant + -y.	cry-cr**ies** carry-carr**ies**
4. Do not change the -y to -i when the base form ends in a vowel + -y.	pay-pay**s** stay-stay**s**
5. Some verbs are irregular in the third-person singular form of the simple present.	be-**is** go-**goes** do-**does** have-**has**

4 Spelling Rules for the -ing Form of Verbs

1. Add -ing to the base form of most verbs.	eat-eat**ing** do-do**ing** speak-speak**ing** carry-carry**ing**
2. Verbs that end in a consonant and silent -e: Drop the -e and add -ing.	ride-rid**ing** write-writ**ing**
3. One-syllable verbs that end in CVC*: Double the final consonant and add -ing. Do not double the final consonant for verbs that end in -w, -x, or -y.	stop-stop**ping** sit-sit**ting** show-show**ing** fix-fix**ing** stay-stay**ing**
4. Two-syllable verbs that end in CVC and have the stress on the first syllable: Add -ing, but do not double the final consonant.	listen-listen**ing** travel-travel**ing**
5. Two-syllable verbs that end in CVC: Double the final consonant only if the last syllable is stressed, and add -ing.	begin-beginn**ing** refer-referr**ing**

*consonant + vowel + consonant

5 Guide to Pronunciation Symbols

Vowels		
Symbol	Key Word	Pronunciation
/a/	hot	/hɑt/
	far	/fɑr/
/æ/	cat	/kæt/
/aɪ/	fine	/faɪn/
/aʊ/	house	/haʊs/
/ɛ/	bed	/bɛd/
/eɪ/	name	/neɪm/
/i/	need	/nid/
/ɪ/	sit	/sɪt/
/oʊ/	go	/goʊ/
/ʊ/	book	/bʊk/
/u/	boot	/but/
/ɔ/	dog	/dɔg/
	four	/fɔr/
/ɔɪ/	toy	/tɔɪ/
/ʌ/	cup	/kʌp/
/ɛr/	bird	/bɛrd/
/ə/	about	/əˈbaʊt/
	after	/ˈæftər/

Consonants		
Symbol	Key Word	Pronunciation
/b/	boy	/bɔɪ/
/d/	day	/deɪ/
/dʒ/	just	/dʒʌst/
/f/	face	/feɪs/
/g/	get	/gɛt/
/h/	hat	/hæt/
/k/	car	/kɑr/
/l/	light	/laɪt/
/m/	my	/maɪ/
/n/	nine	/naɪn/
/ŋ/	sing	/sɪŋ/
/p/	pen	/pɛn/
/r/	right	/raɪt/
/s/	see	/si/
/t/	tea	/ti/
/tʃ/	cheap	/tʃip/
/v/	vote	/voʊt/
/w/	west	/wɛst/
/y/	yes	/yɛs/
/z/	zoo	/zu/
/ð/	they	/ðeɪ/
/θ/	think	/θɪŋk/
/ʃ/	shoe	/ʃu/
/ʒ/	vision	/ˈvɪʒən/

Source: The *Newbury House Dictionary plus Grammar Reference, Fifth Edition*, National Geographic Learning/Cengage Learning, 2014

Unit 3, Lesson 2, Exercise 15, Page 95

Partner B's Schedule

Unit 5, Lesson 2, Exercise 12B, Page 161

B Partner B, look at the ingredients on the list below. Answer your partner's questions about the ingredients. Put a check (✓) next to the ingredients you need to buy. Then write the amount of each ingredient you need to buy on your shopping list.

Partner A: *Do we have* **one and a half pounds of ground beef**?

Partner B: *No, we don't. We have* **one pound**.

Ingredients in Our Kitchen
- a bottle of olive oil ☐
- 1 pound of ground beef ☐
- a head of garlic ☐
- a small onion ☐
- 1 can of tomato paste ☐
- a jar of Italian seasoning ☐
- a container of salt ☐
- a bag of sugar ☐

Shopping List
½ pound of ground beef

C Check with your partner. Are your shopping lists the same?

Unit 6, Review the Grammar, Exercise 4, Page 203

GLOSSARY OF GRAMMAR TERMS

action verb: a verb that shows an action.
- He **drives** every day.
- They **left** yesterday morning.

adjective: a word that describes or modifies a noun or pronoun.
- She is **friendly**.
- Brazil is a **huge** country.

adverb: a word that describes or modifies a verb, an adjective, or another adverb.
- He eats **quickly**.
- She drives **carefully**.

adverb of manner: an adverb that describes the action of the verb. Many adverbs of manner are formed by adding *-ly* to the adjective.
- You sing **beautifully**.
- He speaks **slowly**.

affirmative statement: a statement that does not have a verb in the negative form.
- My uncle **lives** in Portland.

article: a word that is used before a noun: *a, an, the*.
- I looked up at **the** moon.
- Lucy had **a** sandwich and **an** apple for lunch.

auxiliary verb: (also called *helping verb*) a verb used with the main verb. *Be, do, have,* and *will* are common auxiliary verbs when they are followed by another verb. Modals are also auxiliary verbs.
- I **am** working.
- He **won't** be in class tomorrow.
- She **can** speak Korean.

base form of the verb: the form of the verb without *to* or any endings, such as *-ing, -s,* or *-ed*.
- eat, sleep, go, walk

capital letter: an uppercase letter.
- **N**ew **Y**ork, **M**r. **F**ranklin, **J**apan

clause: a group of words with a subject and a verb. See *dependent clause* and *main clause*.
- We watched the game. (one clause)
- We watched the game after we ate dinner. (two clauses)

comma: a punctuation mark that separates parts of a sentence.
- After he left work**,** he went to the gym.
- I can't speak Russian**,** but my sister can.

common noun: a noun that does not name a specific person, place, or thing.
- man, country, book, help

comparative adjective: the form of an adjective used to talk about the difference between two people, places, or things.
- I'm **taller** than my mother.
- Canada is **larger** than Mexico.

comparison: a statement of the similarities or differences between things, ideas, or people.
- Mexico City is **more crowded than** Buenos Aires.

conditional: a structure used to talk about an activity or event that depends on something else.
- **If** the weather is nice on Sunday, we'll go to the beach.

conjunction: a word used to connect information or ideas. *And, but, or,* and *because* are conjunctions.
- He put cheese **and** onions on his sandwich.
- I wanted to go, **but** I had too much homework.

consonant: the following letters are consonants: *b, c, d, f, g, h, j, k, l, m, n, p, q, r, s, t, v, w, x, y, z*.

contraction: two words combined into a shorter form.
- did not → didn't
- I am → I'm
- she is → she's
- we will → we'll

count noun: a noun that names something you can count. They are singular or plural.
- I ate an **egg** for breakfast.
- I have six **apples** in my bag.

definite article: *the*; it is used before a specific person, place, or thing.
- I found it on **the** Internet.
- **The** children are sleeping.

dependent clause: a clause that cannot stand alone as a sentence. It must be used with a main clause.
- I went for a walk **before I ate breakfast**.

direct object: a noun or pronoun that receives the action of the verb.
- Aldo asked a **question**.
- Karen helped **me**.

exclamation point: a punctuation mark that shows emotion (anger, surprise, excitement, etc.) or emphasis.
- We won the game**!**
- Look**!** It's snowing!

formal: language used in academic writing or speaking, or in polite or official situations rather than in everyday conversation or writing.
- *Please do not take photographs inside the museum.*
- *May I leave early today?*

frequency adverb: an adverb that tells how often something happens. Some common adverbs of frequency are *never, rarely, sometimes, often, usually,* and *always*.
- *I **always** drink coffee in the morning.*
- *He **usually** leaves work at six o'clock.*

frequency expression: an expression that tells how often something happens.
- *We go to the grocery store **every Saturday**.*
- *He plays tennis **twice a week**.*

future: a verb form that expresses an action or situation that has not happened yet. *Will, be going to,* the present progressive, and the simple present are used to express the future.
- *I **will call** you later.*
- *We're **going** to the movies tomorrow.*
- *I'm **taking** French next semester.*

helping verb: see *auxiliary verb*.

if clause: a clause that begins with *if* and expresses a condition.
- ***If you drive too fast,** you will get a ticket.*

imperative: a verb form that gives an instruction or command. Use the base form of the verb to form the imperative.
- ***Turn** left at the light.*
- ***Don't use** the elevator.*

indefinite article: *a* and *an;* they are used before singular count nouns that are not specific.
- *We have **a** test today.*
- *She's **an** engineer.*

indefinite pronoun: a pronoun that refers to people or things that are not specific or not known. *Someone, something, everyone, everything, no one, nothing,* and *nowhere* are common indefinite pronouns.
- ***Everyone** is here today.*
- ***No one** is absent.*
- *Would you like **something** to eat?*

independent clause: see *main clause*.

infinitive: an infinitive is *to* + the base form of a verb.
- *He wants **to see** the new movie.*

informal: language that is used in everyday conversation and writing.
- *Who are you talking to?*
- *We'll be there at eight.*

information question: see *Wh-* question.

irregular adjective: an adjective that does not change form in the usual way.
- *good → better*
- *bad → worse*

irregular adverb: an adverb that does not change form in the usual way.
- *well → better*
- *badly → worse*

irregular verb: a verb form that does not follow the rules for regular verbs.
- *swim → swam*
- *have → had*

main clause: (also called *independent clause*) a clause that can stand alone as a sentence. It has a subject and a verb.
- ***I heard the news** when I was driving home.*

measurement word: a word used to talk about a specific quantity of something.
- *We need to buy a **box** of pasta and a **gallon** of milk.*

modal: an auxiliary verb that adds additional meaning to a verb, such as ability or possibility. *May, might, can, could, will, would,* and *should* are common modals.
- *Julie **can** speak three languages.*
- *He **may** be at the office. Call him.*

negative statement: a statement that has a verb in the negative form.
- *I **don't have** any sisters.*
- *She **doesn't drink** coffee.*

non-action verb: a verb that does not describe an action. Non action verbs indicate states, senses, feelings, or ownership. They are not common in the progressive.
- *I **love** my grandparents.*
- *They **have** a new car.*

non-count noun: a noun that names something that cannot be counted.
- *Carlos drinks a lot of **coffee**.*
- *I need some **salt** for the recipe.*

noun: a word that names a person, a place, or a thing.
- *They're **students**.*
- *It's an excellent **hospital**.*

GLOSSARY OF GRAMMAR TERMS

object: a noun or pronoun that receives the action of the verb.
- Mechanics fix **cars**.

object pronoun: a word that takes the place of a noun as the object of the sentence: *me, you, him, her, it, us, them*.
- Rita is my neighbor. I see **her** every day.
- Can you help **us**?

past progressive: a verb form used to talk about an action that was in progress at a specific time in the past.
- He **was watching** TV when the phone rang.

period: a punctuation mark that is used at the end of a statement. It is also called "a full stop."
- She lives in Moscow**.**

phrase: a group of words that does not have a subject or a verb.
- He lives **near the train station**.

plural noun: a noun that names more than one person, place, or thing.
- He put three **boxes** on the table.
- Argentina and Mexico are **countries**.

possessive adjective: an adjective that shows ownership or relationship (*my, your, his, her, its, our, their*). It is used with a noun.
- **My** car is green.
- **Your** keys are on the table.

possessive noun: a noun that shows ownership or a relationship.
- **Leo's** apartment is large.
- The **girls'** books are on the table.

possessive pronoun: a pronoun that shows ownership or relationship: *mine, yours, his, hers, its, ours, theirs*. Possessive pronouns are used in place of a possessive adjective + noun.
- My sister's eyes are blue. **Mine** are brown. What color are **yours**?

preposition: a word that describes the relationships between nouns. Prepositions describe space, time, direction, cause, and effect.
- I live **on** Center Street.
- We left **at** noon.

pronoun: a word that takes the place of a noun or refers to a noun.
- The teacher is sick today. **He** has a cold.

proper noun: a noun that names a specific person, place, or thing.
- **Maggie** lives in a town near **Dallas**.

punctuation: the use of specific marks to make ideas within writing clear, such as commas (,), periods (.), exclamation points (!), and question marks (?).
- John plays soccer**,** but I don't.
- She's from Japan**.**
- That's amazing**!**
- Where are you from**?**

quantifier: a word that describes the quantity of a noun.
- We need **some** potatoes for the recipe.
- I usually put **a little** milk in my coffee.

question: a sentence that asks for an answer.
- Is she a teacher?

question mark: a punctuation mark (?) that is used at the end of a question.
- Are you a student**?**

regular: a noun, verb, adjective, or adverb that changes form according to standard rules.
- *apple* → *apples*
- *talk* → *talked, talking*
- *small* → *smaller*
- *slow* → *slowly*

sentence: a thought that is expressed in words, usually with a subject and verb. It begins with a capital letter and ends with a period, exclamation point, or question mark.
- Karen called last night.
- Don't eat that!

short answer: an answer to a *Yes/No* question.
- A: Did you do the homework?
- B: Yes, I did./ No, I didn't.

simple past: a verb form used to talk about completed actions.
- Last night we **ate** dinner at home.
- I **visited** my parents last weekend.

simple present: a verb form used to talk about habits or routines, schedules, and facts.
- He **likes** apples and oranges.
- Toronto **gets** a lot of snow in the winter.

singular noun: a noun that names only one person, place, or thing.
- They have a **son** and a **daughter**.

statement: a sentence that gives information.
- My house has five rooms.
- He doesn't have a car.

stress: we use stress to say a syllable or a word with more volume or emphasis.

subject: the noun or pronoun that is the topic of the sentence.
> - **Patricia** is a doctor.
> - **They** are from Iceland.

subject pronoun: a pronoun that is the subject of sentence: *I, you, he, she, it,* and *they.*
> - I have one brother. **He** lives in Miami.

superlative: the form of an adjective or adverb used to compare three or more people, places, or things.
> - Mount Everest is **the highest** mountain in the world.
> - Evgeny is **the youngest** student in our class.

syllable: a part of a word that contains a single vowel sound and is pronounced as a unit.
> - The word pen *has one syllable. The word* pencil *has two syllables* (pen-cil).

tense: the form of the verb that shows the time of the action.
> - He **sells** apples. (simple present)
> - They **sold** their car. (simple past)

time clause: a clause that tells when an action or event happened or will happen. Time clauses are introduced by conjunctions, such as *when, after, before,* and *while.*
> - I'm going to call my parents **after I eat dinner.**
> - I called my parents **when I got home.**

time expression: a phrase that tells when something happened or will happen. Time expressions usually go at the end or beginning of a sentence.
> - **Last week** I went hiking.
> - She's moving **next month**.

verb: a word that shows action, gives a state, or shows possession.
> - Tori **called** me last night.
> - She **is** my classmate.
> - She **has** three daughters.

vowel: the following letters (and some combinations of the letters) are vowels: *a, e, i, o, u,* and sometimes *y.*

Wh- question: (also called *information question*) a question that asks for specific information, not an answer with *"Yes"* or *"No."* (See also *Wh-* word.)
> - **Where** do they live?
> - **What** do you usually do on weekends?

Wh- word: a word such as *Who, What, When, Where, Why,* or *How* that is used to begin a *Wh-* question (information question).
> - **Why** are you crying?
> - **When** did they leave?

Yes/No question: a question that can be answered by *"Yes"* or *"No."*
> - A: **Do you live in Dublin?** B: *Yes, I do. / No, I don't.*
> - A: **Can you ski?** B: *Yes, I can. / No, I can't.*

INDEX

Note: All page references in blue are in Split Edition B.

A

A/an
  before adjectives, 23, 312
  consonants and use of, 13, 149, 174, 312
  before count nouns, 149, 150, 174
  before nouns used as adjectives, 316
  before singular nouns, 13, 312
  the vs., 150
  use of, 13
About, 91
Above, 52
Action verbs
  explanation of, G1
  verbs as both linking and, 323
Addresses, *at* in, 52
Adjectives
  to add interest, 339
  and to connect, 23
  comparative forms of, 376–378, 402, G1
  to describe weather, 63
  descriptive, 23
  enough with, 332
  explanation of, 23, 322, G1
  how and *what* questions with, 314
  irregular comparative forms of, 376
  linking verbs with, 323
  to modify nouns, 312, 338
  nouns used as, 316
  possessive, 30, 393, G3
  with same form as adverbs, 324
  superlative forms of, 385–387, 402
  too/very with, 331
Adverbs
  to add interest, 339
  enough with, 332
  explanation of, G1
  frequency, 127–128, 142, G2
  -ly ending for, 324
  of manner, 322, G1
  to modify verbs, 338
  with same form as adjectives, 324
  superlative, G4
  too/very with, 331
Advice, 408, 409
A few, 166
Affirmative imperatives, 106, G2
Affirmative statements
  be able to in, 354
  be going to in, 436, 445
  be in, 6–7
  can in, 345, 415
  explanation of, G1

have to in, 417
indefinite pronouns in, 195, 197
know how to in, 346
me too in, 128
might/may in, 448
in past progressive, 299
in present progressive, 210
probably in, 445
should in, 408
in simple past, 244, 258–259, 274
in simple present, 82
some in, 157
there is/there are in, 180
will in, 445
After, in time clauses, 290, 307, 455
Ago, 245
Agreement, subject-verb, 143
A little, 166
Almost always, 127
Almost never, 127
A lot of, 165
Also, 159
Always, 127, G2
Am, 6. See also *Be*
And
  to connect independent clauses, 361, 371
  to connect two adjectives, 23
  to connect verbs in present progressive, 239
  when to use, 6, 14, G1
Answers. See also Short answers
  be in, 45
  can/could in, 346
  can/may in, 415
  do/does in, 418
  to polite requests, 424
  about possession, 394
  to questions with comparative adjectives, 378
  well to begin, 135
  to *Wh-* questions, 133, 137, 222, 447
  to *Yes/No* questions, 121, 181, 182, 409
Any, 157
Anyone/anybody, 197
Anything, 195
Apostrophes
  with contractions, 7, 16, G1
  with possessive nouns, 31
Are, 14. See also *Be*
Around, 91
Articles
  definite, 150, G1
  explanation of, G1
  indefinite, 150, G2

At
  in addresses, 52
  in clock times, 61, 91
  in general location, 53
Auxiliary verbs
  explanation of, G1

B

Be
  adjectives with, 312
  affirmative statements with, 6–7
  contractions with, 7
  descriptive adjectives with, 23
  forms of, 6
  frequency adverbs with, 127
  guidelines for use of, 38
  negative statements with, 16
  plural noun with, 14, 16
  in present, 6–7, 16, 44, 45
  in present progressive, 210, 212
  questions with, 44, 45, 133, 378
  short answers with, 45
  in simple past, 244, 251–252
  in simple present, 82
  singular noun with, 13
  before *there* in *Yes/No* questions, 181
  where with, 54
Be able to, 354, 370
Because, 282
Before, in time clauses, 290, 307, 455
Be going to, affirmative and negative statements in, 436, 445
Behind, 52
Below, 52
Between, 52
Both, 27
But, 361, 362

C

Can/can't, 334, 335, 346, 415
Can/may, 415
Can you, 424
Capital letters, 275, G1
Clauses
  dependent, G1
  explanation of, 290, 361, G1
  if, 454, 463, G2
  independent or main, 361–362, 371, G2
  time, 290, 292, 306, 307, 455, 463, G4
Commas (,)
  explanation of, G1
  with *if* clauses, 454, 463
  with time clauses, 292, 455, 463
Common noun, G1

Comparative adjectives
    explanation of, 376, 377, G1
    irregular forms of, 376
    more with, 377
    questions with, 378
    use of, 402
Comparison
    comparative adjectives to make, 376–378, 402, G4
    explanation of, G1
    possessive pronouns to make, 393
    superlative adverbs to make, 385–387, 402, G4
Conditional, 454, 463, G1
Conjunctions
    explanation of, G1
    use of, 6, 14, 23, 159, 239, 361, 362
Consonants
    a before, 13, 149, 174, 312
    adjectives ending in consonants + *-y*, 377, 386
    -ed ending and, 259
    explanation of, 13, G1
    plural of nouns ending in consonant plus *-y*, 14, A1
    with superlative adjective ending, 385, 386
Contractions
    for *be*, 7
    explanation of, 7, G1
    for *is* and *are*, 16
    negative (of *be*), 45, 220
    in present progressive, 210, 212, 220
Conversations
    answers to *why* questions in, 282
    can't and *couldn't* in, 344
    contractions *'ll* and *won't* in, 445
    incomplete sentences in, 361
    maybe in, 448
    pronunciation of *going to* in, 436
    questions in present progressive in, 222
    really in, 49, 269
    slow in, 324
Could/couldn't, 334, 346, 370, 415
Could you, 424, 430
Count nouns
    a/an with, 149, 150, 174
    explanation of, 148, G1
    a few with, 166
    how many with, 166
    many/a lot of with, 165
    measurement words with, 156
    some and *any* with, 157
    there is/there are with, 180
    the with, 150

D
Definite article, 150, G1
Dependent clauses, G1
Descriptive adjectives, 23
Did
    with *not* in simple past negative statements, 267
    in simple past *Wh-* questions, 282
    in *Yes/No* questions and affirmative short answers, 280
Didn't
    in simple past negative short answers, 280
    in simple past negative statements, 267
Direct object, G1
Do/does
    know how to with, 346
    in *simple present Wh-* questions, 133
    in *Yes/No questions*, 120
Do not, for emphasis in negative imperatives,107
Don't/doesn't
    in simple present negative short answers, 121
    in simple present negative statements, 90

E
-ed ending
    pronunciation of, 260
    spelling forms with, 259
    for verbs, 259
Enough, 190, 332
-er ending, 376, 377
-es/-s ending. *See -s/-es* ending
-est ending, 385
Everyone/everybody, 197
Everything, 195
Exclamation point (!), 275, G1, G3
Explanations, transition words for, 175

F
Formal language, G2
Frequency adverbs, 127–128, 142, G2
Frequency expressions, 128, G2
Future
    be going to in, 436–437
    explanation of, G2
    if clauses in, 454, 463
    might/may in, 448
    modals to talk about plans in, 462
    with present progressive, 438
    with time clauses, 455, 463
    verb forms and modals to talk about, 462
    will in, 445, 447

G
Go. *See* Irregular verbs
Going to. *See Be going to*
Good/well, 322
Greetings, 4

H
Hardly ever, 127
Have. *See* Irregular verbs
Have to, 417, 418
Helping verbs. *See* Auxiliary verbs
How
    adjectives with, 314
    be going to with, 437
    questions with, 133, 314
    to talk about weather, 63
How about, 95
How far, 346
How many, 166
How many . . . are there?, 182
How much, 166
How much . . . is there?, 182
How often, 133

I
If clauses, 454, 463, G2
I'm, 16
Imperatives, 106, G2
In
    terms for place with, 52
    terms for time with, 61, 91
In back of, 52
Indefinite articles, 150, G2
Indefinite pronouns
    in affirmative statements, 195, 197
    explanation of, G2
    in negative statements, 195, 197
    in *Yes/No* questions, 195, 197
Indentation, paragraph, 115
Independent clauses, 361, 362, 371, G2
Infinitives
    explanation of, 92
    following superlative adjectives, 386
Informal speech, 165
Information questions. *See Wh-* questions
In front of, 52
-ing ending
    for nouns used as adjectives, 316
    for verbs in present progressive, 213, A2
In my opinion, 205
Introductions, 10, 68
Introductory phrases, 205
Irregular noun plurals, 14, A1

Irregular verbs
do, go, have, 84
in simple past, 261, 267–268
It
to talk about time, 60
to talk about weather, 63

K
Know how to, 356

L
Last, 245
Learn how to, 356
Let's + verb, 151
Like
with infinitive, 92
in questions about weather, 63
Linking verbs, 323
Location, 52
Lots of, 165
-ly ending
adjectives with, 324
adverbs of manner with, 322

M
Main clauses, 361, 362, 371, G2
Many, 165
Maybe vs. *may be,* 448
Measurement words, 156, G2
Me too/me neither, 128
Might/may, 448
Modals. *See also* Verbs
can/could as, 344–346, 370
can/may as, 415
explanation of, 344, G2
might/may as, 448
should/shouldn't as, 408, 409
to talk about future plans, 462
will as, 445
More, 377
Much, 165
Must, 417

N
Near, 52
Necessity, 417, 418
Need, with infinitive, 92
Negative imperatives, 106
Negative statements
any in, 157
be going to in, 436
be in, 16
can't/cannot in, 345, 415
don't/doesn't in, 90
explanation of, G2
have to in, 417
indefinite pronouns in, 195, 197
know how to in, 346

me neither in, 128
might/may in, 448
in past progressive, 299
in present progressive, 212, 438
probably in, 445
shouldn't in, 408
in simple past, 244, 267
in simple present, 90–91
there is/there are in, 180
will in, 445
Never, 127
Next, 436
Next to, 52
Non-action verbs, 231, G2
Non-count nouns
a little with, 166
explanation of, 148, G2
how much with, 166
list of common, 148
much/a lot of with, 165
some and *any* with, 157
there are with, 180
the with, 150, 174
No one/nobody, 197
Not, with *be,* 16
No thank you/no thanks, 425
Nothing, 195
Nouns
adjectives to modify, 23, 312, 338
common, G1
count, 148–150, 156, 157, 165, 166, 174, G1
explanation of, 6, G2
with frequency expressing, 128
irregular, 14, A1
non-count, 148, 150, 157, 165, 166, 174, 180, G2
object, 100
plural, 14–16, 31, A1, G3
possessive, 31, G3
proper, 7, 13, G3
as sentence subject, 275
singular, 13, G3
used as adjectives, 316

O
Object nouns, 100
Object pronouns, 100, G2
Objects
direct, G1
explanation of, 99, G3
questions about, 223, 246, 284, 394, 437, 447
Offers
can/could/would in, 425
some in, 157
Often, 127, 142

On
in dates and days of week, 61, 91
terms for location with, 52
One, 376
One of, 385
On weekends, 94
Opinion, 205
Or, 159
Or something, 200
Over, 52

P
Paragraphs
format for, 77
indentation of, 115
Past, simple. *See* Simple past
Past progressive
affirmative statements in, 299
explanation of, 299, G3
negative statements in, 299
simple past vs., 300
Past time clauses
before and *after* in, 290
when in, 292
when to use, 290, 306
Period (.), 44, 275, G3
Permission, *can/may* for, 415
Phrase, G3
Place, prepositions of, 52–53, 76
Please, 106
Plural, 14
Plural nouns
be with, 14
common irregular forms of, A1
explanation of, 14, G3
possessive form of, 31
pronunciation of, 15
spelling rules for regular, A1
use of, 14
Polite offers
answers to, 424
can you/could you/would you as, 424, 430
Polite requests
answers to, 153, 425
can I/could I, 425, 430
would you like, 153, 425, 430
Possession
pronouns and adjectives that show, 393
whose plus noun to ask about, 394
Possessive adjectives
explanation of, 30, G3
use of, 393
Possessive nouns, 31, G3
Possessive pronouns, 393, G3

Prepositions
    explanation of, G3
    of place, 52–53, 76
    of time, 61, 76, 91, 290
Present progressive
    affirmative statements in, 210, 438
    and to join verbs in, 239
    to describe activities in present time, 238
    future with, 438
    -ing for verbs in, 213
    negative statements in, 212
    non-action verbs in, 231
    short answers in, 220
    simple present vs., 230
    Wh- questions in, 222, 223
    when to use, 210, 230, 238
    Yes/No questions in, 220
Present simple. *See* Simple present
Probably, 445
Progressive. *See* Past progressive; Present progressive
Pronouns
    adjectives to modify, 23, 338
    explanation of, G3
    indefinite, 195, G2
    object, 100, G3
    possessive, 393, G3
    as sentence subject, 275
    subject, 6, 30, G4
    use of, 403
Pronunciation
    of *can/can't*, 345
    of *going to*, 436
    of past *-d/-ed* endings, 260
    of plural nouns, *-s* and *-es* endings, 15
    of *-s* and *-es* ending in simple present, 85
    symbols for, A3
Proper nouns, 7, 13, G3
Punctuation
    commas as, 292, 454, 455, 463, G1, G3
    exclamation points as, 275, G1
    explanation of, G3
    periods as, 44, 275, G3
    question marks as, 44, G3

Q
Quantifiers, G3
Question mark (?), 44, G3
Questions. *See also Wh-* questions; *Yes/No* questions
    be going to in, 437
    be in, 44, 45, 54, 133, 378
    can/could in, 346
    explanation of, G3
    have to in, 418

how in, 63
indefinite pronouns in, 195, 197
much, many, and *a lot of* in, 165, 166
about an object, 223, 246, 284, 394, 437, 447
in present progressive, 220, 222, 223, 328
should in, 409
in simple past, 251
in simple present, 120–121
some and *any* in, 157
about a subject, 134, 233, 246, 284, 378, 387, 394, 437, 447
subject and verb order in, 44, 54, 60, 61, 120, 220, 223, 251, 281, 282, 284, 346, 378, 387, 394, 409, 415, 418, 424, 437
superlative adjectives in, 387
this, that, these, those in, 69
about time, 60
about weather, 63
what and *who* in, 223, 284
when in, 61
with *where + be*, 54
with *whose*, 394
will in, 447

R
Rarely, 127
Read, 268
Really, 49, 269
Regular, G3
Regular verbs, 258
Requests, 424

S
Schedules, simple present in, 438
-'s ending, 31
Sentences. *See also* Affirmative statements; Negative statements; Imperatives; Questions
    explanation of, G3
-s/-es ending
    pronunciation of, 85
    for regular plural nouns, 14, A1
    for verbs in simple present, 82, 83, A2
Short answers. *See also* Answers
    be able to in, 354
    be in, 45
    can/could in, 346
    can/may in, 415
    do/does in, 418
    explanation of, G3
    know how to in, 356
    in present progressive, 220, 438
    to questions with comparative adjectives, 378
    should/shouldn't in, 409

in simple past, 251, 280
in simple present, to *Yes/No* questions, 121, 181, 182, 220, 251, 437
Should/shouldn't, 408, 409
Simple past
    affirmative statements in, 244, 258–259, 274
    be in, 244, 251–252
    explanation of, G3
    irregular verbs in, 261, 267–268
    negative statements in, 244, 267
    past progressive vs., 300
    past time clauses with *before* and *after* in, 290
    pronunciation of *-ed* ending in, 260
    regular verbs in, 258
    short answers in, 251, 280
    time expressions in, 245
    Wh- questions in, 252, 282, 284
    Yes/No questions in, 251, 280
Simple present
    affirmative short answers in, 121
    affirmative statements in, 82
    be in, 6–7, 16, 44, 45
    explanation of, G3
    frequency adverbs in, 127
    frequency expressions in, 128
    imperatives in, 106
    irregular verbs in, 84, 268
    negative short answers in, 121
    negative statements in, 90–91
    prepositions of time in, 91
    present progressive vs., 230
    pronunciation of *-s* and *-es* in, 85
    for schedules, 438
    spelling rules for, 83, A2
    to talk about habits or routines, 114
    verbs plus infinitives in, 92
    verbs plus objects in, 99
    when to use, 82, 230
    Wh- questions in, 133–134, 137
    Yes/No questions in, 120–121
Singular, 13
Singular nouns, 13, G3
Slow/slowly, 324
So, 361, 371
Some and *any*, 157
Someone else, 199
Someone/somebody, 197
Something, 195
Sometimes, 127
Spelling rules
    for adverbs ending in *-ly*, 324
    for comparative forms, 376, 377
    for *-ed* form of verbs, 259
    for *-ing* form of verbs, 213, A2

INDEX **I4**

for *maybe/may be*, 448
for regular plural nouns, 14, A1
for simple present, 83, A2
for superlative forms, 385, 386
for *there, they're, their*, 186
Statements, G3. *See also* Affirmative statements; Negative statements
Stress, G4
Subject. *See also* Affirmative sentences; Negative sentences; Questions
   explanation of, G4
   questions about, 134, 233, 246, 284, 378, 387, 394, 437, 447
Subject pronouns, 6, 30, G4
Subject-verb agreement. *See* Affirmative statements; Negative statements; Questions
Suggestions
   how about to make, 95
   let's + verb to make, 151
Superlative adjectives
   explanation of, 385, 386, G4
   irregular forms of, 385
   questions with, 387
   use of, 402
Syllable, G4

T

Take, different uses of, 261
Tense, G4. *See also* specific tenses
Than, 376, 377
Thanks anyway, 424
Thank you/thanks, 425
That, 68, 69
The
   a/an vs., 150
   before superlative adjectives, 385, 386
   use of, G1
The most, 386
There is/there are
   in affirmative statements, 180
   in negative statements, 180
   in *Yes/No* questions, 181, 182
There's one, 182
There vs. *they're* and *their,* 186
These
   general uses for, 68
   questions and answers with, 69
   use of, 68
This, 68
This is, to introduce people, 10
Those, 68, 69
Time
   prepositions of, 61, 76, 91, 290
   questions about, 60
Time clauses
   before, after, and *when* in, 307, 455
   commas with, 292, 455, 463

explanation of, 290, 292, 455, G4
   future, 455
   when to use, 290, 306
Time expressions
   explanation of, G4
   present or future meaning in, 438
   in simple past, 245
Too much/too many, 189
Too/very plus adjective or adverb, 331
To + verb, 386
Transition words, 175

U

Under, 52
Unfortunately, 205
Until, 91
Usually, 127, G2

V

Verbs. *See also* Modals
   action, 323, G1
   adverbs to modify, 338
   auxiliary, 418, G1
   base form of, G1
   -ed ending for, 259
   explanation of, G4
   followed by infinitives, 92
   followed by objects, 99
   in future, 462
   as imperatives, 106, 107
   irregular, 84, 261, 267–268
   linking, 323
   non-action, 231, G2
   regular, 258
   in simple past, 258, 261, 267–268
   in simple present, 92, 99
Very
   to make an adjective stronger, 312, 331
   to make an adverb stronger, 312
Vowels, 13, G4

W

Want
   with infinitive, 92
   vs. *would like,* 153
Was/were, 244, 251, 252, 258, 299
Weather, 63
Well, 135
Well/good, 322
Wh- questions. *See also How; What; When; Where; Who; Whose*
   answers to, 133, 137, 222, 327, 447
   be going to in, 437
   can/can't in, 415
   can/could in, 346
   comparative adjectives in, 378
   do/does in, 418
   explanation of, G4

in present progressive, 222, 223, 438
   should in, 409
   in simple past, 252, 284
   in simple present, 133–134
   superlative adjectives in, 387
   will in, 447
Wh- words, G4. *See also How; Wh-* questions; *When; Where; Who; Why*
What, 60, 63, 69, 387
What for, 282
What kind of, 314
When,
   be going to with, 437
   past time clauses with, 292
   questions with, 61, 133
   in time clauses, 307, 455
Where, 54, 133
Which, 378
Who, 133, 134, 222, 223, 284, 378, 387, 437
Whose, 394,
Who's vs. *whose,* 394
Why, 133, 222, 252, 447
will
   affirmative and negative statements with, 445
   use of, 448
Will not/won't, 445
Would like vs. *want,* 153
Would you, 424
Would you like, 153, 425

Y

Yes/No questions. *See also* Questions
   be able to in, 354
   be going to in, 437
   be in, 44, 45
   can/could in, 346
   can/may in, 415
   comparative adjectives in, 378
   explanation of, G4
   have to in, 418
   indefinite pronouns in, 195, 197
   in present progressive, 220, 438
   short answers to, 121, 181, 182, 220
   should in, 409
   in simple past, 251, 280
   in simple present, 120–121
   superlative adjectives in, 387
   there is/there are in, 181, 182
   this, that, these, those in, 69
   will in, 447
Yesterday, 245
   -y to *-ies,* 14, 83, 377, 386, A1, A2
You, 7, 30

CREDITS

Text and Listening

34: Exercise 10. Source: "A Thing or Two about Twins" by Peter Miller: National Geographic/Features/Photo Gallery, National Geographic Magazine, January 2012. **85:** "Bush Pilots." Source: http://www.ultimathulelodge.com/people/paul-claus. **88:** Source: http://www.scienceclarified.com/scitech/Space-Stations/Living-in-Outer-Space.html. **97:** Source: "Orphans No More" by Charles Seibert: National Geographic Magazine, Sept. 2011. **129:** Exercise 9: Listen & Write. Sources: http://www.viator.com/Bangkokattractions/ Damnoen-Saduak-Floating-Market/d343-a2604; http://www.viator.com/Bangkok-tourism/Visiting-Bangkoks-Floating-Markets/d343-t11629. **136:** "52 Hikes a Year!" Source: http://52hikes52weekends.blogspot.com. **171:** Exercise 2: Listen, Write & Speak. Source: http://blogs.kqed.org/bayareabites/2012/08/07/traditional-ethiopian-coffee-ceremony-brewed-up-by-chef-marcus-samuelsson-and-cafe-colucci. **228:** Adapted from "The Hard Science, Dumb Luck, and Cowboy Nerve of Chasing Tornadoes" by Priit J. Vesilind: National Geographic Magazine, April 2004.

Photo

2–3: ©Adrian Pope/Getty Images; **5:** ©James P. Blair/National Geographic Creative; **9:** ©Stephen Rees/Shutterstock; **11:** ©Beverly Joubert/National Geographic Creative; **12:** ©Beverly Joubert/National Geographic Creative; **19 top:** ©LattaPictures/iStockphoto, **middle:** ©Ingram Publishing/Thinkstock, **bottom:** © Asiaselects/Alamy; **21:** Joel Sartore/National Geographic Creative; **22:** ©Joel Sartore/National Geographic Creative; **25 top:** ©Bobby Model/National Geographic Creative, **middle:** ©Mega Pixel/Shutterstock; **26 top:** ©Andrew Rich/iStockphoto, **middle:** ©Wavebreak Media/Thinkstock, **bottom:** ©Kali Nine LLC/iStockphoto; **28:** ©Erika Larsen/Redux; **29:** ©Erika Larsen/Redux; **32:** ©Tino Soriano/National Geographic Creative; **37:** ©Richard Nowitz/National Geographic Creative; **38:** ©stevecoleimages/iStockphoto; **40–41:** ©Poras Chaudhary/Getty Images; **42–43:** ©James L. Stanfield/National Geographic Creative; **46:** ©Adalberto Ríos Szalay/age fotostock; **49:** ©luoman/iStockphoto; **50–51:** ©Neale Clark/Getty Images; **57:** ©Tyrone Turner/National Geographic Creative; **59:** ©Annie Griffiths/National Geographic Creative; **65:** ©Seregam/Shutterstock; **66:** ©Christophe Boisvieux/age fotostock; **67:** ©Keren Su/Getty Images; **71:** ©AFP/Getty Images; **72:** © epa European Pressphoto Agency creative account/Alamy; **74:** ©Lukas Hlavac/Shutterstock; **75:** ©TonyV3112/Shutterstock; **76:** ©Alistair Berg/Getty Images; **78–79:** ©Lynn Johnson/National Geographic Creative; **80 inset:** ©Minden Pictures/SuperStock; **80–81:** ©James P. Blair/National Geographic Creative; **83:** ©Joel Sartose/National Geographic Creative; **85:** ©Kate Thompson/National Geographic Creative; **87:** © YinYang/iStockphoto; **88:** ©NASA; **89:** ©NASA and The Hubble Heritage Team (STScI/AURA) Acknowledgment: N. Scoville (Caltech) and T. Rector (NOAO); **97:** ©Michael Nichols/National Geographic Creative; **98:** ©Michael Nichols/National Geographic Creative; **102:** ©J.W.Alker Image Broker/Newscom; **103 top:** ©Big Cheese/Thinkstock, **103 bottom:** © Design Pics Inc./Alamy; **104:** Peter Essick/National Geographic Creative; **105:** ©Altaf Qadri/AP Images; **110:** ©Raul touzon/National Geographic Creative; **112 inset:** ©Kelly O/The Stranger, **112 bottom:** ©AlaskaStock/Glow Images; **114:** ©Creatas Images/Thinkstock; **116–117:** ©Luca Invernizzi Tetto/age fotostock; **118–119:** ©Gianluca Colla/National Geographic Creative; **122–123:** ©Anita Stizzoli/Getty Images; **125:** ©Lonely Planet/Getty Images; **126:** ©1000 Words/Shutterstock; **129:** ©MJPrototype/Shutterstock; **131:** ©Sylvain Grandadam/Getty Images; **132:** ©Eric Albrecht/Getty Images; **136:** ©Raymond Gehman/National Geographic Creative; **138 top:** ©Jose Luis Pelaez Inc/Getty Images, **middle:** ©auremar/Shutterstock, **bottom:** ©Thorsten Rother/Getty Images; **142:** ©Richard Nowitz/National Geographic Creative; **144–145:** ©Joel Sartose/National Geographic Creative; **146–147:** ©Richard Nowitz/National Geographic Creative; **152:** ©David C. Tomlinson/Getty Images: **154–155:** ©Nando Pizzini Photography/Getty Images; **155, 1:** ©ffolas/Thinkstock, **155, 2:** ©Petr Malyshev/Shutterstock, **155, 3:** ©Jiri Hera/Shutterstock, **155, 4:** ©Eldin Muratovic/Thinkstock, **155, 5:** © wildlywise/Shutterstock, **155, 6:** ©Picsfive/Shutterstock; **159:** ©Greg Dale/National Geographic Creative; **160:** ©bitt24/Shutterstock; **161:** ©James Baigrie/Getty Images; **162:** ©Tim Hill/Alamy; **163:** ©McPHOTO/age fotostock; **164:** ©Nazzu/Shutterstock; **171:** ©Ton Koene/age fotostock; **172:** ©Stephen St. John/National Geographic Creative; **174:** ©Keri Pinzon/Getty Images; **176–177:** ©Pete Ryan/National Geographic Creative; **178, viajero:** ©zhang bo/Getty Images, **178, Chen C:** ©Asia Images Group Pte Ltd/Alamy, **178, Viet:** ©Martin Valigursky/Thinkstock; **179:** ©Hung Chung Chih/Thinkstock; **184:** ©Fran Lanting/National Geographic Creative; **185:** ©Fran Lanting/National Geographic Creative; **187:** ©tulcarion/Getty Images; **188:** ©Design Pics Inc./Alamy; **192:** © Greg Winston/National Geographic Creative; **193:** ©Boston Globe via Getty Images; **194:** ©UIG via Getty Images; **196–197:** ©Marcio Jose Bastos Silva/Shutterstock; **199:** ©Marjie Lambert/MCT/Newscom; **201:** © John Greim/age fotostock; **203:** L ©Justin Horrocks/Getty Images; **204:** ©Aspen Photo/Shutterstock; **206–207:** ©Henn Photography/Getty Images; **208–209:** Photograph by Brano Beliancin; **211:** ©Jimmy Chin/National Geographic Creative; **213:** ©Jimmy Chin/National Geographic Creative; **214 left:** © Skip Brown/National Geographic Creative, **middle:** © technotr/iStockphoto, **right:** ©Joe McBride/Getty Images; **215:** ©Bill Hatcher/National Geographic Creative; **216 left** and **right:** ©Skip Brown/National Geographic Creative; **218:** ©Stephen Alvarez/National Geographic Creative; **219:** ©Stephen Alvarez/National Geographic Creative; **221:** ©Brian J. Skerry/National Geographic Creative; **225 left:** ©John Burcham/National Geographic Creative, **225 right:** Chris Johns/ National Geographic Creative; **226:** ©F1online digitale Bildagentur GmbH/Alamy; **227:** ©Andrew Zarivny/Shutterstock; **228–229:** ©Cultura Science/Jason Persoff Stormdoctor/Getty Images; **233:** ©Lorenzo Mondo/Shutterstock; **235:** ©AFP/Getty Images; **236:** ©Gordon Wiltsie/National Geographic Creative; **238:** ©Don Bayley/Getty Images

MAP

11, 18, 28, 42, 50, 56, 97, 118, 131, 154, 163, 178, 184, 193, 208, 218, 233: National Geographic Maps

ILLUSTRATION

9, 10, 25, 27, 33, 34, 37, 52, 53, 55, 63, 65, 73, 95, 108, 127, 161, 162, 169, 173, 202, 203, 217: Cenveo Publisher Services